LOCAL ECONOMIC DEVELOPMENT

For my family

LOCAL ECONOMIC DEVELOPMENT
ANALYSIS AND PRACTICE

JOHN P. BLAIR

SAGE Publications
International Educational and Professional Publisher
Thousand Oaks   London   New Delhi

For information address:

SAGE Publications, Inc.
2455 Teller Road
Thousand Oaks, California 91320

SAGE Publications Ltd.
6 Bonhill Street
London EC2A 4PU
United Kingdom

SAGE Publications India Pvt. Ltd.
M-32 Market
Greater Kailash I
New Delhi 110 048 India

Printed in the United States of America

Library of Congress Cataloging-in-Publication Data

Blair, John P., 1947-
    Local economic development: Analysis and practice / John P.
Blair.
        p.   cm.
    Includes bibliographic references and index.
    ISBN 0-8039-5376-3 (acid-free paper)
    1. Economic development.   2. Economic policy.   3. Local
government.   4. Urban economics.   I. Title.
HD82.B5543   1995
338.9—dc20   95-3023

This book is printed on acid-free paper.

    96   97   98   99   10   9   8   7   6   5   4   3   2

Sage Production Editor: Astrid Virding
Sage Typesetter: Andrea D. Swanson

⊠ Contents

A Short and Important Preface   ix

1. Economic Development and Market Logic   **1**
   How Economists View the World   1
   How Markets Work   7
   Economic Development Defined   14
   The Nature of Regions   15
   Summary   20

2. Three Fundamental and Recurring Issues   **22**
   Unemployment and Low Wages   22
   Externalities   27
   Improving the Public Sector   33
   Summary   39

3. Business Location, Expansion, and Retention   **41**
   Locational Factors   41
   The Decision-Making Process   55
   Changing Relative Importance of Locational Factors   60
   Summary   63

4. Market Areas and Economic Development Strategies   **66**
   Demand and Market Areas   67
   Competition for Markets   69
   The Urban Hierarchy and Urban System   74
   An Evaluation of the Central-Place Approach   80
   How to Measure Areas of Influence   84
   Hinterland Expansion Strategies   92
   Summary   93

5. **Understanding Economic Structure**   **95**
    Agglomeration Economies   95
    External-Economy Industries   103
    Comparative Measures of Economic Structure   104
    Other Aspects of Regional Structure   113
    Summary   113

6. **Regional Growth and Development:**
    Fundamental Perspective   **116**
    Stages of Growth   116
    Circular Flow Model   120
    The Export-Base Theory of Growth   127
    Critique of the Export-Base Approach   135
    Supply-Side Approaches   139
    Supply and Demand Approaches Compared   142
    Summary   143

7. **Additional Tools and Perspectives on Economic Growth**   **145**
    Shift and Share Analysis   145
    Econometric and Simulation Models   149
    Importance-Strength Analysis   157
    Input-Output Analysis   159
    Summary   166

8. **Issues in Economic Development Practice**   **168**
    External Benefits From Economic Development   168
    Who Benefits From Growth?   170
    Problems With Local Competition for Economic
        Development   174
    Cumulative Causation   182
    Targeting Development Efforts   184
    Policy and Complex Systems   185
    Summary   187

9. **Resource and Commodity Flows**   **189**
    Models of Trade and Resource Flows   189
    Economics of Migration   193
    Mobility of Capital   198
    Innovations and Ideas   199
    Mobility and Development Policy   203
    Summary   207

10. **Land Use**   **209**
      What Gives Land Value?   209
      The Land Development Process   214
      Land Use Patterns   223
      Change and Growth   228
      Land Use and Economic Development Tools   232
      Summary   236

11. **Housing and Neighborhood Development**   **238**
      Fundamentals of Housing Economics   238
      Residential Location and Neighborhood Change   244
      Housing Policy Debates   256
      Neighborhood Commercial Development   261
      The Informal Economy: An Alternative Strategy   264
      Summary   267
      Appendix   269

12. **Metropolitan Government and Finance**   **274**
      Governmental Functions in a Spatial Context   274
      Size and Scope of Local Governments   278
      Intergovernmental Grants   281
      Guidelines for Evaluating Taxes   285
      Reasons for Fiscal Problems   288
      Fiscal Strategies and Tools   291
      Fiscal Impact and Benefit-Cost Studies   295
      Summary   302

13. **Planning, Futures Studies, and Development Policy**   **304**
      Futurist Perspectives   305
      Planning Perspectives on Development Policy   310
      Planning and Futures Studies Tools   317
      Summary   320

    References   321

    Index   329

    About the Author   345

⊠ A Short and Important Preface

The purpose of this book is to present the economics of economic development in a manner accessible to both economists and non-economists. It is written with an understanding that successful economic development programs require knowledge from a variety of fields, including planning, political science, finance, sociology, and marketing. Nevertheless, economic processes are at the heart of local development efforts. Practitioners should understand how market forces combine with non-economic variables to influence the economic development process.

I have tried to present information in a straightforward manner, minimizing jargon and technical detail. Concepts, theories, and tools are emphasized rather than specific programs because programs change frequently, whereas the fundamentals provide a foundation for strategies, policies, and programs. Theory and practice are given high priority. Theory without practice is sterile. Practice without theory is adrift.

Analytical tools are presented in a "how to" manner. The conceptual foundations and limitations of tools are also discussed so users will be able to understand and modify techniques to fit a wide variety of circumstances. This approach is important because most "real world" applications require some ad hoc modifications of standard textbook techniques.

My motivation for writing an urban economic development book emerged slowly. During nearly 20 years of teaching, consulting, and serving as a planning commissioner, I perceived a widening gap between economic development practice and academic economic interests. In class, I tried to help my students develop tools needed to understand local economic development, but I sometimes felt I was "fighting" the textbook. It was as though academic economics had become so insular that it failed to examine the economy. Local economic development attracted me because the field promised to enhance the lives of people. This book is written in that spirit and hope.

NOTE: This book was supported in part through the Belinda A. Burns Endowed Faculty Scholarship.

Economic Development
and Market Logic

The majority of decisions affecting local economic development are made by private individuals or institutions. These decisions are generally made on the basis of self-interest after consideration of the costs and benefits. Economic development practitioners seek to influence private economic decisions by affecting the real or perceived costs and benefits of decisions. This chapter describes how economists view the economic activities and serves as a point of departure for understanding the development process.

⊠ How Economists View the World

Economists generally agree about the broad outlines of how the economy operates, although they may disagree regarding specific details and policies. In other words, there is general agreement about the appropriate paradigm but some disagreement at the operational level. Students who have not studied economics sometimes fail to understand the role of models and assumptions in economic analysis, the economist's view of individual behavior, and how disagreements about policy can arise. A sketch of these important aspects of the economic paradigm will set the stage for further analysis.

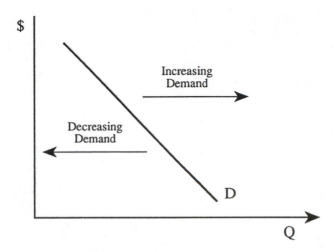

Figure 1.1. The demand curve. The demand curve shows how many units of a product consumers will purchase at various prices. Changes in income, market size, price of other goods, preferences, and expectations could cause the demand curve to increase or decrease.

Models and Assumptions

Economists often build deductive models to help understand economic processes. A model is a simplification of reality to help focus on important components. Most economic models consist of assumptions about a situation and a series of deductions about what behavior will flow from the assumptions. Analysis is the process of breaking a problem into its components. In the process of analysis, it is important to examine the effect of one or two independent variables on a dependent variable. For instance, we might want to consider how quality of life and local wages affect job growth. To focus on how a few variables interact, it is necessary to assume that other variables do not change so as to alter the relationship between the variables that are the focus of the analysis. This is the well-known ceteris paribus, or "other things equal," assumption.

A widely known application of the "other things equal" assumption is the law of demand. It states that if the price of a good falls, the quantity that individuals are willing and able to consume will increase, other things equal. Figure 1.1 is a demand curve consistent with the law of demand. Changes in tastes and preferences, incomes, the price of other goods, expectations, and market size could result in a situation where the relation between price and quantity demanded could appear to violate the law of demand. For instance, price, market size, and quantity demanded could all increase as price increased. Therefore, to express the law of demand properly, it is necessary to make explicit the assumption that everything stays the same except price and quantity.

Students often object to the many assumptions that are incorporated in economic models because the assumptions are unrealistic. In reality, other things do not remain equal, so why do economists assume that they do? The value of the assumptions is that they provide a systematic framework for analysis. The assumptions may be relaxed so the impact of changing assumptions may be analyzed. For instance, the assumptions that the size of the market or incomes do not change may be replaced by the assumption that market size or incomes increase. Then it can be shown that increases will shift the entire demand curve to the right.

Spatial economic models are often predicated upon unrealistic assumptions such as perfect knowledge, profit maximizing behavior, uniform transportation costs, consumers with identical tastes, and homogeneous space. The insights gained from these models can be increased if consideration is given to how the models will be affected if the assumptions were changed. Changing the assumptions of a model provides insights about the variables that were being held constant.

Individual Behavior

For most economists, individuals are the building blocks from which group actions emerge. Let's examine individual decisions. First, economists are careful not to assign to groups motives that reside in individuals. Phrases such as "the city believes in progress" may be a shorthand way of saying that many or perhaps the majority of individuals in the city believe in progress, but we know the city itself does not believe. Also, economists are aware that collective actions are not just the sum of individual actions. For instance, it may be true that anyone may become a millionaire if they work hard enough and/or are lucky enough. However, it is not true that everyone can become a millionaire.

Economists also believe that individuals behave so as to maximize their utility (satisfaction). Most economists believe that benefits for others result from the drive to maximize utility when markets are working properly. Adam Smith expressed this concept as well as anyone when he said,

It is not from the benevolence of the butcher, the brewer, or the baker, that we expect our dinner, but from their own self-interest. We address ourselves, not to their humanity but to their self love, and never talk to them of our own necessities but of their advantages.

According to Smith, a market system creates rewards and incentives that encourage utility-maximizing individuals to do what is in the public interest as if they were guided by an "invisible hand."

Unfortunately, it is impossible to determine directly whether an individual is trying to maximize utility because actions that bring satisfaction to one person may not provide satisfaction for another. Activities that provide satisfaction or utility include acquiring money, gaining prestige, helping others, and so forth. However, economists usually assume that workers and consumers try to maximize utility by trying to achieve an optimal work-leisure balance and making wise consumption choices. Business owners are assumed to maximize utility by maximizing profit.

Economists also assume that individuals are rational in their efforts to maximize utility. The rationality assumption is essential if economic models are to predict behavior. If individuals did not act rationally, then all behavior could be explained as the result of irrational actions.

Students sometimes object to the concept of *utility-maximizing man.* One type of objection is based on the mistaken idea that utility-maximizing behavior is selfish. In fact, economists recognize that altruistic behavior can provide satisfaction to some individuals. The second type of objection to the utility-maximizing man assumption is that it does not examine how tastes and preferences are formed or why individuals differ in how they attain satisfaction. Economists tend to assume that individuals have a set of preferences, but little attention is given to how preferences are formed. It is likely that if economic and social life were different, individuals would have a different set of preferences. Urban and regional economists often rely upon the work of psychologists, sociologists, and planners who are more informed about questions of preference formation.

Policy Debates

Economists explore two distinct types of questions. On the one hand, positive questions inquire into why things are the way they are. They are concerned with describing the world as it is. On the other hand, normative questions inquire into how things should be or ought to be and involve value judgment. It is often useful to determine whether the source of a disagreement is based on different analyses, different value judgments, or both. Economists may disagree about appropriate policies either because of different analyses about how the economy operates or because they have different values.

An agreement about positive analysis but a disagreement regarding values would exist if two economists agree about how the economy operates but disagree about the actions that should be taken. For instance, most urban and regional economists agree that if the population density of an area increased and everything else remained the same, rents would increase. However, they may disagree about whether rents should increase. Some economists might say rents should increase because high rents will efficiently ration a scarce resource and encourage more production. Others might oppose rent increases because of adverse effects on the poor. Those who believe rents should not increase may suggest that the government intervene in the economy to prevent rents from increasing.

Normative agreement and positive disagreement could arise if economists shared the normative opinion that it is unfortunate that rents increase but disagree about consequences of government intervention. One economist might argue that government attempts to lower rents will decrease the supply of housing and hurt the poor, whereas another economist may believe that intervention will successfully shield the poor from paying more rent.

Efficiency, Equity, and Welfare

Equity and efficiency are the principal criteria that economists use to evaluate public policy issues. Efficiency refers to the ability to use resources to produce something of value. If existing resources are used to produce more goods and services using the same level of inputs, the economy may be characterized as more efficient. Efficiency also may be enhanced if a given level of resources is used to produce a different mix of products so that the value of output is increased.

Benefit-cost comparisons are sometimes used to evaluate the efficiency of a change. In a competitive market, the costs of undertaking an activity will reflect the value of resources if they were used in their next best opportunity (opportunity cost). The monetary value of the benefits reflect the value that individuals place on the new output. Hence if the benefit-cost ratio is greater than 1, the monetary value of the goods and services created will exceed the momentary value of the resources used to produce those goods and services. (The value of goods produced will exceed the opportunity cost.) Thus when a public policy change is being evaluated, the benefit-cost comparison provides an indication of efficiency for a given distribution of income.[1]

Sometimes, policymakers are more concerned with economic growth than static efficiency, particularly individuals involved in economic development. A community that operates inefficiently but grows rapidly may be better off in the long run than a community that maintains a high level of static efficiency but does not grow rapidly.

Equity usually refers to fairness. When a policy change hurts some individuals but benefits others, questions of fairness arise. Economists are not very good at deciding which actions are more equitable because such decisions cannot be made on scientific grounds. Nevertheless, the appropriateness of most changes must be decided, at least partly, on the basis of fairness.

Ideological Perspectives

In practice, it is sometime difficult to distinguish between differences in analysis and differences in values because some economists choose their analysis to fit their values. There are two alternative perspectives on economic policy that are within the framework of the traditional economic paradigm: conservative and liberal.

The conservative perspective places a high value on economic freedom and economic efficiency. Many conservatives agree with Friedman (1962) that capitalism is necessary for political freedom. The analyses of conservative economists tend to show that the laissez-faire market works well. When competitive market conditions exist, individuals seeking their own self-interest act in the social interest. Consequently, conservatives tend to oppose government involvement in regional and urban problems. Even when their analysis leads them to believe that the market outcomes are imperfect, conservatives tend to believe that the imperfect market outcome is preferable to government-imposed solutions.

Liberal economists tend to place a high value on economic equity while viewing market operations as sometimes both inefficient and inequitable but still useful. Blinder (1987) referred to the liberal philosophy as combining respect for the free market with concern for those the market leaves behind. Consequently, liberals tend to believe that government action is important to solving urban problems and securing a more equitable distribution of income.

Fundamentally, liberals want to maintain the basic framework of market decision making, but they believe there is substantial potential for government actions to improve market outcomes. In particular, government regulations may help reduce the impacts of externalities through taxes, regulation, and other actions.

Conservatives and liberals constitute the mainstream of economic thinking. Both perspectives rely on the market to provide information and establish the basic incentives that encourage socially desirable behavior. Most of the policy issues discussed in this text are within the liberal-conservative framework.

Radical economic analysis is outside mainstream thinking and often provides interesting challenges to traditional economic thinking. Radical economists are distrustful of the market. Many radical economists believe the market is not an impartial mechanism that helps organized economic activities. Rather, the market is a means of social control. They are less concerned with whether market mechanisms are efficient and more concerned with whose interests the market serves. Government programs that affect economic outcomes often help the wealthy because the same interests that control the market also control government. Radicals tend to see urban problems as a reflection of class conflicts. Greater government involvement in the economy, including direct ownership of productive resources, is seen by radicals as a more preferable solution to problems than either a policy of laissez-faire or government modification of market outcomes.

⌘ How Markets Work

Markets are a process (not a place) through which buyers and sellers conduct transactions. Markets coordinate numerous economic decisions. To emphasize the importance of the coordination mechanism, Milton Friedman (1962) has claimed that no one in the world knows how to make a pencil. He meant that no one knows how to complete all the steps in the process—cutting the trees, mining the graphite, and so forth. Yet the market helps coordinate these decisions and many more.

Another important function of the market is to generate prices for both resources and outputs. Rising prices encourage production and discourage consumption. In addition, prices play a central role in providing information to producers. Suppose, for instance, that consumers want more recording on compact disks and fewer on vinyl. The shift in demand will cause the price of

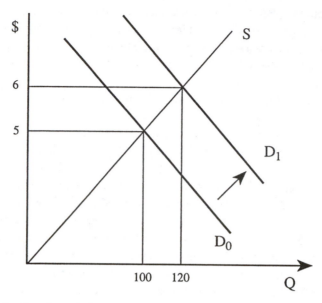

Figure 1.2. Supply and demand. The initial price and quantity for a product are determined by the initial supply and demand curves D_0 and S. Equilibrium price and output will be $5 and 100 units. If demand increased to D_1, price and output of the product would increase to $6 and 120 units.

compact disks to rise. The higher price sends a signal to producers to produce more. The higher prices will enable compact disk producers to purchase the inputs needed for increased production. Similarly, vinyl record producers will produce less and free resources to be used elsewhere in the economy.

Prices also transmit signals from producers to consumers. Suppose the price of gold increases. The cost of producing gold jewelry and other products using gold will increase. Producers would produce less gold jewelry at the existing price, forcing the price up and signaling consumers to conserve on the use of gold.

Supply and Demand

Figure 1.2 illustrates how supply and demand operate. The demand curve shows how consumer purchases will be affected as prices change, other things equal. Similarly, the supply curve shows the quantity of output producers would be willing and able to sell at various prices. The higher prices will induce businesses to produce greater output, other things equal. Higher prices will also allow supplies of the product to outbid producers of other goods for the resources they need.

Price will be determined at the point where the quantity supplied and demanded are equal. If, in Figure 1.2, D_0 is the operative demand curve, the price will be $5. At that price, companies will produce 100 units, and consumers will purchase 100 units. At any other price, there will be either a shortage or a surplus of the product. The $5 price is considered an equilibrium price because once it is attained it will not change unless the supply or demand curves shift. It may take the market a long time to find the equilibrium price, so, at any given time, the actual price may not be in equilibrium.

Suppose that economic development caused the population and incomes of residents to increase. As a result, the demand curve will increase from D_0 to D_1. Price and output will increase. Immediately, we can visualize one of the impacts of economic development on the demand for local products. Similarly, factors that increase the demand for the output of local establishments can contribute to local economic development. For example, if demand for American-made cars increased, communities with automobile product facilities would probably experience increases in employment as the output of automobiles increased.

Supply, Demand, and Efficiency

When there are many buyers and sellers, prices and output levels are determined by the interaction of supply and demand. Competitive markets can be very efficient. Economists believe that the sum of individuals' marginal private benefits (MPB) from consuming additional units of a product determine the demand curve in Figure 1.2. The demand curve slopes downward because benefits from additional units of a product fall as more units are consumed. Furthermore, if the only benefits from the good or service are captured by the person purchasing the good, then the demand of private individuals will reflect the benefits to society, the marginal social benefit (MSB). (The purchaser is part of society.) The price the purchaser pays for a good is equal to the marginal benefit received from the product. Thus individuals will purchase goods up to the point where price equals marginal benefits, $P = MSB = MPB$. The relationship between demand and marginal social benefits in a world where third parties are unaffected by the use of the good is shown in Figure 1.3.

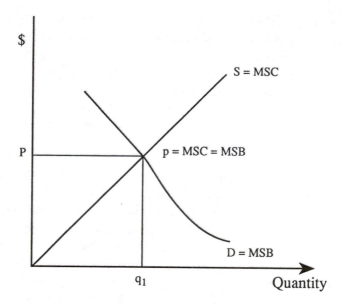

Figure 1.3. Model in an efficient market. When all relevant costs are borne by the principals to a transaction (no externalities), competitive market processes will result in optimum output.

When producers bear all production costs, the supply curve, which represents the quantity of goods that producers will supply, will equal the marginal social cost curve (MSC). The costs paid by producers to make each unit reflect the cost of bidding the needed resources from alternative uses. Those alternative uses are opportunity costs. Therefore, if the producers bear all of the relevant costs of production, then S = MSC = MPC.

In a competitive, free-market economy, the price of each good reflects the value that society places on the resources used to produce it. In Figure 1.3, the market-determined level of output will be q_1. If we assume that all relevant costs and benefits are borne by either the producer or the consumer, then the actual output, q_1, will also be at the point where MSB = MSC. Producing beyond MSB = MSC will result in producing output where the social costs of producing extra units are greater than the benefits, so producing beyond q_1 would be undesirable. If the output level were below q_1, increases in output would be desirable because the MSB would exceed the MSC.

Markets Are Not Always Efficient

If markets worked as effectively as suggested by the analysis underlying Figure 1.3, the role of governments in local economic development would be very small. There would still be an income redistribution role, but interference with market outcomes would be inefficient. However, there are several realities that prevent markets from operating efficiently.

Public Goods

Sometimes, markets will not provide goods that citizens want because there are inadequate payment mechanisms. For instance, how could most roads be provided if not for government? Few individuals would voluntarily pay for roads if they thought they could use them for free. Of course, some toll roads could be built privately and travelers then charged for using the road. However, the cost of collecting tolls would be too high for local collector roads with numerous entrance and exit points, so private businesses would not finance construction of local roads. If they are to be built at all, they must be financed by government. Goods that must be provided by local government include fire protection, health services, police protection, and amenities such as parks.

Externalities or Spillovers

Externalities or spillovers occur when all of the costs and benefits fail to accrue to the principals to a transaction (buyers and sellers). In this case, third parties may benefit (positive externality) or be harmed (negative externality). Often, governments need to intervene to protect third parties. Firms that pollute are an excellent example of a spillover effect. Private providers will often overproduce goods that have pollution as a by-product because the producers will not be concerned with the costs of the pollution that are borne by others. Negative externalities are a particular problem in high-density urban areas because one negative spillover harms so many persons. Pollution is an example of a negative externality. Local governments may also provide, or subsidize, many services that provide positive spillovers to encourage more production than would be provided by the market. Education is a good example because an educated citizenry provides benefits not only to the person receiving the education but to others in the community. Externalities have important economic development implications that are discussed in Chapter 2.

Monopolies

The market will not work efficiently if there is only one or a few producers (or purchasers). Consequently, governments often intervene to control monopolies. The regulation of public utilities is an instance where government has intervened in the market process to ensure that firms do not take advantage of their market power.

Imperfect Information

If some consumers or producers are uninformed, the market will not operate to maximize welfare. Therefore, governments sometimes intervene to improve consumer and producer knowledge. Public relations and advertising associated with economic development are attempts to better inform (or misinform) business about the benefits of locating in a particular area.

The Role of Profits

In the market economy, profits drive production and employment decisions. Producers normally will not hire workers or establish businesses unless they anticipate earning a profit. To understand business decision making, it is important to understand the concept of profit. The formula for profit is

$$P = \text{TR} - \text{TC}, \tag{1-1}$$

where

P = profits
TR = total revenues
TC = total costs

Total revenue equals the price(s) of the output(s) times the number of units sold. One way to sell more output is to lower price. However, if the price decline offsets the increase in sales, then total revenue will fall. If the increase in sales offsets the price decline, total revenue will increase.

Total cost represents all of the private costs of production including the opportunity cost of the owner's efforts and an adequate return on the owner's investment. Thus the owner's time is a cost just as employee wages are a cost. Improving product quality or advertising might increase sales and hence total revenue, but if these steps increase costs more than revenues, profits will decline.

To understand the nature of the profit equations, consider a person who owns a business with the following costs and revenues:

Total revenue	=	$100,000
Cost of material	=	25,000
Cost of hiring workers	=	25,000
Other out-of-pocket costs	=	10,000
Other opportunity costs	=	50,000

The other opportunity costs include foregone income the owner could receive if the capital invested earned a normal interest and if the owner worked for another employer instead of running the business.

To an accountant, this firm would be earning a profit because the accounting costs would be $60,000 (total out-of-pocket costs that do not include other opportunity costs) and the total revenue would be $100,000, so accounting profits would be $40,000. However, the accounting analysis is misleading because the total costs include the opportunity costs of the owner's capital and labor. If the firm were to operate, the investor-owner would give up opportunities to earn $50,000. Thus the opportunity cost of $50,000 should be included to provide a comprehensive total cost estimate. After accounting for all costs, the business actually generates a loss of $10,000.

Equation 1-1 is very useful in understanding business decisions. Suppose a firm is considering a decision to add to its output. Profits would increase only if the additions to total revenue (called marginal revenue) are greater than the additions to total cost (called marginal costs). Conversely, if marginal revenues are less than marginal costs, firms will not undertake the action under consideration.

Economic development practitioners are frequently concerned with attracting business by lowering costs, increasing revenues, or altering the perceptions of costs and revenues. Costs and revenues can be altered both by direct measures, such as business subsidies or infrastructure improvements, and by indirect methods, such as improving the quality of life or enhancing education in the area.

Equation 1-1 has two important limitations. First, there are exceptions to the profit maximizing assumption. Economists usually assume that business managers will behave to maximize profits because maximizing profits is one way to maximize utility. Sometimes, however, business may make decisions that may not increase profits but will enhance the utility of the business manager. For instance, a corporate executive may influence the company to donate a million dollars to a local charity. Such an action could reduce income for the stockholders (owners), but the prestige and community recognition that the manager receives may provide direct utility. Particularly, when managers run companies for stockholders, managers may put their own utility ahead of corporate profits.

Second, future costs and benefits are often not well known, and some things are impossible to know. A business may give to charity because it is good public relations that may increase profits in the long run. Such reasoning may be correct, but it is impossible to quantify. Often, business decisions such as locating a new venture are undertaken on the basis of hunch rather than careful calculation of the marginal costs and benefits. Economic development officials may influence business decisions by describing how an action could increase revenues or lower costs in the long run without having to quantify the impact.

⊠   Economic Development Defined

Economists distinguish between economic growth and development. Growth by itself could be either an improvement or a detriment. For instance, a facility that paid very low wages might open in an area. As a result, the population and overall size of the economy might increase, but per capita incomes might fall, and the quality of life might suffer.

Growth is an important element in the economic development process. It provides jobs and resources that can support many improvements in the quality of life. Without economic growth, there would be insufficient jobs to support even a slowly growing population. Forced out-migration may result.

Economic development implies that the welfare of residents is improving. Increases in per capita income (adjusted for inflation) is one important indicator of welfare improvements. However, economists recognize that income alone is an incomplete indicator of how well residents of a region are doing. Equity is another indicator of economic development. Even if average incomes did not grow, a change from a very unequal distribution of income to one that most people considered more fair could be considered a form of development. Similarly, improvements in the quality of life such as better transportation systems, education, and cultural facilities are also indicators of economic development. Sometimes, indicators of economic development are difficult to quantify, but they are nonetheless important.

Beauregard (1993) correctly pointed out that when we focus on economic development there is a tendency to ignore broader political and social issues that also affect the quality of life in a community. In this book, the theory and tools of economic development focus on production, consumption, and other resource allocation issues. However, we should not lose sight of the fact that local economic development is part of a larger process of community development.

⧖ The Nature of Regions

"Region" refers to a part of an area. In practice, the term is a chameleon, taking meaning from the context of use. For instance, the statement "the region around my house" normally connotes a neighborhood region. However, if someone were to say they lived in a cold region, the phrase would connote a multistate area. As trade between nations increases, international regions are becoming more important and economists are more concerned with multinational regions. In keeping with common usage, both large and small regions are examined in this text.

"Urban" is also a term that has different meanings. An urban area, no matter how it is defined, is a region, although not all regions are urban. Urban places are normally associated with large, high-population-density cities. Yet some places with populations as small as 2,500 are considered urban by the Census Bureau. Thus small villages with only a few stores could be considered urban by the Census Bureau, although such a place might not be considered an urban area as used in everyday conversation.

Many social scientists define "urban" in terms of lifestyle rather than density. Urban society is often contrasted with traditional society. In this sense, urbanization reflects a social change in which diversity, rationality, tolerance, impersonality, functional relationships, and bureaucratic organizations become important characteristics. According to the sociological perspective, the farmer who uses a variety of advanced technologies in production has major capital investments, buys and sells grain futures in a world market, and watches TV broadcasts from around the world via satellite is in the urban sector.

Functional Regions

Functional regions are distinguished by the degree to which they are integrated or the extent to which the component parts interact. If interaction of components within a region is significant compared to interaction with other places, the basis for a functional economic region exists. An area in which local businesses traded with each other more than they traded with the rest of the world would constitute a functional area.

Nodal Regions

Nodal regions are an important type of functional area. A nodal region is based primarily on a hierarchical system of trade relationships. Small business centers may depend on large centers, and both small cities and large centers may depend on a still larger business center for specialized economic goods. The area served by a business center is often referred to as a hinterland, and the larger the hinterland, the larger the business center tends to be. The concept of a nodal region implies that there are regions within regions in the sense that a medium-sized city may have a hinterland of its own even though it is part of the hinterland of a larger city.

Metropolitan Statistical Areas

Metropolitan areas exhibit hierarchical patterns that characterize nodal regions. Specifically, employment and retail activity tends to be concentrated in the central business district and other subcenters throughout the metropolis. The nodes of concentrated economic activity complement contrast with residential areas where the extent of business activity is small. However, the business concentrations and residential areas are dependent upon each other. Many regional policies are best implemented at the metropolitan level because of the interdependence within the region.

The concept of a functional economic area has been operationalized in the statistical construct of metropolitan statistical areas (MSAs). Because of the importance of MSAs to analysis and policy, it may be useful to describe their structure in detail. Central cities are the heart and node of the MSA. Each MSA must include one city with 50,000 or more residents or a Census Bureau-defined urbanized area of at least 50,000 inhabitants and a total MSA population of at least 100,000 (75,000 in New England).

Counties are the building blocks of MSAs. The central county(ies) (containing the central city) plus all contiguous counties that have close economic ties to the central county and are metropolitan in character are included in the MSA. The extent of economic linkage among counties is measured by commuting patterns. The metropolitan character is measured by population density and percentage urban. MSAs in New England are based on groups of cities and towns because there are no counties in New England. However, the intent is to operationalize the same concept of urbanization and integration.

MSAs contain suburbs, or urban communities that are closely linked to the central city. Suburbs include satellite communities and bedroom suburbs. Satellite communities normally have an active local economy, often including a substantial manufacturing base. Frequently, businesses in satellite cities developed independently of the central city. Bedroom suburbs lack an independent economic base. Although a few retail and service stores may be located in bedroom communities, their primary function is to provide a residence for individuals who work elsewhere. Because bedroom communities often provide an environment sheltered from many urban problems, an anonymous wit referred to bedroom communities as a "womb with a view." In addition, there is usually some agricultural activity within the outlying counties of most MSAs. Figure 1.4 presents a stylized picture of an MSA.

An advantage of collecting MSA data by county only rather than by cities or by its urbanized portion is that the geographic boundaries of a county seldom change. Although counties may be added or dropped from particular MSAs, it is relatively easy to establish a consistent time series (data points over period of time) by aggregating data collected for individual counties. In contrast, when city boundaries change or an urbanized area increases, it is usually very difficult or impossible to reconstruct a consistent time series. However, the use of counties as the units from which MSAs are built results in more diversity with the MSA than would be the case if only the most urbanized areas were included.

The rapid growth of metropolitan areas is one of the most important features of economic geography. In the 1950s, about 55% of the U.S. population

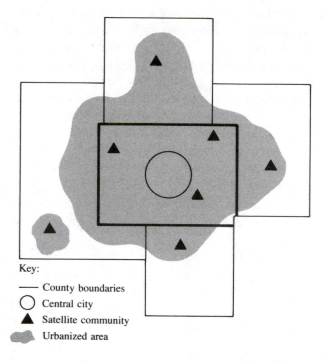

Figure 1.4. Anatomy of an MSA. Metropolitan areas include inner cities, central business districts, various types of suburban areas, and even farms.

lived in metropolitan areas and accounted for only about 5% of the land area. Currently, about 75% of the population of the United States reside in MSAs and account for about 16% of the land area.

Many urban complexes have grown together. As urban areas have over-lapped, commuting and other economic relationships have extended beyond the original metropolitan area.

A consolidated metropolitan statistical area (CMSA) is a combination of contiguous metropolitan areas. It is defined as a metropolitan area that has a population of at least 1 million. The metropolitan components of CMSAs are designated as primary metropolitan statistical areas (PMSAs). For instance, the Cleveland-Akron-Lorain CMSA is composed of the Akron, Cleveland, and Lorain-Elyria PMSAs. PMSAs are similar to MSAs except for their inclusion in a larger metropolitan complex.

Metropolitan growth has also resulted in significant diversity within metropolitan areas. Almost three quarters of the U.S. population lives in metropolitan areas. About 30% of metropolitan residents lives in central cities, and 45% lives in suburbs. Surprisingly, almost one quarter of metropolitan residents lives in areas classified as rural by the Census Bureau. In addition, a large portion of nonmetropolitan residents lives in urban areas. Nearly 40% of the population living in nonmetropolitan areas lives in areas defined as urban by the Census Bureau. The diversity of living arrangements within metropolitan and nonmetropolitan areas shows a further need to unify urban and regional economics.

Homogeneous Regions

Economic development officials sometimes deal with homogeneous regions that are designated on the basis of internal similarity. The many informal belt regions—Corn, Bible, Rust, Sun, Snow, and so forth—are homogeneous regions based on common activities or climate. Likewise, the Appalachian region is distinguished by common economic development problems.

Many neighborhoods are distinguished by ethnic or economic similarity and hence are basically homogeneous regions. The census provides data on census tracts, which are small areas consisting of several blocks. Although the census tracts are not necessarily established on the basis of homogeneity, data on homogeneous neighborhoods are often derived from census tract information.

Administrative Regions

Administrative regions are formed for managerial or organizational purposes. Both private organizations and governments find administrative regions useful. Administrative regions are normally more clearly delineated than either functional or homogeneous regions because administrative regions are formed to clarify spheres of activity for businesses or governments. Administrative regions are also important because they frequently become the basis for policy. Cities, states, and counties are important administrative regions.

Administrative regions are not distinctly different from homogeneous or functional regions. For instance, a company may establish a set of sales districts based on similar tastes for product lines within each district. If

regional offices provide support services for local sales offices, the administrative region will assume characteristics of a functional area as well. Furthermore, once an administrative region is formed, the various components may
develop commonalities that make the region more homogeneous and/or
chains of communication, trade, and control that are characteristic of functional regions may emerge.

The number of governmental regions is numerous. There are approximately 85,000 units of local government in the United States. Within the
Chicago metropolitan area, for example, there are 1,214 units of local government ranging from well-known governments such as cities, counties, and
school districts to many special purpose districts that are nearly unknown to
average citizens, such as water control districts, lighting districts, recreation
districts, and so forth. With so many districts, it is rare that workers in an urban
business will have the same district profile. In the Chicago area, there are 1.7
units of local government per 100,000 population. Many observers believe
that political fragmentation is a major impediment to good government,
whereas others believe that a diversity of governmental units contributes to
wise decision making.

⊠   Summary

The majority of economic development decisions are based on private
costs and benefits. It is therefore important to understand how economists
view economic processes.

Economists build models based on assumptions. "Other things equal" is
one of the most useful assumptions as it allows economists to focus on a few
variables by assuming that other factors are constant. The law of demand
states that as the cost to customers increases, the quantity they will be willing
and able to purchase declines, *other things equal.* The other-things-equal
assumption may be relaxed to provide more complex analysis of how other
variables affect outcomes. Economists also assume that individuals are motivated by self-interest; they seek to maximize utility, or satisfaction. Satisfaction is sometimes interpreted broadly to include such things as emotional
satisfaction or narrowly to include only income or profits.

Market processes coordinate numerous economic decisions between buyers and sellers. Market processes set prices and determine outputs. Price
changes transmit signals to market participants and thereby influence behav-

ior. Supply and demand curves are used to illustrate how prices and outputs are determined in competitive markets. Demand curves show amounts that consumers will purchase at various prices, and supply curves show quantities that producers are willing and able to sell. At the price where supply and demand intersect, the quantity that consumers will buy will equal the amount that businesses produce. Equilibrium will be achieved and price will not change unless either the supply or the demand changes.

The operation of supply and demand, free of governmental restriction, may generate efficient outcomes. However, public goods, externalities or spillovers, monopolies, and imperfect information can result in inefficient markets.

Profits influence business decisions. Profits equal total revenues minus total costs. In a simple case, total revenues equal the price of output times quantities sold. When considering costs, analysts must recognize opportunity cost—alternatives foregone in order to produce.

Economic development includes economic growth but can also include issues of quality of life and income distribution. Qualitative measures of economic development may be difficult to measure, but they are important.

There are various types of regions. A functional region is defined on the bases of the degree of economic integration. Standard metropolitan areas are based on high levels of interaction between the central city(ies), suburbs, and nonurban areas in the region. Counties are the building blocks for MSAs. Homogeneous regions are based on internal similarity. For instance, the Snow Belt represents a homogeneous region. Neighborhoods are often defined on the basis of common characteristics of the residents and may therefore be considered homogeneous regions.

⊠ Note

1. The money value of costs and benefits cannot be determined in the absence of a set distribution of income because the distribution of income affects valuation. For instance, the momentary value of inner-city beautification would probably be larger if inner-city residents were richer.

2

Three Fundamental
and Recurring Issues

Experienced economic development officials recognize that economic development concerns reach into numerous aspects of community life that are not traditionally covered in university economics courses. Perhaps the organization of departments within universities and governments creates an impression that economic development can be separated from other social concerns. In practice, distinctions between social, political, and economic development concerns are fuzzy. Economic development practitioners should recognize that, on the one hand, many issues considered social or political in nature are directly linked to economic development and, on the other hand, traditional economic approaches must be supplemented with ideas from other disciplines to form an effective economic development strategy.

This chapter examines how economists view important urban issues and discusses the limits of traditional economic approaches in developing comprehensive strategies. Three fundamental issues that recur in various forms in development planning are considered: unemployment and low wages, externalities, and public sector decision making.

⊠ Unemployment and Low Wages

Unemployment is a major urban problem, particularly in inner-city areas. Because most families receive the lion's share of their income through work,

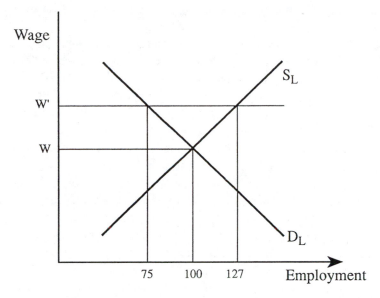

Figure 2.1. A local labor market. There will be no unemployment at wage W. For various reasons, the wage may increase to W', associated with higher levels of unemployment. Efforts to increase the demand for labor will enhance employment and wages.

poverty is often attributed to unemployment and low wages, although there are other causes of poverty as well. Poverty and unemployment are associated with a variety of other urban problems, including poor health, crime, and homelessness. Economists have important insights into the problem of low wages and unemployment.

A Traditional Labor Market Model

Figure 2.1 illustrates a traditional economic employment model. The demand for a particular type of labor in a region is the sum of the demand for labor of establishments. The labor supply curve represents the number of workers in an employment category such as truck drivers. Economists believed that many labor markets are segmented. Workers cannot easily move from one job market to another, so what happens in one job market may have only a weak effect on some other markets. There may be separate labor markets for plumbers, electricians, unskilled workers, and so forth. Because the focus of this section is on low-income earners, the market for unskilled workers is examined.

In the absence of any government involvement in the economy, the level of employment would be 100, as shown in Figure 2.1. The total wage bill for this category of workers would equal the number of labor units hired (100) times the wage rate. If the average income that resulted from the operation of the labor market (allowing for multiple wage earners per household) was below the poverty level, then many individuals in this market would be classified as poor. Currently, a wage rate of $5 per hour, above the minimum wage, would translate to $10,000 per year for a full-time worker employed 50 weeks.

An important wrinkle can be imposed on the traditional model by recognizing that the wage employers pay may be above the equilibrium wage. For instance, the wage rate might be W'. In this case, employers will hire fewer employees and more people would want to work at the higher wage. Unemployment will result. In the case illustrated by Figure 2.1, the level of unemployment at wage W' would be 52 (127 − 75) workers. The higher the wage is above the equilibrium, the greater the level of unemployment will be.

Three explanations for an above-equilibrium wage are common. First, minimum wage laws require an above-equilibrium wage. Minimum wage laws have their greatest impact on unskilled laborers. Whether minimum wage laws hurt or help low- and moderate-income families as a group depends on whether the higher wage effect offsets the lower employment effect. Second, union and other contracts as well as institutionalized wage structures can set wages above equilibrium. Although union wages generally provide an income above the poverty level for those who have jobs, many potential workers are locked out. Third, employers may set wages above the equilibrium level to avoid "shirking" or to induce workers to work harder (Mansfield, 1991). If the level of compensation were set at the equilibrium wage, the workers might not be concerned about being fired because another low-wage job would always be easily attainable. Thus employers may pay above equilibrium to avoid "shirking" or to reduce labor turnover.

Traditional Economic Solutions

Reducing poverty and unemployment is one of the purposes of economic development. In a nutshell, the problem of unemployment and low wages can be addressed by increasing the demand for labor or by preparing workers to enter job markets that they would otherwise be unable to enter.

Job Creation

One of the primary goals of economic development is to create jobs. This goal may be accomplished by encouraging new businesses to locate in the area, encouraging existing businesses to expand, or discouraging existing businesses from decreasing their local activities. Since job creation is a major theme of this book, specific techniques to encourage business are discussed in detail in other chapters. However, the impact of job creation can be thought of as increasing the demand for labor. As the demand for labor increases, the wage rate and employment level will increase. The extent of the wage increase depends on the increase in demand and whether additional workers move into the area, increasing the supply of labor. Wage-induced increases in the size of the area's workforce will dampen the wage effect.

Job creation will address the problem of unemployment and low wages most directly if the jobs that are created match the skill levels of the unemployed and low-income workers or if the unemployed can move into the labor markets where the new jobs are. Evidence indicates that within central cities, most new jobs require high skills that exclude many inner-city residents (Kasarda, 1988). In this case, less-skilled workers either will not benefit from job creation or will benefit indirectly through "trickle down" effects as the direct beneficiaries spend their income.

Governments have also tried direct job creation programs, whereby public sector jobs have been created for low-skilled and unemployed workers. Two problems with this approach have been observed. First, some critics claim the jobs are make-work and have little useful value and may even reinforce poor work attitudes. Second, money that goes into the job creation program may reduce employment elsewhere in the area, resulting in a zero-sum game (one group's gain is offset by another group's loss).

Productivity and Training

Increasing labor productivity will cause the demand for labor to increase. If employees can produce more output and, accordingly, increase the revenues of firms, firms would be willing and able to pay higher wages and possibly employ more workers. Conventional economic theory concludes that workers will be paid their marginal revenue product—the extra revenue attributable to the last worker hired. If the going wage were $6 per hour, but an additional employee could add only $4 per hour to company revenues (net of nonwage expenses), the worker would not be hired. However, if labor productivity could be increased to $7, the firm would hire the additional worker.

Productivity is not always directly recognized. For instance, it is difficult to evaluate the productivity of a school teacher or an economic development official, but it is easy to evaluated the productivity of a piece worker. Because of difficulties in measuring productivity, even effective training may not help some persons. However, for many persons, training may improve their ability to get a job and/or move from a low-paying job to a higher-paying one.

Training programs are one way to increase productivity. Training programs may take the form of teaching direct job-related skills or be aimed more generally at instilling better work habits and teaching basic academic skills or job-hunting techniques. However, there are difficulties associated with most training programs. First, when there are not enough jobs in the economy, there may be nothing to train potential workers to do. A training program that successfully placed its clients might simply bump other qualified workers. A second major problem with training programs is that they often fail to solve behavioral problems that limit employment and income. Journalists and scholars have used phrases like "culture of poverty," "welfare dependency," and "lack of work discipline" to explain why many of the long-term unemployed have failed in the job market even after receiving training.

Reducing Market Barriers and Imperfections

Market barriers and imperfections are an economist's way of saying that markets don't always work according to the perfectly competitive model, which assumes many buyers and sellers, perfect knowledge, resource mobility, and no government interference with the economy. Yet in the real world, such problems abound. The inability of wages to fall is one example of a market imperfection.

Many unemployed workers lack knowledge about available jobs. Lack of knowledge can be a particular problem among the poor who do not have access to suburban labor markets where the opportunities are growing most rapidly. Lack of knowledge about work opportunities also explains why some individuals do not attempt to get as much education as might be beneficial.

Another labor market problem that leads to unemployment is geographic immobility. Often, low-income families are trapped in poor neighborhoods or regions of high unemployment and can't move to growth areas. Such families usually can't afford to move to where jobs are.

Arbitrary discrimination is an "imperfection" that contributes to unemployment. African Americans have about twice the unemployment rate as Whites. Although economists and others have argued about the extent to which Black unemployment is due directly to discrimination and the extent to which it is due to lower education, poor work attitudes, and geographic immobility (these factors may be due to discrimination to some degree as well), there is little doubt that Blacks are discriminated against in attempts to get some jobs.

Economists Don't Have All the Answers

Economists provide important insights into the problems of low wages and unemployment. Job creation, productivity improvements, and reductions in barriers to employment should be important tools in strategies to address employment problems. Nevertheless, a large part of any solution will involve behavioral and institutional changes that are usually outside the traditional sphere of economics. For instance, there is a need to change attitudes and work behaviors among many individuals who are marginally associated with the labor market. Day care, transportation, and health care issues are important. Furthermore, the problem of unemployment and low wages is only part of the larger problem of poverty. Individuals who are unable to work are another group whose problems cannot be addressed through employment policies. Economic development practitioners must be skilled at combining economic insights with insights from other perspectives to realistically address issues of unemployment and poverty.

⊠ Externalities

A variety of urban problems can be subsumed under the heading of externalities, or spillovers. Negative externalities or spillovers occur when costs of activities spill over to parties not voluntarily involved in the transaction. The ubiquity of negative externalities can be appreciated by considering the following spillovers: pollution, sign polluting, nosy neighbors, traffic congestion, unkept properties, and destruction of historic properties. Benefit spillovers are termed positive externalities. The laissez-faire (no government interference) market tends to overproduce goods with negative externalities and underproduce positive externalities. As the quality of life becomes a more important determinant of regional success, development planners will need to increase their efforts to reduce negative externalities and increase positive externalities.

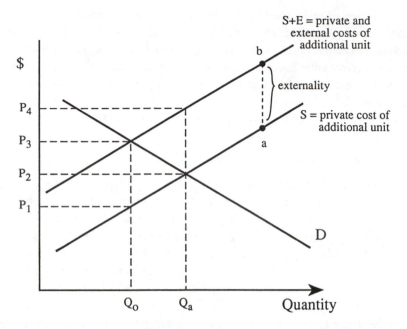

Figure 2.2. Negative externalities. The supply curve represents the private costs of producing additional units. The total social costs including the externalities is represented by the $S + E$ curve. In the absence of government policy, the quantity of output actually produced will exceed the optimal amount because the laissez-faire market will not consider the costs of the negative externalities.

Efforts to increase positive externalities and reduce negative externalities will enhance a region's attractiveness. However, policymakers are more concerned with reducing negative externalities than with increasing positive externalities because negative spillovers are likely to harm others. Negative externalities include various types of pollution and congestion. This section will emphasize efforts to reduce negative externalities. Efforts to increase positive externalities may be treated as a "mirror image" of the negative externality case.

A Negative Externality Model

To understand why negative externalities result in the misallocation of resources, consider Figure 2.2. The supply curve represents the private costs of producing an extra unit of a good. The demand curve represents private value of an additional unit of that good. The units are arranged on the horizontal axis such that the first units are the ones consumers value most and producers can produce at the least cost. High-cost, low-value units are last. The concept of diminishing marginal utility supports the idea that the first units produced and consumed are the most valuable. The concept of increasing marginal costs supports the idea that later units are produced at higher costs.

In a laissez-faire market, output would be Q_a ("a" standing for actual). The private cost of producing the marginal unit, Q_a, is P_2, but production imposes extra costs on third parties of $a - b$. The actual cost of producing the Q_ath unit, including the negative externality, is the private cost of P_2 plus the externality for a total cost $(a - b)$ for a total of P_4.

The optimal level of production is Q_o ("o" standing for optimal). Why is Q_o optimal? On the one hand, at any output level below Q_o, the social benefits from producing an additional unit exceeds the social cost. Therefore, more should be produced because the social gain exceeds the social cost. On the other hand, for any output level above Q_a, the marginal social cost exceeds marginal social benefits. It would be inefficient to produce such units.

The externality model explains why there are too many cars on the roads during rush hour. Imagine there are Q_o cars using the roads and an additional driver is considering a trip. The benefits to the potential marginal driver would be slightly below P_3 as read from the demand curve. The private costs to the marginal driver would include gasoline, automobile depreciation, and time. The private costs would be slightly above P_1. Because the private benefits outweigh the costs, the trip would be taken.

However, the driver would not consider the costs that the trip (the $Q_o + 1$ trip) imposes on others. The two most important external costs are the delays and aggravation imposed on other drivers and the extra pollution. If these costs were considered, the total costs of the trip (private costs plus the negative externalities) would be slightly above P_3. As explained above, the benefits are slightly below P_3. Thus the $Q_o + 1$ trip has higher social costs than benefits. If it is taken, a net social loss will occur.

Positive externalities should be encouraged because the laissez-faire market tends to underproduce goods that provide positive externalities. Education is often cited as a service that provides positive externalities. To the extent that education prepares students to be good citizens or provides uncompensated benefits to society, education provides positive externalities. Under certain circumstances, providing jobs for the unemployed generates positive externalities. Taxpayers, retail merchants, wholesale suppliers, and unemployed individuals may all receive spillover benefits from business expansion.

Density, Population Size, and Externalities

The externality problem increases rapidly as urban density increases, so economic development officials in large cities are likely to be more concerned than their counterparts in rural areas about the need to control negative externalities. A Robinson Crusoe would not have to worry about externalities because there would be no one to impose them. The link between population, density, and negative externalities may be one of the reasons why cities in general and particularly some of the older cities in the eastern and north-central regions are considered to have quality-of-life problems.

To understand why negative externalities escalate at an increasing rate as population size and density increase, consider a simple model developed by Baumol (1967). Assume a given geographic area where as population increases so does density.

Let the number of externality causing events increase in proportion to the population. Thus

$$\text{ECE} = P \times q, \tag{2-1}$$

where

    ECE = externality causing events
    P = population
    q = the number of externality causing events per person

Next, assume that the number of persons affected by each externality-causing event will be a fraction of the population. For instance, on average, each externality-causing event may affect one third of the population. Therefore,

$$\text{PHE} = P \times w, \tag{2-2}$$

where

    PHE = persons harmed per externality
    P = population

w = the fraction of the population harmed per externality

The total number of persons harmed by externalities (TNPH) would equal the number of externality-causing events (ECE) times the number of persons harmed per externality event (PHE). Thus Equation 2-1 may be multiplied by Equation 2-2 to derive the total number of persons harmed by externalities (TNPH):

$$\text{TNPH} = (P \times w) \times (P \times q) = P^2 wq. \qquad (2\text{-}3)$$

Notice that, as population increases, the number of persons harmed increases at an exponential or increasing rate. The increase is due to the fact that additional persons both cause externalities and suffer from those caused by others.

Traditional Economic Solutions

The standard economic solution to negative externality problems is to develop mechanisms that force the firm to bear the externality costs. In so doing, the firm's costs of producing additional units (the supply curve) will increase to the point where the firm's marginal private costs equal the social costs of producing an additional unit. In economic terminology, the cost of the externality becomes internalized. The firm will reduce output to Q_0 in Figure 2.2.

Imposition of taxes on the polluting firm equal to the cost of the externalities is one technique for ensuring that external costs are considered by producers of externalities. The externality tax will increase the producer's private costs. Imagine a tax of $a - b$ per unit imposed on the good or service shown in Figure 2.2. The effect of such a tax would be to increase the curve labeled S upward to the left so that it would equal the curve labeled $S + E$. In effect, the tax would force the producer to consider the costs borne by third parties in the production decision.

Another technique for controlling externalities is to provide transferable externality rights. For example, if a firm pollutes (an externality), it may be required to purchase the "right to pollute" from other businesses. Consequently, a price must be paid for the generation of externalities. Under this system, even if given the "right to pollute" by government, firms still must pay a price to pollute. Those that do not generate significant levels of pollution—perhaps because they practice more effective abatement techniques—may sell their "right to pollute" to others. Accordingly, firms that pollute must either purchase rights to pollute or forego the opportunity to sell their pollution rights.

Taxing externalities and transferable externality rights have an advantage compared to more direct government action. Firms have an incentive not only to reduce production of goods with externalities but also to find new production technologies that will result in fewer negative externalities. In other words, the motive of self- interest and profit maximization can be harnessed to reduce externalities.

Economists generally favor approaches to the externality problem that provide firms with incentives to reduce pollution while at the same time allowing firms the flexibility to address the problem in a variety of ways. Approaches to the externality problem that are generally disfavored by economists are prohibitions, legal limits, and regulatory standards. A law forbidding externality-creating activity is an example of a prohibition. Economists generally believe that there is an optimal level of externalities, so prohibition would result in too little pollution or other externalities. Legal limits would force a firm to reduce externalities, possibly to the optimal level. However, legal limits would not provide incentives to reduce the level of externality beyond the legal limit, even if it could be done at a low cost. Regulatory standards include rules that require how a product should be produced or how by-products should be disposed in order to control externalities. Regulatory approaches assume that governmental officials have substantial knowledge about production and abatement technologies for specific industrial processes. The regulatory approach discourages firms from seeking alternative production techniques that might reduce externalities at a lower cost.

Activities that generate positive externalities may be subsidized. The subsidy lowers the cost to the private party encouraging more output. Thus, to encourage better neighborhood upkeep, a government might subsidize home improvement work. To encourage job creation, which can carry positive externalities, a city may provide job creation incentives to businesses. An important policy principle with respect to externalities is "Subsidize what you wish to encourage, tax what you wish to discourage."

Economists Do Not Have All the Answers

Economic analysts have made significant contributions to policy formulations that will reduce negative externalities and thereby improve market efficiency, the quality of life, and economic development prospects. However, the contributions of economists are limited. One problem with the externality concept is that almost any activity has some associated negative or positive externalities (Rhoads, 1985, p. 188). Social and ethical beliefs and traditional standards are necessary to determine which externalities ought to be addressed. Second, feelings about a community may influence the level of externalities without government intervention. Negative externalities may be reduced in societies where individuals have strong regard for their community and concern for the feelings of other citizens (Swaney, 1981). For instance, in areas where neighbors "look out for each other," many distressing neighborhood externalities, such as noise pollution, speeding cars, and unkept lawns, may be reduced without any government action.

Finally, the concept of optimal level of pollution may be subject to moral and ethical concerns that cannot be quantified in the economic models. For instance, the economic model does not directly address issues of the different impact of externalities on various groups. Pollution affects the poor more than wealthy groups both because the rich will pay more for environments free of negative externalities and because the wealthy have the political power to avoid negative spillovers. Does that mean officials should be less concerned about spillover effects on the poor? Other examples of moral questions not addressed in the traditional economic approach are the following: How should adverse health effects of pollution be valued? How should future generations be considered? Do humans have a moral obligation to care for the earth? Clearly, political and social processes must be used in addressing these and other problems associated with externalities.

⊠ **Improving the Public Sector**

A final area where economic analysis can provide important insights into policy development is improving the operations of the public sector. A well-functioning public sector can encourage economic development in many ways, including providing services to businesses, creating an efficient land use pattern, contributing to a high quality of life, and, in general, providing a good mix of services and taxes. Economists have many useful ideas about improving the efficiency of local governments. Yet, as in the previous two cases, economic theory does not provide the complete solution.

Perverse Incentives: A Public Choice Perspective

Public choice is a branch of economics that studies decision-making processes in the public sector. The public choice perspective provides insights about governmental institutions and incentives that help explain behavior that leads to poor government performance. The public choice perspective has provided theoretical support for many efforts to bring competitive forces into government and make governments operate more like market institutions. The public choice perspective may also assist local development officials in their increasingly frequent attempts to influence state and federal government decisions.

The concept of "economic man" is that individuals are motivated by their own self-interest. Within limits, most economists accept the idea that individuals seek their own self-interest. The laissez-faire market is supposed to work well because the invisible hand directs self-interested individuals to do what is in the public interest. Government action may be required if individuals' pursuit of self-interest conflicts with the public interest. But is there an invisible hand in the public sector?

A naive view of government is that public officials are altruistic in contrast to the selfish motives that dominate the private sector. This view may be supplemented by the contention that public officials know what is good for their community better than does the typical citizen. Thus the naive view leads some to believe that public officials will do what is in the community interest regardless of their self-interest. In contrast, the public choice perspective is that all people act in their self-interest, regardless of whether they are a public official, private sector entrepreneur, or the employee of a business. Therefore, government reward systems must be designed so that when government officials act in their self-interest they will also do what is in the public interest.

Elected Officials

Rather than trying to achieve the public good, elected officials may use their office to maximize their self-interest subject (usually) to legal constraints. Because "self interest" is too broad a concept to be useful in predicting behavior, many public choice economists assume that public officials seek to maximize their chances of being reelected or of gaining higher office. Frequently, politicians will enhance their chances of being reelected by doing what is in the public interest. Thus prospects of reelection serve as an invisible hand. However, there may be instances when self-interest of officials and public interest conflict.

The public choice perspective has significant implication for economic development. Political officials are often judged by their ability to attract high-profile economic development projects. Consequently, insecure or ambitious politicians may feel pressure to provide subsidies to businesses in excess of the amount that is necessary to achieve legitimate economic development objectives. Consider a politician attempting to attract a new business establishment. The political benefits of such developments may accrue in the very short term in the form of favorable publicity and a sense of community progress. Yet the subsidy costs may be incurred in the form of higher taxes spread into the distant future. Similarly, when new public facilities are built, local economic impacts are felt quickly, even before the project is complete in the form of construction jobs. The higher tax costs may be postponed for several years. Many politicians have short-term time horizons; in the extreme, they may look ahead only to their next election. Consequently, a politician may feel the need to provide excessive development incentives to stimulate business activities and employment near election times or if there is a major political need for a success story.

The public choice perspective also explains the power of narrow special interest groups in the economic development process. Most citizens are uninformed and/or don't care about the outcome of most public decisions. The costs (effort) of obtaining information on issues that barely affect them are too high to make it worthwhile. However, the few who are concerned about an issue—citizens who may be directly affected—will be the ones who make their voices heard. Suppose, for instance, that a local plant has threatened to close unless it receives an economic development subsidy. The employees are likely to be organized, vocal, and very focused on the single issue of the subsidy for their plant. Their votes and campaign contributions may hinge on the outcome of that single issue. Citizens not directly affected may have only a vague idea about the costs and related issues. Their votes will not hinge on the outcome of the single issue. To get reelected, it may behoove politicians to decide issues in favor of special-interest groups. The majority of the general population will not know or remember the costly special treatment the business received, but the employees and owners may show their gratitude next election. The strength of special interest groups applies to neighborhood improvement projects, roads, and other public services as well as economic development projects.

Jones and Bachelor (1984) reviewed efforts by Detroit officials to attract the "poletown" automobile plant, which would replace two older facilities in the Detroit area that were being closed. The authors concluded that the incentives offered to General Motors were excessive and not in the public interest. The oversubsidization resulted in a "corporate surplus" at taxpayer expense. The excessive subsidies were the result of General Motor's powerful bargaining position and the mayor's need for an economic development "victory" to help him win an upcoming election.

Bureaucrats

Bureaucrats may also lack incentives to do what is in the public interest. Bureaucrats may seek more pay, better perquisites of office, or hassle-free work environments rather than better serving the citizens according to the public choice view. Public employees often operate under looser constraints than do employees in profit-seeking firms because of the following:

- Public outputs are often difficult to measure (i.e., effective teaching).
- Responsibility for performance is often vague ("buck passing" is likely).
- There is no "bottom line," such as profits, to measure success. Public agencies have been shown to produce some outputs at higher costs than their private sector counterparts, thus providing evidence of inefficiency. For instance, public garbage pickup is more costly than private garbage collection.

Besides their tendency toward inefficiency, public employees may have incentives to expand services beyond the level desired by most citizens. After all, most people would rather be the director of an agency with a $10 million budget and 50 employees than of an agency with a $100,000 budget and a secretary. Consequently, department heads lobby legislatures and local councils for more funds and new programs for their agencies. Essentially, bureaucrats become another special-interest group. Economic development agencies have grown rapidly in recent years. This growth reflects the increasing importance of local economic development, but it may also reflect bureaucrats seeking to expand their authority.

Public workers also constitute an important voting bloc that would probably support higher pay and better working conditions for local government workers. During the early 1970s, the voting power of New York City employees and their relatives was so great an influence on the size of public employment and the wages of employers that this power may have contributed to New York's fiscal crisis.

Traditional Economic Solutions

Efforts to construct an invisible hand in government are suggested by the economic analysis, but how? Currently, some observers have suggested privatizing services previously provided by government. Other reform groups are attempting to make government more responsive by introducing marketlike mechanisms within government. Suggestions for school or housing vouchers are examples. Through public programs such as these, the citizens are given the ability to select the schools or housing types they like best, similar to shoppers. By giving citizens choices, public agencies that do not provide adequate services will lose "customers" and may eventually be terminated. Public officials may receive signals about the kinds of services consumers want as they vote with their vouchers. Vouchers, and other marketlike systems, may also increase the range of "citizen consumer" choice. If the parents of a child have a voucher for his education that they can use at a variety of schools, they will select the school that provides the type of educational strategies and services they want. Thus, through modifications of market models, some reformers are trying to replicate market systems that help make public officials more accountable.

Some observers believe that changes in governmental structure may improve governmental efficiency. One approach is to decentralize government in the hope that local officials will be more accountable than officials in Washington, D.C. or a state capital. Creating small units of government that must compete with each other is another strategy.

Better use of pricing policies is another way that economists have suggested to make the public sector more efficient. Wilbur Thompson (1984) stated that "the failure to use price . . . in the public sector of the metropolis is at the root of many, if not most of our urban problems" (p. 13). Citizens tend to use "free" resources to the point where they derive no more satisfaction from their use. Yet the resources needed to produce the "free" goods are costly. Thus the costs of providing additional units of "free" public services often exceed the value of the benefits received. The popularity of user fees represents another attempt to make the public sector more like a market system. Thompson suggested charging more for downtown parking, particularly "peak hour" parking, and raising fees at public recreational facilities.

Higher prices would discourage the use of overcrowded facilities, thus reducing congestion. Thompson also called for providing different pay rates for teachers and police officers who work in "tough" areas. Differential pay would attract good teachers and police officers to the areas where they are most needed.

Unfortunately, individuals who use public services constitute an important constituency for keeping prices low. For instance, bus riders will pressure politicians to keep bus prices low while most of the public is disinterested. Therefore, there is a tendency to underprice public services. Externalities are also a problem of government coordination. There are many spillovers between local governments in a metropolitan economy. For instance, one community may undertake quality-of-life or economic development programs that will benefit other communities. Under such circumstances, communities may reduce expenditures on amenities and attempt to "free ride" on the spending of other jurisdictions.

Many localities are trying to develop tax sharing and coordinated spending programs to avoid interjurisdictial free riding and ensure that suburban communities work cooperatively to enhance the region's prospects. For instance, in Montgomery County, Ohio, jurisdictions contribute to a common economic development fund. The money is used to encourage economic development throughout the county. Officials recognize that job creation will help individuals living throughout the county, not just residents of the city where the job is created.

Economists Do Not Have All the Answers

Developing an invisible hand in government is a step toward improving government performance by making public officials more responsive and accountable. However, attempts to make governments more marketlike are constrained by many non-economic factors. Governments are intended to do things that markets will not do. Many public decisions involve issues that transcend economic calculus, such as which amenities provide a high quality of life, what values schools should instill, who should be exempt from taxes, and how much effort should be directed toward helping the homeless. Economists lack the tools to determine what the distribution of income should be. Furthermore, to impose a rigorous invisible hand on government officials would require that the costs and benefits of governmental actions on various groups could be reasonably estimated. The tools used to make such estimates are too imprecise. Few citizens want governments to act exactly like a business. The American political tradition is based on the belief that public service and citizenship should be more than exercises in self-interest. To reduce government to nothing more than an arena where self-interest is pursued would rend an important strand in the social fabric. Consensus building often involves political horse trading that is similar to market exchange. Sometimes, groups must be persuaded to forego their self-interest for the benefit of the larger community.

⧓ Summary

Economic analyis can inform policy on a wide variety of urban issues. However, economic analysis by itself seldom provides a comprehensive analysis of any problem. Social, political, ethical, and other factors must be considered to provide a complete analysis and a workable policy. This chapter used three perennial urban issues as springboards to explore the strengths and limitations of economic analysis.

Unemployment and low wages can be analyzed within the context of labor supply and demand curves. Because of the variety of labor, labor markets may be segmented. The problem of low earnings among unskilled workers can be attributed to a low equilibrium wage. The related problem of unemployment can be illustrated as the result of a wage above the equilibrium. Increased labor productivity and job creation will increase labor demand, wages, and/or employment. Improved productivity can also help workers move from one job category or labor market to another. Reducing market barriers and imperfections, such as arbitrary discrimination, can also improve employment and income prospects for some groups.

Economic solutions are useful in addressing low-wage and unemployment problems. Unfortunately, economic analysis does not provide a comprehensive solution. The need to change attitudes and environments as well as providing support services suggests the importance of knowledge outside the scope of economics.

Numerous urban problems can be understood through the concept of externalities. Negative externalities occur when costs of activities spill over to parties not voluntarily involved in the transaction. Positive externalities are a mirror-image of negative externalities. Externalities are a particular problem in urban areas because as population increases so does the number of persons affected by each externality event. A traditional economic approach to negative externality problems is to increase the cost of negative externalities to the offending party, thus discouraging their production. Economists favor approaches to negative externality reduction that provide firms with flexibility rather than prohibitions, legal limits, and regulatory standards.

Economists do not have all the answers regarding how to address externality problems. Because almost any activity is associated with some externality, ethical and political considerations are necessary to determine which and to what degree externalities should be addressed.

The public sector may be improved by recognizing that public officials are motivated by self-interest and structuring incentives accordingly. Privatization, intergovernmental competition, vouchers, and better public pricing are ways to improve governmental efficiency. However, many public decisions involve issues that transcend economic calculus. Most citizens do not want the government to act like a business, nor do citizens want public officials to seek only self-interest.

Business Location, Expansion, and Retention

Economic development officials historically paid overwhelming attention to attracting firms that were either new or were considering a relocation. During the past decade, many local development officials concluded that communities can generate more jobs by encouraging local businesses to expand or at least maintain their current location. Most of the locational factors that contribute to a firm's decision to locate in an area also influence a company's decision to expand.

The purpose of this chapter is to develop a perspective on a firm's decision to locate or expand in an area and to provide development practitioners with a knowledge base for influencing such decisions. Although the chapter emphasizes profit-oriented firms, the discussion has implication for the locational choices of nonprofit organizations.

⊠ Locational Factors

Every organization will be influenced by many of the locational factors discussed below but in varying degrees. When selecting a location, organizations are generally required to make trade-offs among desired locational features. The trade-offs will differ, depending on establishment characteristics. For instance, profit-making organizations will be influenced by profit considerations, political institutions by public opinion, and charitable organizations by particular aspects of their mission.

Inertia

Inertia is perhaps the strongest locational factor, yet it is often unrecognized. Once a firm is established at a location, many forces operate to keep it where it is, even when a new facility is required. First, the reasons for the initial location may not have changed. The same factors that supported the original choice could cause a firm to select that location again. This is particularly true if success has made a new facility necessary to increase capacity.

Second, the economic and social structures of an area may evolve to reinforce the initial choice. In a symbiotic or "coevolutionary" relationship, the firm supports the community and the community develops in ways that support the firm (Norgaard, 1984); they evolve in ways that support (or use) each other. In concrete terms, a firm will develop ties to other producers, buyers, and employees. These ties may be severed or at least not function as effectively if the firm relocates. For instance, a firm may have a local supplier that can accommodate unusual fabrication needs. The business ties may even be cemented by personal friendships. Although similar types of firms may be located in other cities, the reliability and adaptability of alternative suppliers may be uncertain.

Building cooperative working relationships among firms and with local governments can be a powerful business retention strategy for economic officials. In addition, economic development officials have been increasingly concerned not only with the immediate job/income impacts of new facility locations but with the long-range effects on community development.

Third, a firm that relocates will lose some of its workers. While such a loss may not be critical to some firms or other businesses, certain skilled workers may be essential. For instance, a research facility may be hesitant to relocate to another region for fear of breaking up a research team. Key researchers may not choose to move if they like the local environment. The local environment, in turn, may have developed a set of amenities that appeal to high-paid, high-skilled workers via the process of coevolutionary development. The growing two-income families increase the reluctance to move. Schmenner (1982) reported that more than 60% of plant expansions were motivated in part by the desire to keep the management team together rather than risk separations if a larger facility were built elsewhere.

Transportation Cost-Minimizing Models

Transportation costs are the most thoroughly analyzed location factor because manufacturing activities are sensitive to transportation costs and they are relatively easy to quantify. Transportation cost models fit the tools economists have. Products that have high shipping costs (for either inputs or outputs) relative to the value of the final product tend to be sensitive to transportation costs or "transportation oriented."

Market and Material Orientation

Orientation implies a locational tendency that could be altered by other considerations. Market-oriented producers tend to locate near the market in part because the final products tend to be more expensive to ship from the production site to the market. Therefore, it saves transportation costs if the product is produced at the market. Activities that add a resource that is more or less equally available everywhere (ubiquitous) tend to locate near markets. For instance, soft drinks are considered weight gaining because the materials, glass, syrup, and so forth are shipped to the bottler where water, the ubiquitous input, is added. Thus by locating near the market rather than near the sugar cane or some other supplier the producer avoids shipping the water all the way to market. Products that are hazardous to transport, bulky, perishable, or fragile also tend to be market oriented because of the relatively expensive costs of shipping to the market.

Material-oriented activities tend to locate near material inputs. Many material-oriented activities tend to be weight losing—the final product weighs significantly less than the principal input. It makes sense for a sawmill to locate near the forest because, in the process of milling, the inputs lose weight. Likewise, chemical producers that use coal in their production process locate in coal-producing regions because most of the coal burns during production. It is less expensive to ship the chemicals than to transport the tons of coal necessary to produce the chemicals. Meat packing is material oriented because it is cheaper to ship the butchered meat than live cattle. Besides weight-losing products, activities tend to locate near the inputs when the inputs are bulky, heavy, fragile, perishable, hazardous, or otherwise expensive to transport relative to the final product.

End Point and Transshipment Locations

The discussion of material- and market-oriented activities implies that a location at either the market or the material source would be likely. Only if the transportation costs of shipping the material to the market equaled the costs of shipping the product to the market would the transportation costs be equal at the market and material sites and all points in between. Such an equality of transportation costs would occur only by coincidence.

The pull of the market and material sites is bolstered by two additional factors: extra handling costs and nonlinear rate structures. First, a location between the two sites would normally require extra terminal (loading and unloading) costs. If the production site were located between the materials site and the market, the inputs would have to be loaded at the material site, transported to the production site, unloaded, processed, and reloaded at the production site, and the final product transported to and unloaded at the market. Thus a midpoint location requires an extra handling process.

A second factor that favors the market or material site rather than midpoint locations is that transportation systems frequently charge customers less per mile for long hauls than for short hauls. It costs less than twice as much to travel 200 miles as it does to travel 100 miles, even after accounting for loading-unloading costs. Thus it is less expensive to transport a product or input the entire distance between the material site and the market than it is to make two short trips.

Transshipment points represent an important exception to the general locational advantage of market and material sites. They are junctures in the transportation network where loading and unloading cannot be avoided. Because shipments would have to be interrupted in any event, production locations at transshipment points may not increase transportation costs. For instance, before the technology was developed to construct bridges that could span major rivers, goods transported by land routes had to be unloaded and placed on barges to cross the rivers. The transshipment function contributed to the development of St. Louis. Port cities on the East and West Coast also have transshipment functions.

The Principle of Median Location

The tendency for establishments that produce outputs with high transportation costs to locate at the market has been explained. But what if the market itself is dispersed? In that case, such establishments tend to locate in the center of their market. This tendency is known as the principle of median location. An example illustrates the principle. Assume that the production costs, quantity demanded, and price are not affected by location. Transportation costs of the output are assumed to be proportional to distance. This might be

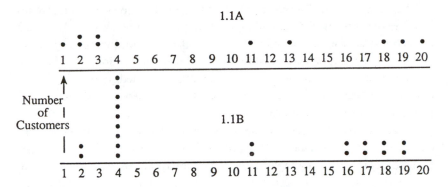

Figure 3.1. The principle of median location illustrates the tendency of market-oriented activities to locate at the point where half of the customers are on either side. A large population cluster tends to attract market-oriented activities even if other customers are not located at the point of the population cluster.

approximated by the case of a pizza parlor that delivers at a uniform price anywhere in an area. Assume the customers, denoted by dots, are distributed as shown in Figure 3.1 and each customer requires one delivery per week. Each numbered hash mark indicates a block. Further assume that each delivery requires one trip—doubling-up to serve both blocks 2 and 4 in one trip is not allowed.

Where should the market-oriented activity locate if segment 1.1A of Figure 3.1 represented the market? Intuitively, many people believe a location on block 11 would be the best choice because it is about in the middle of the market. But that solution is incorrect. Block 4 would be the transportation cost-minimizing location.

To see why block 4 is optimal, suppose the firm relocated from block 4 to 11. On the one hand, the shift would save 5 blocks' travel when serving customers on blocks 11, 13, 18, 19, and 20—a total saving of 30 blocks traveled (6 blocks × 5 customers). On the other hand, an extra 6 blocks of movement would be added for customers on blocks 1, 2, 3, and 4, or a total of 36 travel blocks (6 blocks × 6 customers). Thus the travel costs would increase due to the move. Likewise, any move from block 4 to lower-numbered blocks would increase total travel costs. In general, market-oriented block activities will tend to locate at the median (where half of the customers are on one side and half are on the other side) rather than in the geographic middle of a market.

Segment 1.1B of Figure 3.1 shows the same locational problem, but a "city" exists at block 4. Again, it might seem as though block 11 or 16 would be the most appropriate location. However, the same reasoning used in the previous paragraph indicates that block 4, the median location, would be the minimum transportation cost point for this market-oriented commodity. Large cities tend to be the median location of customers and hence are the locational preference for distribution-oriented firms.

The principle of median location is useful for illustrating locational tendencies of market-oriented firms. However, it is not relevant to some situations because factors such as multiple inputs and multiple markets are not considered.

Road Systems and Multiple Inputs

The above discussion assumed only one input and that the locational choice was limited to a location on a single road. Let's complicate the situation by introducing road systems, multiple input sources, and markets. The concept of locational weights can be useful in analyzing these situations.

The *locational weight of the product* is the cost of shipping one unit of the product one mile. The *locational weight of the input* is the cost of shipping one mile enough of the input to produce one unit of the product.

Figure 3.2 illustrates several possible road systems and shows how the concept of ideal weight can be used to analyze various situations. Case A is an instance where the firm would locate in the middle of the pulls. Moving north of the minimum transport cost point would increase transportation costs per unit by $8 ($5 + $3) per mile while saving only $7 per unit per mile. In contrast, Case B illustrates an instance where the ideal weight at the end point offsets the counterpulls. Moving away from the endpoint would save only $8 ($5 + $3) while costing an extra $10 per unit per mile. Case C shows how a midpoint location may minimize transportation costs if the other weights pull in opposite directions. Case D illustrates the effects of a dominant weight even though there are several small inputs or markets. Case E is interesting because it represents a classic locational triangle, with roads connecting only the tips. In this case, the largest weight, 7, would be sufficient to attract production to that site. In contrast, as a triangle flattens to approach a line, as in Case F, the situation becomes more like Case A, and the midpoint location tends to minimize transportation costs.

Of course, reality presents even more complicated problems than those addressed in Figure 3.2. In practice, a locational planner may have to choose

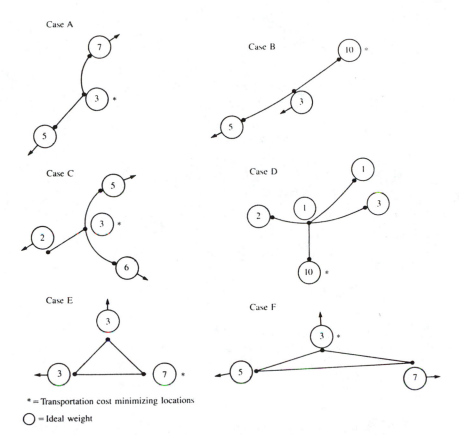

* = Transportation cost minimizing locations

○ = Ideal weight

Figure 3.2. Alternative transportation systems. A fixed transportation system limits possible locations, but ideal weights are still important in determining the transportation cost-minimizing points.

between good and bad roads, alternative routes, and so forth. Nevertheless, the kind of analysis shown in Figure 3.2 provides a foundation for understanding more complicated situations.

Production Costs

Transportation costs have traditionally received more attention than other locational factors because of their importance to many critical manufacturing

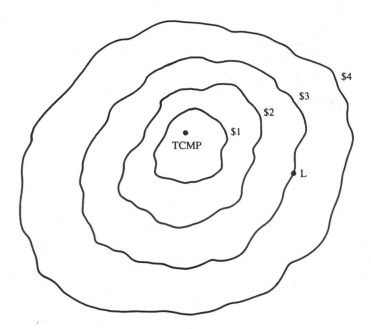

Figure 3.3. Location at a low-production-cost area. Isodopanes show equal transportation cost points above the cost-minimizing site. If production costs can be reduced by more than the increased transportation costs, the alternative location rather than TCMP will be the production site.

processes, such as iron and steel production. The early studies of location placed primary emphasis on the need to minimize transportation costs. However, transportation costs are becoming relatively less important for three reasons. First, manufacturing—which depends heavily on transportation—has decreased in importance. Second, technology has lowered the cost of transportation compared to other inputs. Both direct and manufacturing technologies use inputs that are easier to transport. The greater the product value compared to the cost of shipment, the lesser the importance attached to shipping costs relative to other costs. Finally, the range of variance in other costs of production has become more widely recognized.

Production cost differentials have traditionally been analyzed by examining whether the lower production cost differentials offset the higher transportation costs. In Figure 3.3, the transportation cost-minimizing point is shown as "TCMP." Around the TCMP are lines that show the increased transportation cost associated with moving away from the minimum transportation cost point. These lines are known as isodopanes ("iso" means equal and "dopane" means cost) or isocost lines. Let point L be a low-cost production point. Perhaps energy and/or labor costs are cheaper at L. If the per-unit cost savings are greater than $3, the establishment should locate at L rather than the TCMP. If the savings are less than $3, then the TCMP is the most profitable location.

Labor Costs

Firms that have significant labor costs relative to the value of the final product tend to be labor oriented. Leather, insurance services, and textiles are examples of labor-oriented industries. Currently, many office activities are relocating from the central city to the suburbs to gain access to the "pink collar" workforce that has developed due to the rise of two-wage-earner families.

The Prevailing Wage

A region's prevailing wage rates are an important indicator of labor costs. They represent the wage of a typical worker in a given job category. An area has many prevailing wage rates because there are many different categories of labor. A firm employing unskilled workers would be interested in a different prevailing wage than a firm employing typists. Within a metropolitan area, labor markets are not usually segmented by neighborhood or suburb. Therefore, the prevailing wage for a particular labor type will be the same throughout the metropolitan area. Accordingly, prevailing wage rates affect the choice of region or metropolitan area, but they are not important determinants of the site within the area.

Wage rates alone do not accurately reflect labor costs for several reasons. First, locational decision makers are concerned with the entire compensation package—fringe benefit costs as well as hourly wages. Second, productivity differences can cause labor costs to differ between regions even when hourly compensation is equal. If workers in area A produce twice the hourly output as workers in area B while using equal amounts of other inputs, the compensation rate in A could be higher than in B and yet labor cost per unit of output could be lower in A. Some analysts would argue that labor in some cities is paid more than elsewhere because workers are more productive. Education, work habits, and willingness to cooperate with management are elements of productivity.

Although it is important, labor productivity is difficult to measure, particularly in the service sector. The Department of Commerce publishes data in a useful publication, *County Business Patterns,* that allow researchers to calculate the total dollar value of output divided by the size of the labor force. Although this information can be used to approximate labor productivity, it does not account for different amounts of capital or other inputs used in production. Furthermore, if a region's high productivity is due to better management rather than a capable workforce, the productivity difference will not justify higher compensation for workers.

A third difficulty in using prevailing wage rates as a measure of labor costs is that employers may be able to hire workers at amounts substantially below an area's prevailing wage rate. A study by White (1987) found that workers in Milwaukee who had experienced substantial spells of unemployment were willing to work for wages well below their previous wage and below the prevailing wage in the area. A firm that measures labor costs by the prevailing wage in the industry would overlook the fact that unemployed workers will accept substantially less pay. The weakening of unions in recent years has enhanced the ability of new firms to hire at below the local union wage. Of course, some employers may fear that workers may not remain satisfied with wages below the local prevailing rate. Therefore, firms may choose to assume that wages will increase to the prevailing level. Considerations of future wage levels cannot be rigorously quantified, but neither can they be ignored.

Unionization

Unionization is often mentioned as a locational factor related to labor cost. The common perception is that unions increase compensation and promote work rules that reduce productivity. Both factors increase labor costs. In recent years, states with right-to-work laws (laws allowing employees not to join unions) have experienced more rapid employment growth than those without right-to-work laws. This has been interpreted as indicating that employers believe unionization causes labor costs to increase. In light of several empirical studies, Schmenner (1981) concluded that "right to work laws . . . are often the most effective public policies" for attracting new firms (p. 7). Unionization may be particularly detrimental to branch plant locations where a skilled, flexible, but highly paid workforce is considered less important than a cooperative, low-paid workforce that can perform routine work. Bartik (1984) found that "a 10 percent increase in the percentage unionization of a state's labor force is estimated to cause a 30-45 percent decrease in the number of new branch plants" (p. 19).

Quality of Life

Increasingly, economic development officials believe that if the local quality of life could be improved, economic development would be enhanced. Amenities refer to quality of life enhancing features. Regional amenities include museums, good weather, roads, and schools, and other public services and a variety of other factors that may only indirectly influence production costs. Universities are an especially notable source of life-quality improvement by providing cultural, sports, and educational outlets.

Amenities have become more important because many industries, particularly in high-tech sectors, have become more "footloose" or freed from traditional, cost-oriented locational pulls. A locational decision maker may choose a site with more amenities or a better quality of life if other direct-cost factors are about equal, and many firms will select amenity-rich environments even when other things are not equal.

Amenities may allow firms to recruit more productive workers or recruit workers at lower costs. Technically skilled researchers and creative employees value communities with a good quality of life. Because individuals at the top of their professions can almost always obtain jobs wherever they choose to live, they would work in an area with a poor quality of life only if the wage compensation was substantially higher than elsewhere or if the job was particularly challenging. A good quality of life may help attract and retain less skilled workers at lower wage rates as well.

Amenity-rich areas may experience increases in the demand for property, causing real estate values and rents to rise. In this case, production costs in amenity-rich areas may be high because the company's land rents and taxes (to pay for public amenities) are high. Roback (1982) used weather-related variables such as the number of cloudy days and the number of heating-degree days (days that are cold and require heating) to measure quality of life. She concluded that amenities both lower wages and increase rents. In spite of higher rents, business behavior indicates that amenities exert a strong pull.

Taxes

Traditionally, many economists have not considered taxes a major locational factor because they are a small percentage of business costs. However, several recent studies have challenged this position. Currently, state and local taxes appear to have at least a moderate influence on industrial location and economic growth. Bartik (1992) examined 57 studies regarding the relationship between all types of state and local taxes and local employment growth. He concluded that a 10% increase in taxes will cause a 3.3% decline in job growth in the long run.

There are a variety of taxes that influence where a business will locate, but they do not all have the same impact. Personal income taxes may indirectly affect labor costs as workers require higher compensation to offset higher taxes. Perceived taxes may directly affect the locational decision by influencing the preferred location of high-paid executives who influence the location decision. Wasylenko (1984) and Romans and Sabrahamanyan (1979) have shown that high personal tax rates have detrimental effects on regional growth.

Corporate income taxes directly affect after-tax profits and so may be a more direct locational factor. Bartik (1984) found that capital-intensive industries were particularly sensitive to state corporate profits taxes.

The real estate and property taxes are especially important intraregional locational factors because there are substantial variations in property tax rates within a region (Charney, 1983). Most states and metropolitan regions have both high and low property tax areas.

Business taxes per se are usually a minor portion of overall business costs, so some analysts believe they are not major locational factors. However, taxes are easy to quantify, and sometimes things that can be counted receive more consideration than more important factors that cannot be counted. Examinations of where establishments locate provide some evidence regarding the importance of taxes. Most facilities that relocated chose a new site where site taxes were equal to or greater than the previous location (Schmenner, 1981). However, plants that move long distances (over 20 miles) generally select lower tax locations. Thus taxes appear to be at least a moderately important locational factor. Papke (1987) examined regional tax differentials and found that tax burden differentials are statistically significant and negatively related to the size and location of capital investment.

Government Incentives and Infrastructure

Governments provide a variety of special incentives or subsidies to business to encourage location in an area. Examples of special governmental incentives are state interest subsidies, loan guarantees, regulatory exemptions, sale of land at below-market prices, tax credits, and special infrastructure constructed at public expense. About three fourths of manufacturing locational decisions involve some type of governmental assistance. Special incentives are offered by so many places that they are almost a ubiquity—a locational factor available everywhere. Major downtown hotels or office projects almost always receive special governmental incentives, often from more than one level of government. Like taxes, government incentives are both an intra- and interregional locational factor. There is no strong empirical evidence regarding the effectiveness of direct business subsidies, although most economic development practitioners consider them essential.

Infrastructure developments (roads, water and sewer facilities, telecommunication, public buildings, and so forth) also play an important role in creating an environment that retains and attracts business. A good stock of public infrastructure will make local firms more productive and contribute to economic growth.

Local Business Climate

Recently, business climate has been identified as an important locational factor. Business climate is a somewhat slippery concept because it is intended to include not only tax and expenditure programs but also the less tangible aspects of a community's attitude toward business. Hanson and Berkman (1991) referred to the state business climate as a "poorly conceptually and crudely measured" concept (p. 213). Do public officials make substantial efforts to accommodate business? Are regulations detrimental to business kept to a minimum? Are business executives accorded a place of respect in the community? Are regulations changed without notice? Does the community want business development? The above questions indicate some of the difficult-to-quantify aspects of attitude toward business.

Programs through which local governments attempt to "keep in touch" with existing businesses and monitor their needs through surveys, business round tables, or personal visits are considered useful in creating a good business climate. Such efforts are at the heart of many business expansion and retention programs (Morse, 1990). Business decision makers will tend to remain in an area if they believe that governments listen and are attentive to their needs.

The large-scale, computer-generated, site selection method using business climate has been criticized for three reasons. First, it creates a false sense of rigor (Erickson, 1987). The very concept of business climate is vague, and a good business climate for one industry may not be a good business climate for another. Furthermore, even a state with a very low business climate rating may have regions that are ideal for certain businesses. Second, Skoro (1988) showed that rankings of business climate fail to predict where state growth will occur. If the measure of business climate is unrelated to growth, an analyst must question how well business climate is measured. Third, only easy-to-quantify data are generally used in the early stages; thus locational factors that may be important to particular firms may be ignored. Nevertheless, large-scale computer winnowing is an accepted practice and is used to some degree even among individuals who recognize the limitations.

Site Costs

The cost of a particular site may be expressed in terms of rents or purchase price of a building. Site costs include land and building. Site costs are not an important interregional locational factor because almost all regions offer a variety of sites at a wide range of prices, but site costs are a major factor in the competition among jurisdictions within a region. Warehouses and office facilities are particularly sensitive to site costs.

Political Climate and Stability

National political stability is a locational factor that is generally the same in regions throughout a nation. As the world economy becomes increasingly interdependent, establishments are considering sites throughout the world. One of the most important considerations a foreign investor has is whether the government is stable and the political climate compatible with a satisfactory return on investment. Currency stability is also important. The political stability of the United States and Canada partly explains the dramatic increase of foreign investment flowing into these countries during the 1980s.

Political factors may also help one area within a country compete with other regions, particularly for establishments that do business with the federal government. In such cases, the strength of the region's congressional delegation may be a very important factor, as businesses that deal with the government have occasion to request assistance in obtaining government business. The choice of Texas as the site for the multi-billion-dollar supercollider has been attributed to that state's political strength.

Energy Costs

Energy prices directly affect transportation costs and, consequently, affect the location of transportation-oriented activities. Energy is also a direct input in the production process. Carlton (1983) examined births of new branch plant locations and concluded that electricity prices were a major locational factor.

Energy costs are highly regulated, and many development officials hope to attract business by keeping costs as low as possible. However, there are important quality dimensions to energy that should also be addressed. For instance, businesses may be concerned with the availability of some energy sources. Can they get natural gas, or will they be subject to blackouts or brownouts? As businesses rely increasingly on computers, the quality of electrical energy, including the minimization of surge, is an important locational consideration.

⊠   The Decision-Making Process

The locational choice can be complex because the decision may involve a variety of motives and affect a substantial portion of the workforce. This section examines the motives of locational decision makers and the corporate decision-making process.

Motivations

In economics, the most widely used motivational assumption is that businesses seek to maximize profits. Because profit maximization is a cornerstone for understanding behavior, it is appropriate, at least as a first approximation, to assume it is the main criterion in choosing a location. However, there are three instances where profit-maximizing explanations will fail or provide only part of the explanation.

First, the profit-maximizing assumption fails to account for choices of nonprofit institutions. Fire stations and other public facilities are located on the basis of quick service and the political pulls of citizens in various parts of the city. Politics can be a very important locational determinant for many facilities such as military bases.

Second, profit-maximizing behavior fails to account for occasional conflicts of interests that can occur between the owners of corporations—the stockholders—on the one hand, and the individuals who make the locational decisions, on the other. Many corporate officers may own such a small amount of their company's stock that a profit-maximizing location may not significantly enhance their wealth. Consequently, some managers may choose to locate a facility in an area that has a good climate, low personal tax rates, or other advantages that have personal appeal.

In other words, managers may place their personal interest above stockholder interests (which is not surprising if you believe that managers maximize utility and have some insulation from being fired if profits are not maximized).

Third, business owners and managers may prefer safe locations (a high probability of generating satisfactory profits) rather than high-risk/high-return locations; if the high-risk location fails, the managers may be fired or the business may fail.

Practical Limitations on the Choice Process

The amount of time and study devoted to locational decisions varies drastically. At one extreme, an individual may open a business after comparing rents among few buildings and making sure there are no competitors in the area. It may be rational not to devote much time, effort, or money to a locational decision if the profitability of the enterprise is not sensitive to location. After all, even profit maximizers want to maximize profits *net* of locational search costs. However, other locational decisions involve extensive analysis. The location of retail chain stores and large manufacturing plants usually involves substantial analysis. Activities that require large, long-term investments generally devote substantial resources to determine the most appropriate location. However, even in cases that are studied intensively, the final decision normally requires substantial judgment on the part of the decision makers. Locational analysis is far from a pure science because of the complexity of factors that must be considered, the uncertainty of the future, and the variety of motives of the participants.

New businesses are less likely than branch plants to engage in careful, profit-maximizing analysis of locational choice. New businesses often locate where the founder lives, which suggests that personal factors may be as important as locational factors that might increase profits. However, a successful and enduring business site may have attributes of a profit-maximizing location, even if it was initially selected based on personal factors. Locations based on purely personal choices in areas that cannot support satisfactory profits will perish. As Hoover (1948) put it,

> A good analogy is the scattering of certain types of seeds by the wind. These seeds may be carried for miles before finally coming to rest, and nothing makes them select spots particularly favorable for germinations. . . . Because of the survival of those which happen to be well located, the resulting distribution of such plants from generation to generation follows closely the distribution of favorable growing conditions. (p. 211)

Hoover's analogy is appealing but probably overstates the case. Nonoptimal locations may or may not be quickly eliminated. In fact, bad locational choices could remain in place for decades. The local economic environment could change in ways that support the initially suboptimal location. As the process of coevolutionary development continues, an initially suboptimal location could become a very suitable location.

Steps in the Corporate Site Selection Process

Although there are a variety of motives involved in selecting a location, large businesses tend to follow similar steps in the site selection process. Schmenner (1982) has identified five basic steps.

Need Recognition

Locational decisions are seldom *only* location decisions. They are usually part of a broader corporate planning process and occur at critical junctures in a firm's life cycle. The search for a new location may be due to an abrupt change in corporate strategy, say, a decision to abandon one product line and enter another. The search could also be prompted by a routine process, such as accommodating projected increases in demand.

A corporate planning office or a division of a multidivision firm may begin the locational process with a forecast of future demand. The forecast may be ad hoc or, more typically, part of a company's ongoing corporate planning process, such as a rolling five-year plan. If a capacity shortage is anticipated, officials must decide how to address the issue. Expansion at one or more of the company's existing sites normally will be one option. Increasing the product price or subcontracting work to other producers could be other options. If a new facility is determined to be the best way to address the projected capacity shortage, a site selection team will be formed.

Establishing the Selection Team

The organization of the company affects the nature of the site selection process. Corporations with a centralized staff will generally form a team at the corporate level. Team members will include representatives from key corporate departments, such as transportation, distribution, personnel, engineering, real estate, or planning. Decentralized companies, such as loosely organized conglomerates with relatively strong divisions or subsidiaries and weaker corporate staffs, may carry out the locational study at the divisional level. For small companies, the CEO is more directly involved in the decision because the small company cannot afford a team of "in house" specialists. Small companies also normally search within short distances of their existing plants, so information costs may not be as significant.

Several consulting firms specialize in locational decisions. They can often conduct a site analysis cheaper than in-house staffs because they have access to data on a great many sites throughout the United States. Consulting firms are used in about one third of the locational decisions of *Fortune* 500 companies. The proportion may be even higher for small- and medium-sized firms that do not have the internal staff needed to conduct a locational study. Additional advantages of employing consulting firms rather than doing the work in-house include the insulation of the site selection team from internal pressure and greater anonymity for the company. Companies usually do not reveal that they are seeking an alternative location until they are far enough into the selection process to start negotiating for specific terms on land, locational incentives, and so forth.

Developing Criteria

The site selection team will develop a list of important locational "must have/want" characteristics for the new facility. The role of the proposed facilities in the overall corporate strategy will be considered in developing and revising the list of criteria. Desires to penetrate new markets, to segregate or integrate corporate functions, or to increase a firm's visibility may be important elements in the locational decision. The "must have/want" list will include both quantitative and qualitative locational factors. The locational factors may be weighted to indicate which locational features are most important.

Some trade-off occurs in developing criteria between information that is ideally desired and information that is available. No firm could use a locational model that included every factor that could possibly influence profits. The information needed to make such a model operational would be too costly. Consequently, much of the data needed to make informed locational decisions is unpublished and must be gathered from expensive site visits. Secondary data already collected by governmental agencies or by local chambers of commerce are usually inexpensive but may only approximate the specific information that decision makers require. Secondary data may also be several years old by the time they are collected and disseminated. Therefore, most firms focus on a few important factors that are necessary and a few desirable factors.

Winnowing and Focusing

Once the criteria have been established, the search for a site begins. The search is normally made sequentially. The first stage involves the choice of a multistate, state, or urban region. Over half of all locational studies make their "first cut" at a multistate level, although the first cut is often at the metropolitan level. Once a region or state has been selected, a more microgeographic focus is taken, culminating in the short list of one or a few communities. At this stage, the search for an exact site begins. Individual suburban and central city jurisdictions within a metropolitan area often compete with one another as well as with sites in other regions.

In selecting a broad region, the site selection team focuses on labor, state taxes, climate, proximity to customers and suppliers, and other features that may have significant interregional variation but are similar almost everywhere within the region.

Locational factors that are similar within large regions, such as climate and energy costs, are termed macrolocational factors. Locational factors that vary at the microgeographic level of detail, such as land costs, access to major roads, and good local schools, are less important in the initial winnowing stage because satisfactory accommodations can generally be found somewhere within almost all major regions. Hence microlocational factors become more important when selecting a specific community within a region or a specific site within the metropolitan area.

Several consulting firms use large-scale computer models to aid in the winnowing process, particularly in ranking states and metropolitan areas. In constructing such a model, weights are first assigned to the "must have/want" list of characteristics. The more important the attribute, the higher the weight. A score for each locational factor is also assigned to each region. The better the regional attribute, the higher the score. By multiplying the weight times the region's location score and summing the results, an overall desirability index can be obtained. A computerized score for each region can be generated by this process.

Once a few regions have been identified, a specific site must be found. At this stage, computer models are less useful than the telephone and legwork. Information costs limit the number of sites that can be examined in detail. Normally, a firm making a major locational decision will gather detailed information on 10 to 25 specific sites. A company may make its requirements or needs known to state or local agencies and let them respond by describing the assets of particular communities. Regional and city planning agencies, local utilities, banks, railroads, and chambers of commerce are all sources of information. Features of each site are compared against the "must have/want" list. Sites will be eliminated as more detailed and difficult-to-obtain information is gathered on remaining sites after each elimination round. Site visits and collections of nonstandard or unpublished data help narrow the field of prospective sites.

Discussions with local public officials regarding potential problems and incentives may begin as the locational choices are narrowed. Most communities are anxious to attract new economic activity because they believe it will create jobs and increase the tax base. The firm may require assurances from local officials that zoning or other land use regulations will not become impediments if it decides to locate in the area. The firm's consultants may also want to feel that they will be welcome members of the community. Increasingly, firms are asking for and receiving special incentives to locate in a particular area. Incentives include tax abatements, below-market-price land, and a variety of indirect subsidies.

Reaching a Final Decision

The final decision is normally formalized in the firm's capital budget. Preliminary estimates of land acquisition and construction costs are developed for inclusion in the corporation's capital budget. In a large corporation with several divisions, each unit may have to compete with other divisions for a share of the capital budget. A feasibility analysis must normally show that the proposed facility will earn a sufficient rate of return to justify the construction costs.

⊠   Changing Relative Importance of Locational Factors

Various locational factors were discussed previously, but their relative importance was not assessed. Numerous scholars have questioned corporate decision makers to determine the most important locational factors. It is difficult to generalize from these studies because each study used a different research design. The differences in the studies include the types of locational factors examined, the time period examined, the types of businesses analyzed, and the techniques used to draw a conclusion. Nevertheless, a useful perspective on the relative importance of various locational factors can be gained by reviewing previous surveys.

The Use of Surveys

Before reviewing the results of surveys, four methodological problems regarding their use should be sketched. First, questions must be designed carefully to avoid ambiguous responses. For instance, quality of life has been found to be important in many surveys, but researchers are still not clear as to what a good quality of life is. Second, respondents may provide answers that they believe will influence policy in their favor or that they believe the surveyor wants to hear. Taxes, for instance, are often ranked high on surveys even though they are not a major cost element for most activities. Possibly this is because respondents believe that, if taxes are considered "important," governments will reduce taxes. Third, only existing firms can be surveyed. Firms that made bad choices and went out of business cannot be contacted. Finally, the choices given by the survey researcher can affect the response. Suppose all the labor-related locational factors—labor cost, productivity, cost of skilled labor, fringe benefits, changes in the wage rate, presence of clerical workers, unionization, and right-to-work laws—were listed in great detail. Possibly, no single factor would be considered important by more than a few respondents. However, every firm might respond that "labor" was an important factor if labor were a choice by itself. This problem makes comparison of findings very difficult.

Survey Findings: Past to Present

Early location theory treated transportation costs as the dominant locational factor. Later, Morgan (1964) examined the results of 17 locational studies conducted prior to 1963. He found four significant factors: markets, labor, raw materials, and transportation. Other factors such as taxes, quality of life, and financial incentives were not found to be significant. The direct, cost-oriented locational factors exerted the dominant influence on industrial location. Morgan's study is dated, but it provides an excellent reference point for examining how locational factors have changed since the mid 1960s.

More recent surveys (Fortune, Inc., 1977; Grant & Co., 1985; Heckman, 1982; Kieschnick, 1981; Premus, 1982; Schmenner, 1982) indicate that many additional factors affect locational choices. Four important generalizations can be made by contrasting the recent finding with surveys conducted prior to 1970.

First, the traditional locational factors—markets, labor, new materials, and transportation—remain the most important location factors.

Second, the relative importance of the traditional locational factors has diminished compared to other locational factors. For example, unlike studies in the 1940s and 1950s, most of the recent locational studies found factors such as education, unionization, personal reasons, business climate, energy and familiarity with local conditions on the "must have/want" list. In contrast, in his review of 17 location studies conducted prior to 1963, Morgan (1964) found the traditional locational factors to be practically the only ones that mattered.

Third, the primary impact of technological change has been to reduce the significance of proximity to raw materials and transportation costs as locational factors. Technology increased the number of steps in the production process, reduced the importance of raw materials, and lowered transportation costs. One consequence has been a shift in the growth of manufacturing activities from the resource-rich Midwest to areas of the country where markets are expanding, such as the Southwest and Far West.

Fourth, studies have found that state and local taxes have had an important effect on business location, particularly within metropolitan areas where business property taxes can vary substantially among jurisdictions. Thus, contrary to what the earlier literature suggested, it would be imprudent to ignore taxes as one of the important factors that influence the industrial development of regions (Grant & Co., 1985; Heckman, 1982). Nevertheless, the preponderance of evidence shows that state and local tax policies *alone* will do little to change the economic fortune of regions.

Future Locational Factors

Corporate facility planners deal with issues that influence company assets 25 to 100 years into the future. Consequently, planners must consider locational factors that could become important in the future as well as factors that affect operations today.

The speed with which locational factors can emerge as important can be understood by examining changes that occurred during the past decade. During that period, quality of life, environmental concerns and the emergence of super regional airports became locational concerns. In the realm of policy, numerous states strengthened their economic development efforts through a variety of assistance programs. The research park, the urban highway loop, metropolitan government, and other planning and zoning concepts were implemented. Technological changes, such as global satellite communication and mass transit technologies, have also influenced locational choice.

In the future, rapid changes in important locational determinants can be similarly anticipated. But it is more difficult to anticipate what the changes will be. Table 3.1 summarizes some well-informed speculation about some transportation, political and technological factors that will influence future locational choices. Clearly, no one can anticipate all potential changes that can affect a locational choice. But some potential changes will be critical to firms in industries that will be directly affected. It is an interesting exercise to ask how different industries will be affected by each of the changes. Because of the long-term nature of facility location, locational planners are future oriented.

⊠ Summary

Locational factors affect a community's ability to attract and retain economic activity. Every organization will be influenced by a variety of locational factors but to differing degrees, depending on the characteristics of the organization.

Inertia is a major but often unrecognized locational factor. The reasons why the firm located in the area in the first place may continue to be important, and economic and social structures that may evolve will tend to reinforce the initial choice. When a firm moves out of an area, it risks loss of business contacts and valuable workers. Building cooperative working relationships among businesses can be a business-retention strategy.

Transportation-cost-minimizing models are based on the idea that firms will locate at a transportation-cost-minimizing point. Market-oriented firms produce finished products that are expensive to transport, so they locate near markets. Material-oriented activities locate near materials because the materials needed in production are expensive to transport. The principle of median location explains location tendencies of market-oriented firms serving several markets.

Low production costs may encourage a firm to locate away from the transportation-cost-minimizing point. Principal production cost factors are

TABLE 3.1 Factors Influencing Future Locational Choices

Most Significant Before 2000	*Most Significant After 2000*
Transportation	
Piggyback services between trucks, trains, ships, and freight helicopters	30 minutes air service between the United States, Europe, and the Far East
Corporate internal airlines	Private commercialization of space
Collision-avoidance avionics will reduce airport congestion problems	Computer controlled cars driven on selected express freeway routes
Computer controlled sails on ocean-going vessels	Newspapers will be delivered by facsimile printing in home
Government-subsidized tax: fleets as feeders to rapid transit systems	
Political-Legislative	
Global agreements to allow more data and information transfer	Laws may regulate use and behavior of robots
International agreements regarding control of multinational corporations	A world monetary unit will be adopted to facilitate international trade
Water conservation legislation will limit development prospects	Leading cities will be multiloop cities, having two or more perimeter routes
A national land use policy will be enacted	Urban parks will be enclosed and climate controlled
No urban or industrial construction on prime agricultural land will be permitted without state or federal approval	
Technology	
Permanently manned space stations will be in orbit	A child will be born in space
A process for economically desalting sea water will be in use	Energy will be plentiful and inexpensive
Product life cycle will get shorter, requiring shorter amortization periods	The human brain will be linked to a computer
Acquisition, strategy, and distribution of body parts will be a fast-growth industry	Large scale agriculture using untreated sea water will be possible

SOURCE: McKinley Conway, *A Technology Review and Forecast for Development Strategists* (Atlanta, GA: Conway, 1986).

labor costs (including prevailing wage, productivity, and unionization), quality of life, taxes, government incentives and infrastructure, political climate (including stability), local business climate, site costs, and energy costs.

Economists normally assume that profits drive locational decisions. This is generally true. Nevertheless, profits may fail to account for the choices of nonprofit institutions. Profit-maximizing models also fail to account for possible conflicts of interest between corporate managers and stockholders. Finally, decision makers may prefer safe locations (a minimum nearly guaranteed profit) to high-risk, high-expected-profit locations.

The corporate decision process can be divided into five steps. First, a need for a new location must be recognized. Location decisions are seldom *only* locational choices but are often associated with other business changes. Second, a site selection team will be formed to include key corporate officers and possibly locational consulting firms. Third, a "must have/want" list will be developed. Locational factors may be weighted according to relative importance. Fourth, a winnowing and focusing stage, which may use computer models, will narrow the locational choices. Negotiations with local policymakers over details such as costs and subsidies may also be necessary to reduce the short list to a particular site. The final decision will be recognized in the company's capital budget.

The most important locational factors continue to be transportation costs, access to materials, access to markets, and labor costs. However, the list of important locational factors has increased significantly in recent years. Consequently, the relative importance of the "big four" has declined. The nature of locational factors will continue to change as technology and other factors change the production process.

Market Areas and Economic Development Strategies

Economic development officials need to understand the linkages between their communities and surrounding areas. The relationship of city to other areas both provides and limits economic development opportunities. This chapter shows how individual locational choices of firms may result in the formation of cities that are linked into networks of cities. The logic of a system of cities will be built based on economic concepts. The urban patterns that result from the theoretical approach sometimes differ from observed patterns because the assumptions set forth in the model may not square with reality. Nevertheless, the chapter describes important tendencies that influence urban development.

First, demand for products is presented in a spatial context. The analysis is different from traditional discussions of demand because the further a consumer is from the producer the more costly the delivered price and hence the smaller the quantity demanded. Competition among producers also affects the size of market areas. Market areas for goods and services produced in a city, in turn, determine the area's hinterland. Central-place theory is described in the next section. It shows how producers who locate in the center of their particular market areas contribute to the development of a hierarchical system of cities. An evaluation of central-place theory is presented in the fourth section. The final sections describe some techniques that can be used to measure the extent of market areas and discuss hinterland expansion strategies.

⊠   Demand and Market Areas

A market area is the region in which a product is sold. This section examines the nature of market areas. To focus on the principal economic forces that shape a product's market area, it is useful to assume the following:

1. An economy exists on a homogeneous plane. In other words, natural resources and other locational features such as climate and population density are the same.
2. The plane is initially populated by self-sufficient families. That is, they produce all their own food and clothing and do not rely on outside producers.
3. Transportation costs are equal in all directions and proportional to distance.

After considering the implications of this restrictive model, assumptions may be relaxed. As the assumptions are relaxed, a framework will exist to help understand the importance of geographic irregularities.

Under the above conditions, production would concentrate at particular places due to economies of scale in production. Some of the original self-sufficient families would specialize, producing products at lower costs than their neighbors. The area in which they sold their output would constitute their market area. Producers would be the only sellers within their area. The market area would be limited because the larger the area serviced the greater the transportation costs at the market fringe. Thus, unless economies of scale were substantial, transportation costs would prevent one site from servicing the entire nation. To see how the above implications are derived from the initial economic assumptions, it is useful to first understand how demand is affected by distance.

Demand in a Spatial Setting

The nature of market areas can be better understood by examining demand in a spatial setting. Traditional demand analysis as described in most economics textbooks states that the demand curve shows the quantity of a good that consumers would be willing and able to buy at each price in a range of prices during a given time period. The stability of the demand curve requires that consumer tastes, income, prices of related products (complements and substitutes), market size, and expectations do not change. When any one of these factors changes, the entire demand curve shifts. Regional economists make the spatial dimension explicit by showing how location

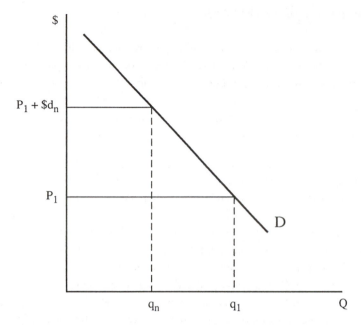

Figure 4.1. Demand with and without transportation costs for a consumer living distance d from the plant.

influences product demand. Figure 4.1 shows a typical demand curve for an individual. The typical consumer will purchase q_1 units per period at price P_1.

Suppose a producer operating on the "homogeneous plane" initially priced a product at P_1, as in Figure 4.1. The price represents the selling price at the establishment's point of sale. A consumer buying the product must pay the point-of-sale price plus the transfer costs. Transportation costs include monetary and nonmonetary costs. Thus time and aggravation are "transportation costs" just as gasoline and automobile depreciation are. There are two important implications from the existence of transfer costs. First, transportation costs drive a wedge between the cost to consumers (the price plus transportation costs) and the revenue received by producers. Second, the cost to consumers will differ depending on how near to the producer they live even though the point-of-sale price may be equal for everyone. The further they are from the producer, the greater their cost.

Consumers located next to the store or plant may be assumed to have no transportation costs. Therefore, an individual next to the plant could be expected to purchase q_1 units following the traditional economic analysis of demand. However, consider a customer located distance D_n from the plant. Let $\$d_n$ equal the transportation costs for someone living distance D_n from the plant. Thus the person living at D_n will bear a total cost of P_1 (the point-of-sale price) plus $\$d_n$. Clearly, individuals living further from the point of sale will purchase fewer units, q_n in this case. The inclusion of distance in traditional demand analysis helps us understand that two things happen when a firm lowers its price. First, customers within the existing market will consume more. Second, the size of the market area will increase as new customers travel longer distances to make purchases.

Implications

The fact that distant customers pay higher total costs the further they are from the point of sale has implications for individual businesses and for economic development officials. Businesses should recognize that they must compete harder for distant customers. To attract distant consumers, some businesses target them in their advertising. Special sales may be designed to offer lower prices to distant consumers. Charging different point-of-sale prices to different customers is a form of price discrimination. Various forms of price discrimination are a common business practice and are perfectly legal.

Development officials should recognize that many business clusters, such as neighborhood shopping centers, may need assistance when competing for distant customers. Improving access to neighborhood shopping areas by improving roads and parking may be helpful. Sometimes, perceptions of travel may be as detrimental to attracting customers as actual travel time. For instance, when potential customers fear that they may be assaulted or hassled, they may view travel costs as high. (Perceived inhospitable downtown areas are a major problem in central business districts.) Local efforts to make shopping more convenient and safe can reduce the perceived shopping costs.

⌧ Competition for Markets

Suppose a producer is successful in an enterprise and earns excess profit. (In economic terminology, "excess profits" are profits in excess of what could be earned if the resources were employed in comparable investments.) The producer may also have established a market area and will have some monopoly power within that market area. Figure 4.2a shows the average cost curve and demand of the producer. Because the price at the profit-maximizing level of output is above the average cost of producing the output, the firm is earning excess profits. (In keeping with the economic tradition, "normal profits" are included as a cost in the average cost curve.) Figure 4.2b shows the corresponding market area for the producer. Notice that initially there are no nearby competitors.

Will the excess profits remain in the long run? Assuming that other potential producers have knowledge of market opportunities and the ability to open similar facilities, new producers will enter the industry in search of excess profits. Producers will initially locate away from each other to avoid competition. Thus new producers will carve out their own market areas and earn profits similar to the representative firm. However, as still more producers enter the industry, they will squeeze the initial producer, thus reducing the excess profits and market area. New firms will reduce the demand for the original producer's product. Figures 4.2c and 4.2d show the situation. In this case, profits will be reduced, but they may still attract other producers. As more producers start businesses, the landscape will become increasingly crowded. Eventually, profits will fall to a level at which no more firms enter the industry. One possible equilibrium is shown in Figures 4.2e and 4.2f.

Hexagons, as shown in Figure 4.2f, are an efficient shape for filling an area. However, they are not the only possible outcome of spatial competition. Suppose every firm was earning very slight excess profits when the market areas were tightly packed so that an additional producer would not be able to operate profitably. This situation may represent an equilibrium. Therefore, there is a degree of indeterminacy about market size. The important point is that as firms enter the industry in search of excess profits, profits of existing firms drop and the size of market areas shrink.

The equilibrium shown in Figure 4.2e is similar to the outcome suggested for firms in monopolistically competitive industries. Even if all producers sold identical products, the spatial perspective indicates that demand for the product would be downsloping—not horizontal as suggested in the traditional discussions of the purely competitive industry. The spatial analysis indicates that monopolistic competition may better depict markets that would otherwise be classified as competitive. Essentially, producers are differentiated by location. Consumers have preferences for producers' locations just as they have preferences for particular brands of very similar products.

Figure 4.2a Costs

Figure 4.2b Market Area

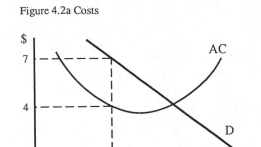

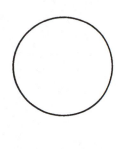

Competition Arises and Profits Decline

Figure 4.2c Costs

Figure 4.2d Market Areas

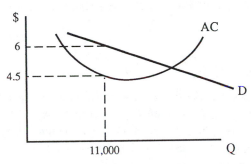

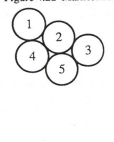

Further Competition Reduces Profits to Normal Levels

Figure 4.2e Costs

Figure 4.2f Market Areas

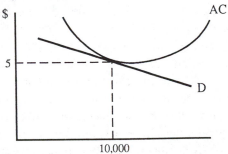

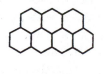

Figure 4.2. Costs, competition, and market areas: A spatial monopolist.

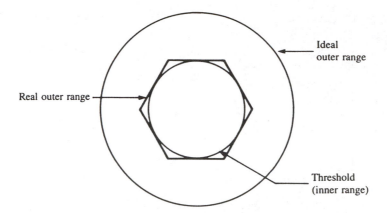

Figure 4.3. Threshold and range. The threshold is the market size that will allow a firm to break even. The ideal outer range is the distance at which the transportation cost makes the product prohibitively expensive. The actual outer range represents the actual market area.

Threshold Demand and Range

"Threshold" and "range" are useful concepts for understanding market areas. The threshold demand is the minimum quantity a producer must sell to earn at least normal profits. It may be thought of as the break-even quantity. Figure 4.3 shows the geographic threshold associated with quantity demanded 10,000 (the breakeven output in Figure 4.2 when the firm was earning just sufficient profits to stay in operation). Assuming that individuals consume roughly equal amounts regardless of where they live, the threshold quantity can be associated with a threshold population. For instance, if the typical individual consumes 10 units per year at a price of $5, the threshold population associated with Figure 4.2 would be 10,000/10 or 1,000. The threshold population is also associated with a threshold geographic market sometimes called the inner range. For a firm producing an amount just sufficient for the inner range, the price, average total cost, and average revenue are equal.

Variations in threshold size explain why some economic activities are more common than others. Activities with very low demand thresholds, such as filling stations, convenience food stores, churches, and restaurants, are more common than activities with high thresholds, such as undertakers, public accountants, and specialized physicians.

The "ideal outer range" of a good is the maximum distance that individuals are willing to travel to purchase a good at the lowest possible average cost. At the parameter of the ideal outer range, consumer cost (including transportation costs) are so high that demand for the product is zero. Competition from other producers normally reduces the distance that a consumer will travel below the ideal outer range. The "real outer range" is the maximum distance a customer will travel in a competitive environment. It is the actual market area of a firm.

The real outer range describes the firm's actual market area. In Figure 4.3 the firm has an opportunity to make excess profits because the real outer range is larger than the threshold level. Of course, if the producer is inefficient and produces at above the minimum necessary average costs, the opportunity to earn excess profits will be lost. When threshold and real outer range are equal, only normal profits (normal return to owner) are possible even if the producer operates efficiently.

Determinants of Market Size

Three factors determine the size of the market area for a particular product:

1. If *economies of scale* are significant, producers will be able to offset some or all of the additional transportation costs of serving distant markets. Thus establishments in industries with significant economies of scale will have large market areas. Economies of scale are often associated with high fixed costs.

2. *Demand density* is the quantity demanded per unit of land area or the quantity demanded per person times the population density. The larger the demand density, the greater the number of producers that can operate in a given area. Hence high-demand-density products will have smaller market area.

3. The effect of *transportation costs* on market size is ambiguous. On the one hand, if scale economies exist and transportation costs decline, the product could be provided cheaper everywhere, including beyond the market fringe. Thus the decreased transportation costs would allow firms and consumers to take advantage of both scale economies and lower transportation costs by expanding the market. On the other hand, if the representative firm faces increasing cost conditions, a decrease in transportation costs will increase profits *initially* and may eventually attract more firms into the industry. In this case, the combination of increasing production costs may offset the lower transportation costs so that it becomes more expensive per unit to serve an expanded market. Accordingly, smaller market areas may result.

Forces are continually operating to change the size of market areas. For instance, there has been a long-term tendency for incomes and population to increase. As a result, market areas for some products, particularly retail goods, have become smaller. At the same time, economies of scale have increased in some manufacturing industries, tending to increase the market areas for some products.

⊠   The Urban Hierarchy and Urban System

The previous section described the formation of market areas for a single product. This section shows how the overlap of market area centers for numerous products leads to the development of cities and trading patterns among cities. Cities will form. Some cities will be small because they are the production points of only a few products with few economies of scale. Large cities will be the home of many producers. Furthermore, economic forces will impose an order on the size of, spatial distribution of, and relationships among cities. This section shows how a hierarchy of central places will develop and a system of cities will emerge.

Central Places

To understand the development of cities of various sizes, it is necessary to recognize the economic advantages that accrue when two or more plants locate together. These advantages are termed "agglomeration economies" (see Chapter 5). Producers will trade off some of the advantages of locating near their customers to gain advantages from locating near other producers. Examples of agglomeration economies include shared parking among retail stores, shared roads, and other shared public infrastructures. Fixed transportation systems and geopolitical barriers will reinforce the tendency of establishments to share market areas. Thus different activities may have similar but not identical market areas; yet they may find it advantageous to locate together and serve the same market. Accordingly, there will be fewer market areas than products.

Assume that there is a fixed number of different market sizes reflecting the trade-off between ideal market areas and agglomeration economies. Market sizes will range from small areas for convenience goods to markets that include entire regions or multiregion areas. Commodities or services with similar threshold markets will locate together and market areas will tend to be standardized. Furthermore, assume that some of the producers with small market areas locate in the same place as producers serving large market areas. This assumption will economize on the number of cities, reduce infrastructure needs, and make other agglomeration economies possible.

A hierarchy of central places will result from the sharing of common locations. Many cities will be the site of only a few producers serving small market areas. These first-order central places—hamlets—will provide such services as grocery and drug stores, churches, and so forth. The rural population is the hinterland (market area) for the first-order central places. Second-order central places will provide all the services provided by first-order places because residents and the rural population near the second-order cities have a demand for these goods. In addition, second-order central places will provide services that have larger threshold markets. Clothing and furniture stores are examples of additional functions that might be offered by second-order central places. The market area of the second-order goods and service producers will include several first-order places. For example, if a resident of a first-order central place needed a new suit, it might be purchased in the nearest second-order city. First-order places are part of the second-order central place's hinterland.

Second-order cities will be part of the hinterland of third-order cities and so on up the hierarchy. The largest cities will be the production centers for establishments with the largest market areas, but they will also provide lower-order functions. A functional regularity exists in the system of cities. Higher-order cities will provide some services to lower-ordered places in their hinterland. Table 4.1 illustrates a hypothetical distribution of activities according to the rank of the central place. Of course, in reality, the functional separations will not be so regular. Some higher-ordered cities might have missing functions—say, they may lack a grain elevator—and some lower-ordered cities might have functions that particular larger cities do not have. A scalogram, as shown in Table 4.1, is useful in identifying activities that might be appropriate for development in an area. For instance, if a function is unexpectedly absent and a more detailed study fails to uncover any reasonable explanation for the absence, that activity might be a successful new business possibility that could be encouraged.

There will be a spatial regularity to city systems as well as a functional regularity of output. If establishments in first-order central places have market

TABLE 4.1 Hypothetical Hierarchy of Urban Functions

Economic Function	Order of Central Places					
	6	5	4	3	2	1
Minimum convenience						
Filling station	x	x	x	x	x	x
Grocery store	x	x	x	x	x	x
Full convenience						
Eating places	x	x	x	x	x	
Hardware store	x	x	x	x	x	
Drug store	x	x	x	x	x	
Low-order specialty						
Laundry		x	x	x	x	
Clothing store	x	x	x	x		
Appliances	x	x	x	x		
Hotel, motel	x	x	x			
Shoe store	x	x	x			
Sporting goods	x	x	x			
High-order specialty						
Radio		x	x			
Paint store	x	x				
Music store	x	x				
Antique store	x	x				
Wholesale						
Lumber supplies	x					
Professional service equipment	x					
Groceries	x					
Bulk oil	x					
Number of cities in class (nesting factors = 3)	1	3	9	27	81	243

NOTE: Higher-order cities have more functions than lower-order central places.

areas of radius *r*, then first-order towns will be 2*r* apart. Higher-order places will be further apart than first-order places because some of the producers in these cities serve larger market areas. Furthermore, each second-order city includes some first-order cities in its hinterland. Likewise, because first-order cities have smaller market areas, more first-order places will exist than second-order places.

Figure 4.4 is a stylized map of a system of cities in our theoretical urban hierarchy. It shows villages, towns, metropolitan areas, and one capital. In other words, there are only four different market sizes, and producers locate

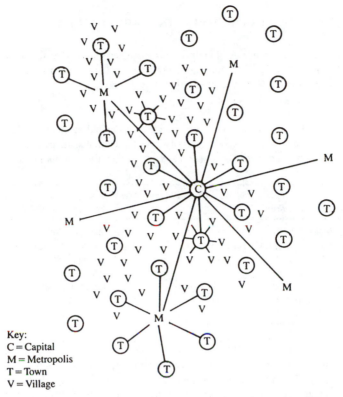

Figure 4.4. Spatial distribution of cities. Central-place theory describes an ordered region with snowflakelike symmetry.

according to the size of the area they serve. The market area of higher-order places are also identified. Each town has 6 villages in its hinterland; each metropolis has 6 towns and 36 villages in its hinterland. The largest city is the "capital" of the region. Its hinterland includes 6 metropolitan areas, 36 (6 × 6) towns, and 126 (36 × 6) villages (not all of the villages are pictured).

Population size can also be understood within the framework of the central-place model by assuming that local population is a function of employment; employment depends on output, which in turn is determined by the size of the market served by the central place.

PERSPECTIVES ON MARKET SIZE

The geographic size of markets was examined empirically by Leonard W. Weiss (1972). He defined a market area as the radius from a plant within which 80% of a plant's output was shipped.

Weiss concluded that

- there are wide variations in market size, depending on the product.
- manufacturing goods generally have large, multistate market areas.
- only a minority of markets are unequivocally national in scope.

Radius of Market Areas

Product (Radius in Miles)	Product (Radius in Miles)
Soft Drinks (68)	Soap and Detergents (572)
Concrete Products (144)	Flour and Grain Products (682)
Ice Cream (158)	Truck Trailers (780)
Brick (200)	Fertilizers (828)
Metal Cans (362)	Tires and Inner Tubes (833)
Malt Liquors (370)	Cigarettes (1,108)
Railroad Cars (542)	

Berry and Garrison (1958) examined market size in terms of the minimum population needed to support an economic activity in Snoholmish County, Washington. They defined threshold size as the smallest population size of a community in which the function exists. Their findings are summarized below:

Function (Threshold Size)	Function (Threshold Size)
Filling Stations (196)	Furniture Store (542)
Churches (256)	Veterinarian (579)
Taverns (282)	Apparel Stores (590)
Elementary School (322)	Bank (616)
Appliance Store (385)	Florist (729)
Auto Dealer (398)	Local Taxi (762)
Dentist (426)	Shoe Repair Shop (896)
Drug Store (458)	Sheet Metal Work (10,176)
Meeting Hall (525)	Hospitals (1,159)

SOURCES: Leonard W. Weiss, "The Geographic Size of Markets in Manufacturing," *Review of Economics and Statistics* 54 (1972): 255-57; Bert L. Berry and W. L. Garrison, "Functional Bases of the Central-Place Hierarchy," *Economic Geography* 34 (1958): 304-22.

Changing Urban Patterns

Once an urban system has developed, the central-place model can be used to examine forces that cause it to change. Because the system of cities is based on market systems, the same factors that cause market areas to change will cause the hinterlands of cities to change. Thus changes in transportation costs, scale economies of production, and demand density (per capita spending and population density) are important influences on the urban hierarchy.

In general, when the optimum size of a market area declines because of increases in income, increases in population density, decreases in optimum plant size, or increased transportation costs, activities will shift toward lower-order central places. Economic activities will shift down the hierarchy, and goods previously provided exclusively by larger places will now be provided by lower-order places. In effect, the dominance of higher-order urban places will be weakened. For instance, when video cameras were introduced, they could be purchased only in specialty shops located in large metropolitan areas. As consumer acceptance increased (increasing demand density), they became available in lower-order central places. When market areas increase, possibly due to improved transportation or increases in economies of scale, the site of services will shift upward and lower-order central places will be weakened compared to larger cities.

When one or a few functions become available at a different level of the hierarchy, the economic functions of cities will change. If the location of a large number of economic activities shifts upward or downward, an entire category of central place could disappear. Stable and Williams (1973) documented the disappearance of some intermediate places that lost their role in serving smaller areas in the Saskatchewan area. The rural ghost towns—or near-ghost towns—apparent in many parts of the Midwest may be attributable to the tendency of farmers to bypass grocery and other service establishments in small hamlets, preferring the greater variety and other advantages of shopping in towns only slightly further away. Improved transportation and the mechanization of agriculture (lowering demand density) probably contributed to this phenomenon. Within metropolitan areas, improved transportation due to belt ways have contributed to the rise of regional shopping centers and the decline of neighborhood stores.

The changes discussed above should not obscure the overall stability of the urban hierarchy. If we examine a region over a period of one or two years, we would find little change in the relationship among central places. It is unlikely that a central place would disappear or that a new place would emerge. Although cities will grow at different rates, it is very rare that the primary or highest ranking city will change. The system of cities changes slowly, partly because of inertia and the long economic life of capital investment, particularly infrastructure, and partly because new activity will tend to belocated in the existing urban grid.

The stability of places in the urban hierarchy may also be explained by the establishment of channels of interdependence. Once urban or regional linkages are created, they transmit growth from one place to another. Cities lower in the hierarchy may grow, but as they do, opportunities for growth among linked cities within the hierarchy will be created. Roads and wire connections (telegraph and telephone) are important physical linkages that support economic linkages. The hierarchy of cities was less stable in the Southeast than in other regions both before and after the Civil War. Pred (1977) attributed the lack of stability to the fact that southeastern cities were not yet members of a regional city-system. Most southeastern cities were linked directly to New York or Philadelphia, so southern cities lacked established hinterlands. Consequently, growth opportunities occurred without going through channels of the urban hierarchy, so cities in the South did not benefit from growth of other southern cities.

⊠   An Evaluation of the Central-Place Approach

The patterns generated by the central-place model are highly regular. Let's review the key outcomes of the theoretical model:

1. There are as many size classes of cities as market sizes.
2. Cities of the same order have equal hinterlands, offer the same services, and have the same population size.
3. Higher-order cities provide all of the goods and services that lower-order cities provide, plus functions of producers serving the next-larger-sized market.
4. Smaller cities with smaller hinterlands are more numerous and closer together than larger cities.
5. Central places of the same order will be equal distance from one another.
6. Although residents of lower-order cities may purchase goods and services from producers located in higher-order cities, commodities will not flow from lower-ordered places up the urban hierarchy.

A casual observer will recognize that the predictions of the central-place approach have some validity, but there are many exceptions.

Considerations Extraneous to Central-Place Theory

Central-place theory described a well-ordered region with snowflakelike symmetry that does not exist in reality. The conclusions, however, follow from the model's initial assumptions that emphasized economic factors operating on a homogeneous plain. The combined results of the assumptions are market-oriented locational decisions by firms. Accordingly, cities are also market oriented. This section explains why the patterns described by central-place theory may not match reality.

Spatial Differences in Production Costs

The abstract central-place model implicitly included the assumption that the cost of production was the same at all locations. Therefore, firms located primarily to be near their markets. In fact, as discussed in Chapter 3, some areas are more suitable as production sites than others. Production processes requiring raw materials may tend to locate near the materials, firms may locate near suppliers or purchasers, and land has different levels of productivity.

Some producers of products having large market areas may operate most profitably in small towns because of lower labor costs, access to raw materials, and so forth. In this case, goods made in smaller places will be sold to larger cities. Manufacturing activities are particularly sensitive to spatial cost variations. Richardson (1978) described the location of manufacturing activities as "wild cards" within the hierarchy because large manufacturers may locate in small towns as well as major cities. Central-place theory is more applicable to activities that are market oriented in location than to activities that are cost oriented. Thus central-place models describe the location of service centers (where activities such as retailing, wholesaling, and business dominate) much better than the site selection of manufacturing.

The locational factors excluded from central-place theory can create a situation where two towns have similar hinterlands and similar functions except that one of the towns may be the site of a manufacturing plant with a very large market area. Thus the manufacturing town will be larger than the other place, even though, with the one exception, they are similarly situated in the urban hierarchy.

Transportation Cost Variations

The central-place model includes the assumption that transportation costs are uniform in all directions. In reality, transfer costs are cheaper along established routes and market areas extended along transportation routes. Discontinuities in transportation costs will arise due to disruptions in the transportation system caused by rivers, mountains, and other geographic features. For instance, a mountain may raise transportation costs and cut off part of what would otherwise have been part of a city's hinterland. Accordingly, actual urban systems will not always reflect the ideal central-place pattern.

Transport companies often charge block rates rather than continuously increasing rates. Consequently, a producer located 50 miles from a village may experience the same transportation costs as a firm located 150 miles away. This can lead to market overlap and indeterminate market boundaries because producers may deliver a product at the same price. Long-haul economies may also contribute to market overlap.

Seller Rate Absorption and Price Discrimination

Sellers may absorb some of the transfer costs themselves so as to extend their markets, or they may price-discriminate by charging distant customers a lower price. An example of rate absorption would be a producer who sold a product at a uniform delivery price to all customers in the region instead of charging full cost for delivery. A seller could use this technique to price-discriminate against nearby customers so as to offer lower prices to distant customers. There may be promotional or advertising advantages to offering uniform prices to all customers. A furniture store may offer "free" delivery anywhere in a metropolitan area to attract distant customers, even though some very distant customers may have delivery costs so high as to make the sale unprofitable. When many firms practice freight absorption, market overlap may occur. Furthermore, distant consumers are more likely to be near other sellers than customers located near the facility. Thus producers will have an incentive to charge lower prices to distant customers.

Institutional Factors

Numerous political factors can affect the urban networks. Liquor stores may be underrepresented in a state with stringent laws or high liquor taxes, whereas a cluster of similar stores may be found on the other side of the state border. Interstate commerce within the United States is relatively free of barriers to trade—but not entirely. "Buy at Home" campaigns, tax policies, licensing, and inspection regulations are a few institutional impediments that affect market area.

Institutional factors are more important in international commerce. Languages, tariffs, quotas, customers, and differences in legal systems are just a few impediments that prevent a firm located in one country from extending its market area abroad. Some regions, such as European Economic Community countries, are trying to reduce institutional impediments. However, progress is slow. There is a tendency for products with larger market areas and export impediments to locate near the center of a country's population to avoid border problems.

Product Differentiation

The abstract model included the assumption that products were undifferentiated, so it was reasonable to assume that consumers would buy the least-cost item. If all firms charged the same price, the nearest producer would be the least-cost supplier. However, if consumers have a preference for one brand over another, some customers would be willing to pay a premium to purchase the brand preferred. Thus market overlap is likely to occur. The more intense the brand loyalty, the greater the extent of market overlap.

Nonemployment Residential Locations and Commuting

Central-place theory suggests that large production centers will be large cities because of the implicit assumption that people live where they work. However, cities can grow for reasons unrelated to employment. Retirement and amenity oriented communities in the South and Southwest are examples of growth outside the central-place framework. Likewise, "bedroom" communities can grow because of the increase in commuters who work in other central places outside the local area.

Empirical Evidence

How well does empirical evidence support central-place theory? There are many more small cities than large ones, as suggested by central-place theory. Larger cities are further apart and provide a greater variety of services than smaller places. These generalizations support central-place theory. However, whether the theory explains economic geography sufficiently depends on individual judgment rather than a definitive statistical test.

One of the first empirical tests was undertaken by Losch (1954), who used 1930 Census data to analyze urban places in Iowa. He divided cities into various orders and found that the central-place model predicted the number of places in each order, the size of centers, and the distance apart. Since Losch's, numerous other empirical studies of central-place theory have been reported. Central-place theory even explains settlement patterns in communist (Skinner, 1964) and traditional (Steponaitis, 1981) economies. The consensus of these studies is threefold:

- Central-place theory explains the size and spatial distribution of cities in homogeneous agricultural regions, such as the Midwest. It does less well in explaining urban patterns in complex regions, such as the megalopolises of New York-Washington D.C., because places of work are often separated from places of residence.
- The distribution of service activities can be explained by central-place theory reasonably well. Manufacturing, extractive, and governmental activities are not explained by central-place theory. These goods and services are likely to move up as well as down the urban hierarchy.
- The central-place model has also been tested using data from shopping centers in metropolitan areas (West, Von Hohenvalken, and Kroner, 1985; Morrill, 1987). The researchers obtained the expected hierarchies of shopping centers, although they observed stores of the same type replicated in the same centers, possibly due to the economics of comparison shopping. When similar stores are located together, consumers may economize on trips by comparison shopping in an area with many competing stores.

⊠   How to Measure Areas of Influence

The concepts of market area and hinterland are similar. Market area refers to the region in which a particular product is sold. The size of a market area, of course, depends on the product. An urban hinterland refers to the areas in which one central place dominates. Just as the distribution point of a product tends to be near the center of its market area, the city is near the center of the region it serves and the city's influence weakens the further the hinterland area is from the central place. It is sometimes useful to measure a city's hinterland as distinct from the market for individual products.

Survey Techniques

There have been numerous attempts to measure the range of a city's hinterland. Early efforts examined the circulation of major daily newspapers between New York and Boston, reasoning that newspapers accurately reflect retail trade patterns and social orientation among residents between New York and Boston. Thus a city could be placed in New York's hinterland if New York newspapers had a larger circulation than Boston ones. Today, television coverage may be as good an indicator as newspapers.

Green (1959) also examined the border between New York and Boston. Besides newspaper circulation, he examined other indicators of influence, such as railroad ticket purchases, freight movement, telephone calls, origin of vacationers, addresses of directors of major firms, and associations of hinterland banks. Green found that the various indicators did not give a constant definition of the hinterland. For instance, Springfield would have been classified in Boston's hinterland when newspaper circulation was the criterion but was in New York's sphere of influence when freight movement was the basis of classification. A generalized sphere of influence does exist, but it should be considered a composite of a variety of indicators.

Shopping patterns are an important indicator of the hinterland. Surveys have been used to determine shopping patterns within a metropolitan region or for specific products. The market area for single products or shopping centers can also be found directly by examining sales patterns. Direct measurement is particularly easy when producers have records of their customers' addresses.

Several generalizations can be drawn from the direct empirical studies:

- The proportion of consumers shopping at a central place varies with distance from the shopping area. The closer that individuals are to a shopping area, the greater the proportion of individuals who will shop there.
- The distance that consumers are willing to travel increases as the size of the shopping area increases.
- The distances that consumers travel vary for different types of products. The greater the cost, the longer the travel distance.
- The "pull" of any shopping area is influenced by the nature of competing shopping areas (Huff, 1963).

The first two generalizations are similar to the law of gravitational attraction. The pull of gravity decreases with distance and increases with the size of the object. This similarity has given rise to gravity models of spatial interaction as described below.

Reilly's Law of Retail Gravitation

William J. Reilly (1931) was the first to apply a gravity model to determine the scope of a city's hinterland. Similar techniques have been used to estimate traffic flows between various points. Although Reilly's Law is dated, the initial formulation serves as the basis for modern techniques for measuring spheres of influence. Simply stated, the model postulates that an individual's tendency to shop at center A will increase as the size of place A increases and will decrease as the square of the distance between the customer and center A increases.

The Law of Retail Gravitation states that the breaking point where trade is equally divided between two cities runs through a point where the ratio of the distances squared equals the population ratio:

$$\frac{P_a}{P_b} = \frac{D_a^2}{D_b^2} , \qquad (4\text{-}1)$$

where

P_a = population of city A
P_b = population of city B
D_a = distance from city A to intermediate place
D_b = distance from city B to intermediate place

The breaking point is where the influence of the two cities is equal. If Reilly's Law were applied to the situation depicted in Figure 4.5, the break point would be 56 miles from A. Reilly's Law may be restated to express the distance between a major city, say A, and the outer limit of its trading area:

$$S_a^h = \frac{D_{ab}}{\left(1 + \sqrt{\dfrac{P_b}{P_a}}\right)} ,$$

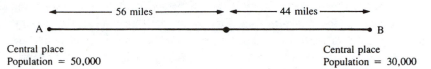

Figure 4.5. Generalized sphere of influence. The attraction of an area increases with size and decreases with distance. Using Reilly's Law of Retail Gravitation, the point at which half the trips are to A and half are to B can be estimated.

where

S_a^h = scope of A's hinterland (distance from A to the breaking point)

D_{ab} = distance from A to B, where B is the nearest competing city

In terms of the hypothetical cities shown in Figure 4.5, the breaking point for A's sphere of influence would be

$$56 \text{ miles} = \frac{100 \text{ miles}}{\left(1 + \sqrt{\dfrac{30,000}{50,000}}\right)}.$$

The breaking point is closer to B than A because A is the larger city. Thus individuals equidistant between A and B would make most of their trips to A. After all, consumers could probably purchase anything in A that they could purchase in B and purchase some things in A that could not be purchased in B. Reilly's Law has been applied principally to determine the breaking point between the cities of approximately the same order with the urban hierarchy. Thus, Reilly used his Law to test the break points between Pittsburgh and the following major cities: Cleveland, Youngstown, Canton, and Steubenville in Ohio; Wheeling and Clarksburg in West Virginia; Cumberland in Maryland; Erie, New Castle, Johnstown, and Altoona in Pennsylvania; and Buffalo in New York. Obviously, there are small cities that have market areas within Pittsburgh's larger hinterland. However, Reilly's study focused on Pittsburgh's hinterland for higher-order services.

The label Law of Retail Gravitation incorrectly implies that Reilly's formula is almost universal in applicability and generates highly accurate results. This is not the case. It does not have the precision of a physical law.

Furthermore, development officials should be aware of three shortcomings that weaken the model's practical use. First, the model implies a sharp break point. In reality, a central place's influence tapers off and hinterlands overlap. Second, the distance parameters (the squares of distance) may not be the same for all types of shopping trips. Third, travel time or cost may be more appropriate than miles as a measure of trade barriers. Some of these criticisms have been addressed by the development of more sophisticated statements of Reilly's Law.

Probabilistic Models

Without modification, Reilly's Law is limited by the inherent uncertainty of consumer behavior. Huff (1963) developed a probabilistic model to determine the influence of shopping areas within metropolitan regions. He estimated the likelihood that an individual in place i would shop at a particular central place j. The probability depended on the distance (usually expressed in time) between the consumer and the destination (j), the number of competing central places, and the size of the central place (j). The measure of size is not necessarily population. Because Huff's model is often used to measure the attractive pull of a retail shopping center within a metropolitan area, the number of square feet of shopping space may be a better size indicator. His formulation may be expressed as

$$P_{is} = \frac{\dfrac{S_s}{(T_{is})^b}}{\displaystyle\sum_{i=1}^{n} \dfrac{S_j}{(T_{ij})^b}} ,$$

where

P_{is} = probability of an individual in place i shopping at the subject center

s_j = size of central place j (subject central place and competitors)

T_{ij} = distance between i and the j expressed in time

T_{is} = distance between i and the subject center expressed in time

b = an exponent (similar to the squared term in Reilly's Law but allowed to vary, depending on what exponent will provide the best fit)

S_s = size of the subject center

Ideally, a survey of customers should be conducted to determine the value of b, depending on the particular type of goods available in the central place.

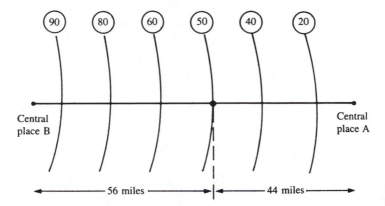

Figure 4.6. Retail trade areas determined by probability contours. Probability contours show the probability that a shopping trip for a resident located anywhere on the "map" will be to A. The closer to A the shopper is, the higher the probability of shopping at A.

The need for a survey is a major impediment because of the extra time and cost involved. However, studies have found that b equals about 2 for most general merchandise goods. Goods and services for which individuals are willing to travel longer distances will have lower coefficients (lower-distance discounts). Often, distance is measured in terms of time rather than miles because time is more relevant in urban travel decisions. In empirical studies, time is usually measured by dividing the hinterland into 5-minute time zones: within 5 minutes, $T = 1$, between 5 and 10 minutes, $T = 2$, and so forth. Huff's probabilistic model results in retail trade areas defined in terms of probability contours as shown in Figure 4.6. The point of 50% probability is the same as Reilly's break-even point.

Retail Spending

The model is often extended to estimate total retail spending that would occur at a shopping center and thus is an important tool for commercial developers and planners. To understand how a real estate planner might use the model, assume that the number of potential customers at each location, POP_i, is known (locations are often defined as census track areas within a given MSA, so the data are available). Assume also that the annual expenditures per person per year for the types of goods sold by the center equals E. These variables can be determined from surveys or published sources. Estimates on annual household budget by product category for various levels of income are available from data published by the U.S. Bureau of Labor Statistics. The "Survey of Buying Power," published by *Sales Management* contains similar data. Total spending of individuals located at i shopping at area j would equal the probability of shopping at i, P_{ij} times total spending:

$$TS_{is} = P_{is} \times POP_i \times E .$$

By summing the total spending for all areas, i, an estimated total spending at a particular location may be derived. Thus gravity models are useful for market-oriented locational decisions.

An Example

To see how the model can be applied, assume that a developer is planning to construct a small neighborhood shopping strip of 10,000 square feet in census tract j, as shown in Figure 4.7. There are two existing centers, A and B. What is the likelihood that an individual located in census tract i will shop at the proposed center? Assume that the distance measure, T_{ij}, increases by 1 for each 5 minutes' distance increase. Applying the probabilistic gravity model yields

$$P_{is} = \frac{\left(\dfrac{10,000}{2^2}\right)}{\left(\dfrac{10,000}{2^2}\right) + \left(\dfrac{15,000}{3^2}\right) + \left(\dfrac{20,000}{4^2}\right)} .$$

Thus the probability of an individual in area i shopping at the proposed center is .46. One may interpret this result as 46% of the population in i shopping only at the proposed center, or, more realistically, the average shoppers will make 46% of their trips to the proposed center in i. (This assumes that the point in the center of the customer area represents the location of all consumers in i.)

The estimate of the likelihood of shopping at the proposed center must be supplemented with additional data before the volume of retail trade can be

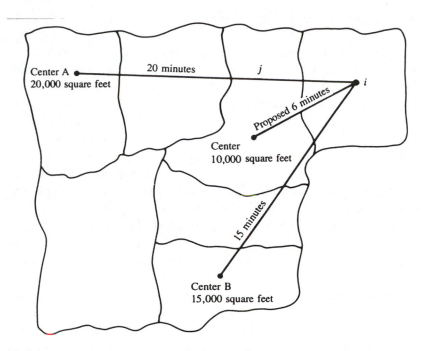

Figure 4.7. Location of customers and competitors. The size and location of other establishments should be considered when estimating the likelihood that a resident located at *i* will shop at the proposed center.

calculated. Specifically, one would need to know the population size of area *i* (POP$_i$) and the annual expenditures per capita (*E*).

To estimate retail trade at the proposed center, assume that the population of census track *i* is 8,000, and the average family in *i* spends $700 per year on the type of retail goods anticipated for the proposed center. Then, the amount of trade estimated for the proposed center from area *i* would equal

$$.46 \times 700 \times 8,000 = \$2,576,000 .$$

The above example indicates only the sales likely to come from individuals in area *i*. To develop an estimate of total sales, the same procedure would have to be followed for every area in the region.

⊠   Hinterland Expansion Strategies

Areas of urban influence are elastic. Urban development officials may increase relative sales in their area by expanding the distance over which individuals will travel to make purchases. Hinterland expansion may be particularly beneficial to merchants in small- or medium-sized cities in agricultural regions where many families have choices (albeit limited) about which city will be their primary market center. Similarly, managers of shopping centers in metropolitan areas may engage in hinterland expansion strategies to increase the scope of the local business sector. Neighborhood and suburban merchants may also benefit by increasing the distance that individuals will be willing to travel to shop in an area.

The theoretical models suggest that the principal levers for increasing an area's hinterland are improving transportation and increasing the variety of goods offered for sale. Accordingly, policymakers should be particularly attuned to ways of improving transportation along routes traveled by customers who may express indifference between shopping in their area and another. Policymakers should also seek to encourage new merchandising lines that are absent in the hinterland area in which they hope to expand. Efforts to expand a district's hinterland may include changing perceptions as well as changing reality.

One approach to hinterland expansion is to change perceptions of distance or travel time. If individuals are familiar with an area, including how to get there, where to park, and which stores can best serve their needs, they may perceive the area as being closer than a place that is an equal distance but unfamiliar. Generally, the more frequently individuals travel to an area the more familiar they feel about it. Sometimes, a cumulative process can occur whereby trips to an area diminish the perception of distance, which then contributes to additional trips. Following this line of reasoning, cities may sponsor festivals or other special regional events designed to attract shoppers who might otherwise be unfamiliar with an area. Simply creating a welcoming attitude will also help. Small rural towns offering services that competing towns do not have may use the advantage to expand their hinterland. Because individuals must travel to the town on some occasions if they wish to purchase particular items, their level of familiarity will increase. Hence communities may extend their market area by building on uncontested products or services.

Consumer perceptions of size and the variety of goods available are also susceptible to influence. Suburban shopping centers have frequently attempted to attract customers beyond their initial market area by promotions that emphasize the variety of goods available or the number of stores at their location. Small towns and urban neighborhood shopping areas have similarly tried to promote themselves as offering a large variety of merchandise. For instance, many communities have developed specializations in crafts, dining, antiques, automobile sales, and so forth. Hence such communities have successfully extended market areas by building on specialties.

⊠ Summary

This chapter described relationships between urban places. When demand is considered in a spatial context, both price and distance from customers determine a firm's sales. If a producer is earning excess profits, other firms will enter the industry, decreasing existing profits. At the same time, the spatial market area of the original firm will decline.

The minimum geographic area that a firm must serve to break even is the inner range. The real outer range is the firm's actual market area. If a firm's actual market area is larger than the inner range, the firm may earn excess profits. Three factors operate to determine market size: economies of scale, demand density (population density and per capita spending), and transportation costs.

Market areas for producers of different products overlap. The overlap allows firms to locate in the same area to achieve agglomeration economies as producers locate near each other. Central places are centers of one or more market areas, with producers locating at the centers. Large cities will be the home of many producers, including some with very large market areas. Smaller cities are the production site of fewer firms with a smaller market area. Market areas form the basis of an urban hierarchy of cities.

Factors that change market areas will alter the system of cities and the hinterland for individual cities.

Evaluations of the central-place model have concluded that the predictions of the model have some validity. However, there are many exceptions to the pristine, symmetrical conclusions. Spatial differences in production costs, transportation cost variations, price discrimination, institutional factors, product differentiation, and nonemployment residential choices are some of the factors not accounted for by the theoretical model.

The empirical evidence suggests that urban patterns in homogeneous agricultural regions fit the theoretical predictions better than activity patterns in dense coastal regions. The model explains the distribution of service and retail activities better than the distribution of manufacturing activities. The theoretical model also explains some shopping center patterns within metropolitan areas.

There are several methods for measuring areas of influence. Such techniques are important because developers, planners, and others may wish to estimate the attraction of new enterprises. Models based on three principles have been useful: Areas of attraction increase with its size, diminish with distance, and diminish with intervening competitors.

An urban hinterland expansion strategy may be a useful economic development tool. Such a strategy could be based on changing the reality or perceptions regarding travel costs to the area and the goods and services available in the area.

Understanding Economic Structure

Repulsion among competing firms was a principal economic force described in the discussion of market areas. However, cohesive forces also operate in regional and metropolitan economies. Production and marketing interdependencies, which tend to attract firms toward each other, are critical to urban development. Economic development officials need to understand existing linkages between firms, how to strengthen existing linkages, and how to establish new, beneficial relationships among firms.

⊠ Agglomeration Economies

Agglomeration economies are cost reductions that occur because economic activity is carried on at one place. Isard (1975) stressed the importance of agglomeration economies: "An understanding of the development of cities and regions cannot be acquired without a full appreciation of the forces of agglomeration and deglomeration that are at play" (p. 113). But although economists acknowledge the importance of agglomeration economies, they generally agree that agglomerative forces are not well understood. This section will focus on the importance of agglomeration economies but will also discuss some conceptual ambiguities. There are several types of agglomeration economies, ranging from savings that accrue to only one establishment to agglomeration economies that spread throughout an entire region.

Internal Agglomeration Economies

Internal agglomeration economies are per-unit cost reductions that accrue to a firm that expands its activity at a particular place. For instance, the expansion of a plant could result in internal agglomeration economies. Because the firm that expands also receives the benefits of the expansion, the agglomeration economies are "internal"; that is, the benefits are captured by the firm engaging in the expansion.

The spreading of fixed costs over a larger output is an important reason for internal agglomeration economies. Other sources of internal agglomeration economies include greater division of labor, potential for using alternative technologies, and saving through bulk purchases. Better use of a manager's time or better use of specialized machinery can result in lower average costs due to increased output. The concentration of General Motors' headquarters activity in Detroit undoubtedly allows a substantial internal agglomeration economy.

Linkages Between Pairs of Businesses

The tendency for firms that trade with each other to locate in the same region is one of the most important causes of industrial agglomeration. Interindustry agglomeration occurs through forward and backward linkages. A forward linkage involves suppliers attracting buyers; a backward linkage involves buyers attracting suppliers. For instance, if a metal fabricating plant was located in an area and a farm implement manufacturer decided to operate nearby to be close to its suppliers, a forward linkage would be the dominant locational factor. Conversely, a backward linkage would exist if the metal fabrication facility was attracted to the farm implement producer.

The question of whether forward or backward linkages are generally more influential is important to development planners. If forward linkages are more important, then a regional policymaker might choose to concentrate on development of primary production activities, such as oil, raw materials, and agriculture. The primary activities could then be expected to attract establishments that will use their inputs. If backward linkages are more effective, then an economic strategy might focus first on the development of final products, such as apparel or food canning. Once established, these activities would induce further growth through backward linkages, attracting suppliers.

Hirschman (1972) argued that underdeveloped countries (and by implication, underdeveloped regions) are characterized by weak interdependencies and linkages. That is, firms in underdeveloped areas do not trade with each other. Agriculture and extractive activities, which are major products in less developed countries, have few backward linkages almost by definition. Furthermore, Hirschman argued that the few forward linkages—principally, refining of raw materials—that might be generated by these activities do not encourage significant development that spreads elsewhere in the economy. Therefore, oil, mineral, and agricultural products are often exported without encouraging additional local economic activity. Likewise, activities that merely put finishing touches on imported products—packaging or making minor modifications—have ineffective linkages that do not generate further growth. Hirschman recommended governmental activity to encourage the development of large-scale industries with significant backward linkages. Forward linkages were not ignored, but they were not considered as effective as backward linkages in inducing further growth.

Hirschman's analysis would suggest the establishment of an automobile assembly facility in a less developed region. Initially, engines, tires, chassis, and other inputs in the assembly process would have to be imported. But Hirschman suggested that some of the imports would eventually be replaced by local products. Locally produced inputs would have a competitive advantage over imported inputs because transportation costs would be less and proximity to the purchaser could improve communications so that locally produced inputs could be more responsive to the needs of the assembly plant. The development of an automobile production complex around a Honda facility in Marysville, Ohio, is an example of growth as the assembly plant attracted suppliers.

Most economists now believe that generalizations about whether forward or backward linkages are more effective are inadequate. Whether forward linkages are more powerful than backward linkages depends on the industry pairs and the specific sets of circumstances. The issue of how to use linkages in the development process calls for additional empirical research.

Localization Economies

Interindustry linkages among direct trading partners are a special type of localization economy, but locationalization economies can encompass much broader based agglomeration economies. Localization economies occur when increases in the output of an entire group of firms at a particular place result in lower costs for firms in that industry at that location. Economic development officials often develop strategies designed to create a cluster of closely related industries in order to attract further growth from firms seeking the benefit from localization economies (Sternberg, 1991).

An enhanced labor pool, specialized machinery, imitation, and the chance to comparison shop are important sources of localization economies.

Labor Pool

First, if many firms in the same industry locate together, they may contribute to the development of a skilled labor pool. Labor market advantages from agglomeration are particularly useful when firms have unstable labor demands, as in the case of many consulting firms concentrated in New York, Boston, Washington, D.C., and California's Silicon Valley. If such firms are in a large center of qualified labor, they can expand their workforce quickly, even when skill requirements are specialized. Labor agglomeration has been considered an important factor in the location of biotechnology firms (Haug and Ness, 1993).

Employment fluctuations may increase the advantage of a concentration of skilled labor. If only one or two firms in an industry were located in the same region, they might have difficulty in hiring specialized workers during periods of peak demand, particularly if both firms had simultaneous increases in demand. Hiring peaks might even out, however, if many firms in similar and competitive businesses were located together. Furthermore, if a local industry had unique skill requirements that were sufficiently large, it might even be feasible to develop a school or a college major to train workers. Such a training program would not only improve the quality and availability of labor but could also enhance the ability of workers to adapt to industrial change. Thus two-year colleges often have excellent training programs designed to meet unique labor market requirements in their district.

Specialized Machinery

The ability to share specialized machinery and other factors of production is another source of localization economies. For example, an area may start developing as a distribution and warehousing center. When the area attains a large enough volume of activity, the market may be sufficient to support a distribution equipment firm that sells, produces, or modifies loading and handling equipment (notice the backward linkage effect). As a consequence of the improved availability of specialized distribution equipment, all distribution and warehousing firms in the area may operate more efficiently. In this example, the specialized distribution equipment firm could not have achieved sufficient size to operate efficiently in an area that had only a few distribution and warehousing establishments. Currently, specialized air cargo shipment facilities offer a similar type of specialization.

Imitation, Modification, and Innovation

Firms in the same industry may be able to imitate and copy one another more readily if they are located together. Therefore, they may be able to respond to changes in their industry quicker than if they were isolated from their competitors. Of course, the firm that is copied may be harmed, so it would be better off in an isolated location where copying would be more difficult. However, managers may not know which firm will develop leading innovations. Therefore, the cluster of firms as a whole may benefit from locating together even though individual firms may be disadvantaged at one time or another. In industries with numerous and scattered innovations, such as the fashion industry, all firms may be better off if they have locations that allow them to imitate quickly. Furthermore, a firm that copies two changes is in a better position to innovate yet another change, perhaps by combining or modifying changes that were taken from other firms. Thus, particularly in fast-changing industries, economies from industrial imitation, modification, and innovation tend to be important sources of localization economies.

Comparison Shopping

Another localization economy can be traced to the desire of individuals to compare products. Individuals may prefer to shop for shoes in a regional shopping mall because they can compare the merchandise in four or five different stores. Firms selling similar products may repel one another under most circumstances, but when consumers have a demand for display variety, similar competing establishments may agglomerate. An additional shoe store in a regional shopping mall may actually benefit all the shoe stores by making the mall a more desirable place to shop for shoes. The additional store may lower the percentage of mall shoe shoppers who purchase at each existing store, but total sales may increase due to the greater number of shoppers.

Households are the direct beneficiaries of display variety because their shopping costs are reduced. But some of these advantages may be captured by retailers due to greater sales. Shopping center owners may also benefit if they can charge retailers higher rents because of the popularity of the shopping center.

Display variety agglomeration is most likely to occur for products that are differentiated and have price variations sufficient to make comparison shopping worthwhile. Few of us would comparison shop for oatmeal or other grocery items, so grocery stores do not tend to agglomerate. Automobile alleys and urban restaurant areas are examples of agglomerations based on display variety. Centers of agglomeration that are national or international in scope include sales conventions (i.e., television executive meetings are often buying conventions for TV programs), New York's Fifth Avenue jewelry stores, and Kentucky horse auctions. Individuals come to these events from around the world to comparison shop.

Retail establishments selling complementary products also tend to cluster. For instance, a theater and a restaurant often locate together, reflecting the fact that people like to eat out before or after seeing a movie. Yet are the theater and restaurant in the same industry? Perhaps if the industry is defined as an "evening's entertainment," they could be considered to be in the same industry. Industry is a slippery concept. Agglomeration clusters may have similar outputs, similar production techniques (but different outputs), or similar input requirements.

Urbanization Economies

Urbanization economies, the most diffuse type of agglomeration economy, are cost savings that accrue to a wide variety of firms when the volume of activity in an entire urban area increases. The firms that share in urbanization economies may be unrelated. Urbanization economies may be attributed to several sources.

Infrastructure

First, urbanization economies may result from economies of scale in public infrastructure. Most publicly provided goods, such as roads, sewers, and fire protection, and some private goods, such as recreation and health facilities, can be included in the concept of urban infrastructure. A region's infrastructure becomes inputs into a wide variety of private production and consumption activities. When significant economies of scale exist in infrastructure provision, increase in size of an urban area allows lower per-unit infrastructure costs. These cost savings may be passed on to producers and consumers, perhaps in the form of lower taxes. However, there need not necessarily be a fixed relationship between the size of an urban area and the size of the units producing the infrastructure. A small area may, in some cases, purchase infrastructure from larger producers to achieve the necessary economies of scale.

The transportation sector is an important component of the urban infrastructure. Firms using transportation facilities will benefit from locating near transportation modes. The larger the number of establishments the better the transportation facilities are likely to be, and all firms using those facilities will benefit. For instance, as the number of air passengers increases, the number and diversity of flights will increase and almost all air travelers will benefit. Likewise, as more highways are constructed, transportation costs will fall for firms shipping by truck, salespeople traveling by car, and tourists visiting regional attractions.

Division of Labor

Urbanization economies may also result from a more extensive division of labor made possible by greater size and activity. In a small town, many aspects of production and distribution must be carried out within the plant because the local market cannot support specialty firms. Activities that cannot be carried out within the plant must be purchased from elsewhere or not performed at all. The extra costs of importing will tend to place the firm at a competitive disadvantage relative to other producers.

Internal Economies

Establishments that sell to a variety of firms and households may also achieve cost reductions as the urban area expands because larger markets will allow firms to achieve internal economies of scale. Internal economies may be passed forward to customers or backwards to the factors of production.

Averaging of Random Variations

Larger urban markets allow for an averaging of variations in economic activity. A drop in sales to one customer or group of customers may be offset by new orders from other customers. Mills and Hamilton (1984) summarized this aspect of agglomeration economies:

> [The] most important of such agglomeration economies is statistical in nature and is an application of the law of large numbers. Sales of outputs and purchases of inputs fluctuate . . . for random, seasonal, cyclical and secular reasons. (p. 18)

Thus, to the extent that business ups and downs are uncorrelated, a firm in an urban area will have fewer scheduling production problems than if it were located in a smaller place. Similarly, labor changes can be accommodated more easily in a large urban area. If a chief financial officer or a tax accountant quits, finding a replacement will be a more significant problem in a small town than in a metropolitan area.

Urban Diseconomies

As the size of an economic concentration increases, diseconomies appear. Urbanization economies may be partially offset by urban diseconomies. Some social scientists believe that crime, anxiety, and loneliness are personal costs of high-density living. Examples of urban diseconomies are the inconvenience, delay, and aggravation associated with congestion in metropolitan regions. Competition for locations near the center of large agglomerations increases rents, which, in turn, repels some firms. The higher wages paid in large cities may reflect compensation necessary to offset negative psychological costs of working in congested areas. Businesses are unequally affected by urban diseconomies, so some firms are repelled from large cities before others.

However, there does not appear to be a size so large that overall urban diseconomies outweigh the economies associated with size. For instance, productivity generally increases as metropolitan size increases. Therefore, urbanization economies tend to outweigh urban diseconomies over the range of city size observed in the world today.

Recap

The impacts of agglomeration economies range from specific to diffuse. The most specific agglomeration economies accrue to a plant. Agglomeration economies affecting pairs of firms are also rather specific. Economies that result when an industry or an industrial cluster expands are slightly more diffuse. Urbanization economies are the most diffuse type of agglomeration economy. They depend on the size of the entire urban area, and the benefits of the agglomeration are shared by a wide variety of businesses.

⊠　External-Economy Industries

Industries composed of firms that are dependent on many diffuse agglomeration economies with other nearby establishments are referred to as external-economy industries. Firms in external-economy industries receive spillover benefits when related establishments locate in the area. Examples of external-economy industries are fur goods, handbags, children's coats, dresses, and book publishing. These are generally rapid-change industries. Firms in these industries must purchase a variety of inputs from other firms. The inputs often must be obtained quickly, and rapid changes in the product, such as style changes, make flexibility important.

External-economy industries tend to concentrate in large urban areas because of the diversity of products and information available. Over 90% of all U.S. jobs in paints and varnishes, periodicals, security and commodity brokerage, millinery, and aircraft are in large urban areas. The concentration in production in such activities is much greater than could be explained based on market orientation.

Lichtenberg (1960) examined industries that he considered as highly dependent on external relationships and found that nearly all of the external-economy industries were overrepresented in the New York area. The high location quotients for New York in publishing and apparel (see Table 5.1 next section) indicate that Lichtenberg's findings are still relevant. New York accounted for about 10% of all national employment at the time of his study, but the region accounted for a much higher percentage of employment in the external-economy industries. Furthermore, he found that New York-based firms in the external economy industries tend to be smaller than similar firms located elsewhere. Lichtenberg attributed this size difference to the ability of the New York-based firms to purchase inputs and obtain services quickly at reasonable costs outside the firm. In contrast, firms located in smaller cities were more likely to produce inputs internally rather than purchasing from vendors. Therefore, external-economy firms located in smaller cities require more "in house" capacity.

⊠   Comparative Measures of Economic Structure

Although agglomeration economies is an important theoretical concept for understanding economic structure, we also need means to measure and analyze economic activities. This section describes some of the important empirical tools used by urban and regional economists, beginning with the description of a widely used way of categorizing industries. Next, location quotients are explained, and then techniques for using location quotients for estimating exports are illustrated, followed by a discussion of the coefficient of specialization.

Standard Industrial Classifications

The Standard Industrial Classification (SIC) system is the most commonly used means of labeling economic activities. It is a uniform identification procedure used by most U.S. agencies that collect and analyze data on economic activity. Industries listed in Table 5.1 are identified by a numerical SIC code as well as industry name. A SIC code is assigned to each business establishment. The code reflects the specific activity at that site and places the establishment within a larger industrial group. For instance, a meat-packing plant would have a SIC number of 2011. The first two digits indicate that it is a food processing establishment. All meat products establishments are in SIC 201. Thus the meat-packing designation indicates that the activity is part of the meat products industries, which are themselves part of the food products group.

The major industrial categories (sometimes referred to as "one digit industries") are agriculture, forestry, and fisheries; mining; construction; manufacturing; wholesale and retail trade; finance, insurance, and real estate; services; transportation, communication, electric, gas, and sanitary services; and government.

A firm may have several plants or establishments producing a variety of products. The SIC system classifies establishments (i.e., plants) rather than firms or companies. In most instances, the establishment is a facility at a single location. If a diversified company makes several different products at different sites, it will have plants in different SIC categories.

TABLE 5.1 Location Quotients in Four Major Urban Regions, 1990

SIC		*Chicago*	*Houston*	*Los Angeles*	*New York*
Manufacturing					
20	Food products	0.956	0.524	0.099	0.356
23	Apparel	0.310	0.062	2.352	2.345
24	Lumber or wood	0.265	0.210	0.464	0.133
25	Furniture, fixtures	0.826	0.177	1.637	0.477
26	Paper and allied products	1.137	0.287	0.648	0.447
27	Printing and publishing	1.369	0.544	0.942	1.719
28	Chemicals	0.584	2.480	0.663	0.409
29	Petroleum or coal	1.109	4.207	1.713	0.045
30	Rubber and plastic	1.374	0.667	0.953	0.223
32	Stone, clay, glass	0.598	0.555	0.752	0.192
33	Primary metals	0.965	0.473	0.691	0.146
34	Fabricated markets	1.447	1.066	1.159	0.303
35	Machinery except electrical	1.230	1.180	0.728	0.158
36	Electronic equipment	1.380	0.333	0.953	0.270
37	Transportation equipment	0.279	0.206	2.511	0.092
38	Instrument and related	0.862	0.449	1.621	0.285
Transportation, etc.		1.058	0.250	0.982	1.212
Wholesale		1.226	1.159	1.186	1.111
Retail		0.874	0.888	0.794	0.832
Finance, insurance, and real estate		1.226	1.010	1.060	2.104
Services		1.007	1.025	1.081	1.293

If a single plant makes more than one product, the establishment is classified according to the dominant product. For example, suppose a plant produced construction machinery (SIC 3531) and mining machinery (SIC 3532). The first two digits indicate that the establishment is in the "machines, except electrical" category. The first three digits indicate "construction and related machinery." If over half of the output (in terms of sales) were in construction machinery, the entire activity would be considered as SIC 3531.

Because more than one product can be produced by a single establishment, the SIC system may lead to an underestimation of the variety of goods and services produced in a region. Furthermore, changes in the internal operations of a plant can cause an establishment to be reclassified by a different four-digit code. Consequently, it is sometimes difficult to distinguish between an internal change in production, on the one hand, and the death of one firm and the establishment of another, on the other.

Although the four-digit code provides considerable detail, a variety of separate activities are still lumped together within one four-digit designation. For instance, SIC 3729, "aircraft engines and engine parts," includes about 50 separate manufactured items, such as "starting vibrators" and "rocket motors."

Information on community economic activity is limited by the disclosure rule. Data will usually not be released if they can be traced to a particular establishment. For instance, if there is only one bakery (SIC 205) in a county, no information on that industry will be disclosed. However, bakery information may be included in the description of the food products sector (SIC 20). The disclosure rule is a particular problem for small-region data collection. Even in large regions, disclosure problems will occur at the three- and four-digit level of detail.

Location Quotients

The location quotient (LQ) is a technique for assessing a region's specialization in an industry. The industrial composition of a local economy may be better understood by comparing the local industrial structure with other cities or with the country as a whole than by examining a local economy in isolation. For instance, suppose it was determined that fabricated metals accounted for 12% of total employment in a community. Although this information may be useful for some purposes, it does not tell us whether the economy is highly concentrated in metal fabrication compared with other cities.

The employment location quotient is the ratio of the percentage of regional employment in a particular industry to the comparable percentage in a benchmark area. The country is usually the benchmark area, although states or similar regions may also be used as reference points. Accordingly, the location quotient for industry i is generally expressed as

$$LQ_i = \frac{\dfrac{e_i}{e_t}}{\dfrac{US_i}{US_t}}, \qquad (5\text{-}1)$$

where

LQ_i = location quotient for industry i

e_i = local employment in industry i
e_t = total local employment
US_i = national employment for industry i
US_t = total national employment

Quotients can vary among regions due to differences in consumption and production. The term LQ = 1 for a particular industry means that the region has the same percentage of employment in that industry as found nationally. The term LQ < 1 implies that the area has a less than proportionate share of employment in a particular industry, whereas the term LQ > 1 implies a greater than proportionate concentration of employment.

Location quotients can be useful tools for identifying industries in which a region has a disproportionate level of employment. The reasons for a community having concentrations of employment in particular industries can often be traced to a current or historical locational advantage. If an industry is underrepresented locally, a development planner might investigate why employment is low and what can be done to increase it. This is not to say that communities should strive to develop economies with structures that are identical to the U.S. average. Therefore, good judgment is important in determining how to interpret location quotients.

Table 5.1 shows the location quotients for several major metropolitan regions. They are roughly consistent with our casual knowledge of these regions. For instance, New York has high location quotients in apparel, printing, and FIRE (finance, insurance, and real estate). The Los Angeles location quotient in transportation equipment reflects the area's heavy concentration in aerospace production. The dominance of petroleum and chemicals in Houston is consistent with our perception of the Texas economy.

The picture of industrial structure given by the location quotient can change depending on the level of industrial detail used in the calculations. For instance, the data in Table 5.1 reflect the two-digit level of industrial detail. Houston is obviously highly concentrated in the chemical industry when the classification is limited to two digits. However, Houston does not have high concentrations in all aspects of chemical production. If the two-digit chemical industry were divided into more narrowly defined sectors, three-digit industries, Houston would be seen to have LQs significantly less than 1 for some chemical activities and a very high LQ for petrochemicals.

Location quotients are a versatile tool. Although employment is the most frequently used measure of the extent of economic concentration, value added, sales, and other measures of activity have also been used. The formula shown in Equation 5-1 used industrial employment as the specialization variable and total employment as the reference variable. However, the specialization variable need not even be the same as the reference variable. We might refer to a location quotient for linked activities, LQ_L. For instance, grain storage facilities could be used as an indication of specialization with reference to grain production:

$$LQ_L = \frac{\frac{gs}{gp}}{\frac{GS}{GP}},$$

(5-2)

where

LQ_L = location quotient for linked activities
gs   = local grain storage in cubic feet
gp   = local grain production
GS   = U.S. grain storage in cubic feet
GP   = U.S. grain production

In this case, a very low location quotient for grain storage facilities might lead a development planner to attempt to encourage a grain storage business enterprise. Clearly, the LQ can be a very useful tool for development officials seeking to target industries.

How to Estimate Export Employment[1]

The difference between export activities and activities that serve local consumers is an important structural distinction. The purpose of this section is not to describe the role of exports in the growth process but to show how location quotients can be used to estimate regional exports.

To establish the link between location quotients and export employment, the following assumptions are necessary:

1. There is no cross hauling of goods (i.e., if automobiles are exported from Detroit, automobiles will not simultaneously be imported).
2. The output employment ratio is identical in all regions.

3. Consumption patterns throughout the country are identical.
4. The product of each SIC industry is identical in each region.
5. There is no international trade.

Under these circumstances, an LQ > 1 means that the region has more individuals employed in the particular industry than would be expected based on benchmark patterns. A possible explanation for a higher than average proportion of regional employment in a particular sector is that some of the sector's workers are producing exports—products that are sold outside the region. If this explanation is valid, an LQ > 1 means that some portion of the employees in that industry is producing for export. Conversely, an LQ < 1 means that the product is underproduced locally and hence must be imported. Exact self-sufficiency is signified by the LQ equaling 1.

Export employment can be estimated using a variant of location quotient. If LQ = 1 means exact self-sufficiency, then export employment in an industry would be the excess employment above the number necessary to satisfy local needs. Self-sufficient employment would be the number required to bring the location quotient to 1. Let s_i equal the self-sufficient employment level. Then,

$$1 = \frac{\dfrac{s_i}{e_t}}{\dfrac{US_i}{US_t}} \tag{5-3}$$

or

$$s_i = \frac{US_i}{US_t} \times e_t , \tag{5-4}$$

where

US_i = United States employment in industry i
US_t = the total employment in the country
e_t = total local employment

Equation 5-3 may be modified to estimate export employment in industry i, x_i:

$$x_i = e_i - s_i \qquad (5\text{-}5)$$

or

$$x_i = e_i - e_t \left(\frac{US_i}{US_t} \right). \qquad (5\text{-}6)$$

Total export employment is the sum of the export employment in the individual sectors. Therefore, total regional export employment x_t may be expressed as

$$x_t = \sum x_i . \qquad (5\text{-}7)$$

Critique

Unfortunately, the location quotient is not a precise indicator of the extent of importing and exporting. Consequently, the LQ technique often underestimates exports. When the initial assumptions are examined, other explanations for the size of location quotients become apparent.

First, when analysts assume that an LQ of 1 implies exact self-sufficiency, they overlook the possibility of cross-hauling. If cross-hauling existed, an area with an LQ = 1 could be exporting and importing a product simultaneously.

Second, if workers in a region are more productive than workers elsewhere, an $LQ_i < 1$ might be appropriate for a community, even though the industry was an exporter of the product. Conversely, an unproductive sector could have a high LQ_i, even though it produced only for local consumption. To minimize the problem of worker productivity differences, value-added or total output could be used to develop the location quotient.

Third, if there are significant regional variations in the level of demand, the location quotient will not necessarily reflect the extent of exports or imports. For instance, Southern cities have had a disproportionate level of employment in air conditioning maintenance. However, this difference is due to greater local demand compared to the rest of the United States rather than to significant exportation of such goods and services.

Fourth, the estimated level of exports depends on the level of industrial detail and product differentiation. As pointed out previously, when broad industrial categories are examined, the LQs tend to be closer to 1 than when more detailed industries are examined. A region could have a low location quotient in manufacturing, indicating no exports, but some sectors within manufacturing may be exporters. Similarly, Detroit is a net exporter of automobiles, but it also imports models of cars not made in Detroit due to product differentiation. Because of the existence of cross-hauling, the volume of exports estimated by the LQ technique will be subject to error. Cross-hauling of identical products could even occur under some circumstances. Generally, the more detailed the industrial breakdown, the greater the export-ing sector will appear. Thus the direction of bias due to the failure to disaggregate completely or due to product differentiation is predictable.

Fifth, a location quotient of 1 indicates self-sufficiency only in a closed national economy. However, the United States imports products from the rest of the world. Hence the average community with a location quotient of 1 for a particular good or service may still be exporting or importing some of the commodity.

Rebuttal

The criticisms above suggested that the location quotient approach to determining exports would not result in an exact estimate of export activity. Empirical studies indicate that the number of individuals in the export sector is normally underestimated when location quotients are used to estimate exports. However, the technique has three important advantages that are responsible for its continued popularity.

First and foremost, location quotients are an inexpensive way to describe a region's exports because they can be constructed from published data. Second, location quotients can help estimate indirect exports. For instance, a city that exports computers may have a high location quotient in molded plastic parts because the plastic is embodied in the computer and indirectly exported. If the plastic parts manufacturers were asked directly, they might respond that their products were sold within the local economy and not exported. However, they are, in fact, indirect exports. Unfortunately, the LQ technique does not allow determination of whether products like molded plastics are exported as part of computers or whether they are exported directly. Third, the LQ technique applies equally to commodities and services. How can a service be exported? A service can be considered an export when nonresidents enter the region to purchase a service. In this sense, Orlando, Florida, is an exporter of entertainment services because vacationers go to Disney World.

The Minimum Requirements Technique

Some analysts believe that a more accurate picture of the local export sectors can be obtained by the minimum requirements (MR) technique. Whereas the LQ technique normally uses the entire national economy as a benchmark, the MR approach bases the self-sufficient employment level on analysis of similar areas. For instance, suppose you wish to determine the export employment for a region with a population of 100,000. The MR approach could involve examination of, say, 20 cities of similar size. The cities might be selected based on other common characteristics such as location or per capita income. The city with the smallest location quotient in an industry (i.e., smallest percentage employment) would be presumed to represent the minimum requirement needed by a city to satisfy its domestic needs. Thus it represents the self-sufficient level. The MR approach normally results in a higher level of estimated exports than does the LQ technique. A variant of the MR technique might use some other threshold, such as the fifth smallest location quotient, as the minimum requirement for self-sufficiency. Export employment would be all employment above the MR threshold.

Coefficient of Specialization

Many local development officials are concerned that the coefficient of specialization measures the extent that a region's industrial structure differs from some standard, such as the national industrial structure. Table 5.2 indicates the coefficient of specialization for the East North Central region (Ohio, Indiana, Illinois, Michigan, and Wisconsin) in terms of employment by major industrial categories. In 1991, the East North Central region had a specialization coefficient of .054, due largely to the high concentration in manufacturing.

The first two columns in Table 5.2 show the percentage employment in each of the sectors. The third column shows the differences between the proportion of U.S. employment from each sector and the comparable regional percentage. For the region, the positive differences in some sectors must be offset by negative percentages in other sectors. The sum of the positive differences (or the absolute value of the negative differences) is the coefficient of specialization. The more detailed the industrial structure, the larger the coefficient of specialization will be.

A coefficient of zero would indicate that the region had exactly the same percentage of employment or other variable from each sector as found

TABLE 5.2 Coefficients of Specialization: East North Central Region, 1991

	% of Total [a] Employment		
Industry Group	*United States*	*East North Central*	*Difference*
Construction	.043	.037	.006
Manufacturing	.169	.218	−.049
Transportation	.053	.049	.004
Wholesale and retail trade	.233	.238	−.005
Services	.264	.244	.020
Government	.169	.152	.017
Sum of positive differences			.054

NOTE: a. Totals will not add to 100% due to rounding.

nationally. The maximum coefficient would approach 100; for instance, residents of a region might receive all their income from sources not available elsewhere in the United States. A coefficient of specialization is high or low by comparison with other areas.

Like location quotients, the coefficient of specialization is a versatile tool. It can be used to examine sales, value-added sales, and so forth. The coefficient of specialization could be used to determine the extent to which the demographic pattern of a region—age, sex, and/or race—fits the national average.

⊠ Other Aspects of Regional Structure

The economic perspective is traditional and widely used among regional economists. However, the structure of a local economy includes more than industrial composition. A detailed understanding of an area's structure might include the occupational, demographic, ownership, market, political and social structure as well. All of these factors may influence the course of economic development.

⊠ Summary

Economic development officials need to understand existing linkages between firms and industries within a local economy, so they can strengthen existing linkages and help build new ones. This chapter examined cohesive forces that tend to link firms within a region and quantitative tools that can be used to understand local economic structure.

Cost reduction due to spatial concentration of economic activity are termed agglomeration economies. Internal agglomeration economies are attributed to an increase in one firm's activities at a single place. Firms that trade with each other often benefit from locating in proximity. Localization economies accrue to firms in a particular industry from expansion of an activity cluster in an area. They have been attributable to development of a qualified labor pool, specialized equipment, imitation/modification/innovation, and comparison shopping. Urbanization economies are the most diffuse type of agglomeration economy, resulting from an expansion in overall economic activity in an area. Shared infrastructure and economies from averaging random variations are sources of urbanization economies.

The Standard Industrial Classification system is a widely used way of organizing information about industries.

Location quotients are a popular technique for comparing the size of a local industry to that industry's importance in the national economy. The location quotient formula is

$$LQ = \frac{\% \text{ of local employment in industry } i}{\% \text{ of national employment in industry } i}.$$

Location quotients may be used with sales, value added, or other measures of activity in addition to employment.

A location quotient greater than 1 indicates that the industry is more dominant in the local economy than nationally. Given a set of very strict assumptions, the location quotient has been used to estimate export employment. Although location quotients are an imperfect tool for describing a local economy and estimating exports, they are widely used because they are an inexpensive technique, reflect indirect imports, and apply to both goods and services.

All employment above the level necessary to set an industry's location quotient to equal 1 can be considered export employment. Alternatively, the minimum requirements technique uses the minimum location quotient from a group of similar cities as a benchmark. All employment above the level for the benchmark location quotient is considered export.

The coefficient of specialization shows the extent to which an area's industrial structure differs from the nation or some other point of comparison.

This chapter was primarily concerned with industrial structure. However, economic development analysis should be aware that other types of structure can influence an area's economic future.

⊠ **Note**

1. In urban and regional economics, the term "export" normally means that the product is sold outside the area, not outside the country.

6

Regional Growth and Development

Fundamental Perspective

Previous chapters addressed the issue of economic growth indirectly. The implications of various models for urban and regional growth have been very near the surface. Local growth is affected by location and expansion decisions of firms, the area's place in the system of cities, and its economic structure. This chapter presents fundamental theories of urban and regional growth. Chapter 7 then builds on the fundamentals by developing additional models and perspectives.

⊠ Stages of Growth

Thompson (1968) and Jacobs (1969) observed that cities pass through stages as they develop. Although there are differences in the terminology, emphasis and details, the similarities between their descriptions are striking. Table 6.1 summarizes the stages of growth described by Thompson and Jacobs.

The stages of growth indicate that metropolitan areas initially export one or a few products. The initial export becomes the foundation for additional activities. During the second and third stages of the development process, the local economy becomes more complex. Exports become more diversified, and goods previously imported into the area may be produced internally (import

TABLE 6.1 Stages of Urban Growth

Thompson's (1968) Stages of Growth	*Jacobs's (1969) Stages of Growth*
1. Export specialization: "The local economy is the lengthened shadow of a single, dominant industry" (pp. 15-16).	1. Expanding market for a few exports and suppliers of the export.
2. Export complex: "Local production broadens and/or depends by extending forward or backward" (pp. 15-16).	2. Suppliers begin exporting directly.
3. Economic maturation: "The principal expansion is in the direction of replacing imports" (pp. 15-16).	3. Goods initially imported into the area are produced and sold locally.
4. Regional metropolis: "The local economy becomes a node connecting and controlling neighboring cities" (pp. 15-16).	4. The city's enlarged and diversified local economy becomes a potential source of exports. The exports increase the volume of imports.
5. Technical-professional virtuosity: "National eminence in some specialized economic function is achieved" (pp. 15-16).	5. New work is constantly developed. An "economic reciprocating system" results in new skill or businesses.

substitution). For instance, Chicago's manufacturing activities began as small operations designed to serve the local market. Products originally intended to satisfy local customers may make the product unique and help establish an export demand. Also, the increases in variety of goods that the locality exports may cause the number of suppliers to the dominant exporter to increase. Development of new economic activities is a critical element for continued growth. In the fourth stage, the area becomes a regional center by developing a hinterland that depends on the city for a variety of goods and services. As cities grow, they improve their ability to develop or improve products and production processes as well as to copy what others have done. The service sectors such as education, banking and real estate become important in generating new products and attracting new industry. This innovative and imitative ability contributes to further growth in the fifth stage.

Once an area reaches a critical mass, the local economy has resources to develop new work. Thompson (1968) referred to an "urban size ratchet" because he believed that once a threshold was reached urban areas could muster the resources—public and private—to maintain their local economies:

> If the growth of an urban area persists long enough to raise the area to some critical size, power, huge fixed investments, a rich local market, and a steady

supply of industrial leadership may almost ensure its continued growth and
fully ensure against absolute decline. (p. 24)

The strength of the urban size ratchet can be overstated. During recent years,
many cities and even some metropolitan areas have declined, even after
attaining dominance within a region. The fact that larger and more complex
cities have abilities to generate new economic activity is important to understanding the development process.

Industrial Filtering (Life Cycle Model)

The theory of industrial filtering helps explain the necessity for metropolitan areas to generate new exports. In Thompson's view, metropolitan
areas have a pioneering role in the development process. Larger urban areas
tend to be the location of firms when their industries are in the early stages of
their life cycle. Activities eventually filter down from their urban birthplace
to the less urban hinterland. During the early stages of industrial development,
firms often require advanced technical skills, support of other business, and
production flexibility. Later, after the production process has become more
routine, the need for skills, business support, and flexibility may decrease and
other locational factors become more important. Firms engaged in routine
work may relocate or expand in less urban areas in search of lower production
costs. Thus urban areas are on a treadmill, developing new economic activities
as old activities filter down to lower-production-cost areas. Also, larger
metropolitan areas may retain control of research and development functions
within an industry even as the routine functions are dispersed to low-production-
cost sites.

Adding New Work to Old

Jacobs (1969) used the phrase "adding new work to old" to describe what
she believed was a key element in the movement through the developmental
stages. Cities do not grow by simply doing more of what they have done
previously. Economies expand by developing new kinds of work. New work
results in more diversified exports products, many of which started production
simply to replace imports; but new work is usually an extension or modification of previous activities. The process of adding new work to old is so
pervasive that it is often overlooked, as when a day care center offers a

"sick-child care service" in addition to normal service. The cumulative impact of such activities is vital to development. New work often increases the specialization of labor. A manufacturer of kitchen equipment, a delicatessen, a cheese importer, and a nightclub might all have resulted from new work being added to an original restaurant. Creating new work also helps conserve old work. As a product spins off from an old activity, the new product may be a supplier or a purchaser supporting the "mother" activity.

Jacobs (1969) indicated that larger areas have an edge in the ability to add new work to old:

> The greater the sheer numbers and varieties of division of labor already achieved in an economy, the greater the economy's inherent capacity for adding still more kinds of goods and services. Also, the possibilities increase for combining the existing divisions of labor. (p. 59)

Many instances of service duplication and congestion that urban critics claim are inefficiencies of large places are defended by Jacobs, who believes they contribute to the innovative climate that encourages new products and processes. Thus the analysis of how new work develops contributes to our understanding of the process of urban innovation.

Movement Between Stages and Policy Implications

How do cities move from one stage to the next? Theories regarding stages of growth (including the theories of Jacobs and Thompson) are weak in answering this question. To Jacobs, the key is the ability to add new work to old. But why do some areas move to the next stage and others do not? According to Thompson (1968), momentum gained during an early stage of development may help propel an area to the next stage. At each stage, the growth stimulus must be sufficient to lift an area to a level complex and large enough so that additional products can be developed and produced locally. To continue to move up the urban hierarchy, momentum must be considered relative to other cities, particularly for areas striving toward the regional metropolis stage.

Economic development officials should consider what stage of growth their area has attained as they draft development strategies. For instance, a small community may be well served by a focus on direct export expansion. Planners in larger areas may seek ways the area may benefit from a diversified economy. However, both the Jacobs and Thompson models suggest that

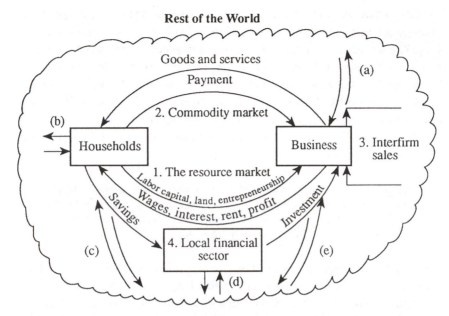

Figure 6.1. A local circular flow model. The circular flow diagram shows major sectors of an economy and how they interact. The main difference between the nation and a regional economy is the importance of monetary inflow (exports) and outflow (imports).

complex urban economies must develop new products and processes to grow. Accordingly, a focus on innovation and entrepreneurship is indicated.

⊠ Circular Flow Model

A circular flow model is illustrated in Figure 6.1. The circular flow is not a theory of *how* a region grows because it implies no causal relationships. Rather, it is a stylized picture of some important linkages and money flows. It is the basis for several important theories of growth discussed later.

Elements of the Circular Flow Model

In the highly simplified circular flow model, the economy is divided into households and businesses. These categories overlap because the same person can be in the household category while also fulfilling a business role. Specifically, the same individual may be in the business sector when purchasing factors of production and in the household role when purchasing goods and services.

There are five important types of markets in the circular flow model:

- *Resource Market.* The lower portion of Figure 6.1, the resource market, shows that businesses purchase factors of production from households. In return for the factors of production, households receive wages, rents, interests, and profits. Notice that profits are not retained by businesses in this model. If none of the households earn income outside of the community, the sum of payments received by households from area businesses would equal total regional income.

- *Commodity Market.* The local commodity market is the second subsector of the model regional economy. In this market, households purchase goods and services from local businesses. If we assume no nonlocal customers, local households spending will account for the net (excluding local firms selling to each other) business receipts.

- *Interfirm Sales.* Interfirm sales are an important category of local transactions. Establishments within an area sell intermediate goods and services. The role of interindustry transactions is described in detail later.

- *Local Financial Sectors.* The fourth set of transactions occurs within the local financial sector. Some local household savings flow into the local financial sector. In Figure 6.1, all savings is by households, implying that businesses do not retain earnings. Even if a household saves by putting money in a sock rather than in an established savings institution, that transaction is considered savings in the local financial sector. Household savings take two forms. A part of the local savings is invested locally. Other savings flow out of the area and are presumably deposited in outside financial institutions or invested directly in outside business ventures by local households. Savings invested outside the area are treated as monetary outflows.

- *Exchanges With the Rest of the World.* The fifth set of transactions is necessary because of the region's interaction with the rest of the world. Exchange with the rest of the world—other regions within and outside the country—are important to the local economy model. Some aspects of an open economy were previously described in the discussion of financial transactions. Monetary inflows and outflows constitute a relatively small but growing percentage of economic activity for the United States as a whole. Exports constitute about 10% of the U.S. gross national product (GNP). However, for a region, monetary inflows may account for well over half of business receipts or, expressing the idea in real terms, exports may account for over half of business sales. Normally, the smaller the region the more open the economy and the more important money inflows and outflows are. Notice that households, businesses, and the local financial sector are all shown to interact with the rest of the world. These interactions result in monetary inflows and outflows.

Segment a of Figure 6.1 represents business sales to nonresidents that result in a counterflow of money into the area. Businesses also make purchases outside the area. Segment b represents household transactions outside the area, such as the direct export of labor as would be the case of someone working outside the area, and segment c represents direct investment on savings placed outside the area. The return on such investments constitutes a counterflow. Segment d represents financial exchanges with the rest of the world that flow through the local financial sector. Outside investments made directly to local businesses and the return on such investments are represented by segment e.

Money flows into a region for a variety of reasons: gifts from relatives, payments for services performed for nonresidents, payment for goods sold to nonresidents, governmental transfer payments, interest on nonlocal investments made outside the area, and so forth. A portion of the monetary inflows would go directly to households, immediately increasing household income if households sold labor services. Another portion accrues to businesses. This would be the case when businesses sell goods and services to nonresidents. Businesses also receive money inflows when nonresidents make investments in local businesses.

Money inflows that accrue to local business may become income to households as businesses pay the households for the factors of production used in producing the goods and services.[1] However, only a portion of business sales becomes income to local residences. Suppose a nonresident purchased a $3,000 stamping machine from a local business. How much income will accrue to households? If the machine were produced entirely within the area, then the full $3,000 will flow to households in the form of wages, rents, interest, and profits. But it is unrealistic to suppose the entire machine was produced locally. More realistically, some of the materials necessary for the production of the stamping machine were purchased from another area outside the region. In this case, the firm making the stamping machine might spend a portion of the $3,000 purchase price, say, $1,000, to replenish the inventories from outside used in production. Only $2,000 would accrue to local households. Local households may be perceived as receiving the value added locally, not the total value of exports. Accordingly, the sale of an item for export may be viewed as a net monetary inflow equal to the total value of the product less the cost of the components purchased from outside the community.

Monetary outflows refers to money that leaves the local economy. Monetary outflows occur when households purchase goods or services from outside the area, pay taxes to nonlocal governments, make interest payments to nonresidents, invest in business outside the area, and so forth. Many consumer imports are indirect. For instance, if a person purchases a hat from a local haberdasher, a portion of that expenditure may be attributed to the import of the hat that was made elsewhere. Only the local value added will accrue to household income. As described in the above discussion of the stamping machine, businesses contribute to monetary outflows when they purchase inventories and parts from outside the area.

A model is intended to simplify reality. It is tempting to add details in order to make the model more realistic. However, too much added complexity defeats the purpose of a model, which is to highlight key factors. Perhaps the elements shown in Figure 6.1 may already be too complicated to be a good model. Nevertheless, it is usually a worthwhile exercise to examine what has been excluded from models and to ask whether the simplifications seriously distort the reality the model represents.

Equilibrium and Change

The difference between the size of monetary inflows and outflows is critical to local economic growth. Monetary inflows can cause the entire volume (or velocity) of money circulating within a city to increase. This, in turn, may increase incomes and employment.

Payments for goods produced in the area and sold elsewhere are a major source of income for the community. For example, when a Detroit-made automobile is sold to a resident of Chicago (or more accurately, when the Detroit-made automobile is sold to an auto dealer who expects to sell it to a Chicago resident), money flows into the Detroit area and becomes income. The inflow of money does not by itself increase real output. However, monetary inflows increase the ability of residents to command additional goods and services and may attract additional resources to the area or stimulate the use of previously unemployed local resources. Sales of goods and services to nonlocal customers are often referred to as "exports." Other nonlocal sources of community income include interest payments from outside corporations, government transfers such as Social Security, gifts received, and investments by nonresidents.

Monetary outflows shrink an area's circular flow and consequently decrease local income and employment. For example, when residents of one area increase their purchases from neighboring regions, the outflow represents foregone income to local business—money that could have been paid to local households in subsequent transactions. Purchases of goods and services from nonlocal sources are called imports. The term "imports" applies to all purchases made outside the city and not just to international transactions. Thus the resident of Chicago who purchases a car from Detroit causes an outflow of funds from Chicago and an inflow of dollars to Detroit (assuming auto retailers maintain their inventories by replacing the car they sold).

What is the equilibrium condition of the model represented in Figure 6.1? When monetary outflows equal monetary inflows, the community income level will remain constant. The equilibrium condition can be proven mathematically, but it can also be grasped intuitively by using the bathtub analogy. The amount of water in the tub will remain constant only when the water flowing from the faucet equals the amount that leaves through the drain.

The Multiplier

To illustrate the multiplier, suppose a business increases its sales by increasing exports to a business in a nearby state. A portion of the increase will accrue to households as payment for labor and other services involved in producing the output. Households will spend a fraction of the increased earnings in local establishments, thereby expanding the local consumer market and allowing businesses to purchase additional factors of production. However, businesses and households will also purchase from outside the area and cause monetary outflows. Therefore, the process of local spending and respending will not continue at the same level indefinitely.

Figure 6.2 illustrates what might happen if a major convention were held in a city. Suppose the convention resulted in increased spending by nonresidents of $260,000. Assume that of the $260,000 in increased spending, $160,000 went to outside suppliers and to a nonlocal corporation that owns the major hotel. Consequently, $100,000 of the initial spending would go to residents who provided services for the conventioneers. Of the $100,000, local residents might spend $80,000 locally. The remaining $20,000 would flow outside the city as households spent or invested outside the local area. Carrying the process further, of the $80,000 spent at local businesses, $50,000 might be used by local businesses to replace inventories (purchased outside

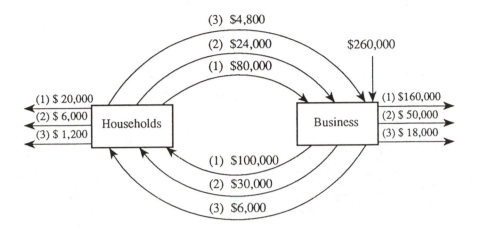

Figure 6.2. A community income/expenditure pattern. The multiplier works through respending of income. Totals after all of the increase leaks out: leakages, $260,000; business receipts, $370,000; income, $143,000.

the city) and $30,000 may be returned to residents in the form of wages, rent, interest, and profits. Thus the $260,000 of additional spending resulted in an increase of $100,000 in local income initially and $30,000 of income in a second round of spending. In this instance, because of imports of local businesses, the marginal propensity to consume locally would be $30,000/$100,000, or .3. If the process were to continue, after a few rounds the original $100,000 would leak out of the community in the form of outside business and consumer spending—imports. Because of successive rounds of local spending, about $43,000 of household income would be created in addition to the initial $100,000.[2] The larger the leakages per transaction, the smaller the total increase in household income.

The multiplier has a different effect if the monetary inflow occurs only once compared to a permanent increase in income. To distinguish between temporary and permanent increases in exports, assume that local convention business increased permanently by $260,000 annually. An extra $100,000 would be earned by households every period. Community income would be increased by $130,000 in the second period—the $30,000 second-round

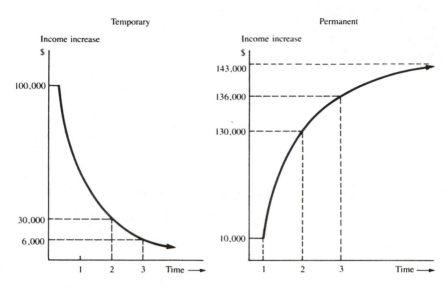

Figure 6.3. Income paths from temporary and permanent increases in monetary inflows. A temporary increase in monetary inflows will increase income by successively smaller amounts. A permanent increase in monetary inflows will permanently increase income by a multiple of the original increase.

increase shown in Figure 6.2 plus the extra $100,000 earnings from the first-round spending of the second year. In the third period, total income would rise to the sum of first-round Year 3 income ($100,000), second-round Year 2 income ($30,000), and third-round Year 1 income ($6,000), or $136,000. Thus the permanent increase in inflows would cause annual community income to rise permanently by $143,000. Figure 6.3 compares the income effects of a temporary and permanent increase in monetary inflows.

The fact that households receive only temporary increases in income from "one shot" money inflows has important implications. Many public construction projects and other temporary infusions cannot be a source of a long-run increase in incomes. Of course, even a temporary increase in income is nice. However, a business that permanently increases its exports will increase community income to a new, higher equilibrium. Thus local development officials may prefer a project that promises a continuous inflow of funds over a one-shot injection associated with many public works.

⊠ The Export-Base Theory of Growth

The export-base theory of growth is grounded in the idea that a local economy must increase its monetary inflow if it is to grow and the only effective way to increase monetary inflow is to increase exports.

Tiebout (1962) described the fundamental relationships posed by the export-base theory:

> Export markets are considered the prime movers of the local economy. If employment serving this market rises or falls, employment serving the local market is presumed to move in the same direction. When the factory (export) closes, retail merchants (local) feel the impact as laid-off factory workers have less to spend. Because of the prime mover role, export employment is considered as "basic." Employment which serves the local market is considered adaptive and is titled "non-basic." (p. 10)

The export-base theory may be expressed in terms of either income or employment:

$$\Delta T = k\Delta B \qquad\qquad (6\text{-}1)$$

or

$$\Delta Y = k\Delta E , \qquad\qquad (6\text{-}1')$$

where

T = total employment
Y = total income
B = basic (export) employment
E = export earning
k = export-base multiplier
Δ = change

The key concept of the export-base theory is that export activity is the engine of growth. Income originally earned by the export sector is spent and respent locally, creating additional income through the multiplier. Export industries generate the money that flows into the city. A portion of the export-earned dollars are spent locally by the export workers, creating local service jobs. Employees serving the local economy, in turn, spend much of their earning locally thus supporting additional jobs. The size of the multiplier depends on the propensity of individuals to spend money in the local economy rather than spending it outside the local area.

It is vital to distinguish between two meanings of "service." Services are a type of economic output as in the phrase "goods and services." In this sense, services are critical to the growth process. Services can be a source of export earnings and therefore a part of the region's basic activities. Services can be exported from the region either when local residents travel outside the area to provide the service or when nonresidents come from outside the area to purchase services, as when individuals travel to Williamsburg, Virginia, for a vacation. When sales by the local service sector bring outside dollars into the local economy, they are basic and should be considered as sources of economic growth. Gillis (1987) has argued that services play these important economic development functions: serve as exports, substitute for existing imports, and provide services to local residents. In the export-base literature, "local service activities" refer only to economic activities that serve local residents. In this sense, service is synonymous with nonbasic.

Recent studies have documented the extent that service activities are export earners. Ashton and Sternal (1978) found that 20% of New England's service-producing industries export more than half of their sales to individuals outside the region. Similarly, Beyers and Alvine (1985) found that about 40% of the services originating in the Puget Sound region in Washington are sold to users outside the state. Keil and Mack (1986) identified 22 of 53 service categories as having strong or moderate export potential. Accordingly, service activities can be a source of export earnings and an important part of an area's economic base.

Proponents of the export-base theory recognize that many businesses serve both local customers and nonresidents. The use of location quotients to determine the export and service sector was discussed in Chapter 5. For the remainder of this section, simply assume that one can distinguish between exporting and activities serving the local economy.

The Formal Income Model

The export-base theory can be derived from the circular flow model. Income rather than employment is usually the focus of formal presentations of the export base theory. Income may be expressed as

$$Y = C + \text{MI} - \text{MO}, \qquad (6\text{-}2)$$

where

Y   = total income
MI = monetary inflows
C   = consumption spending by local residents
MO = monetary outflows

Equation 6-2 states that income of local residents is equal to consumption (C) plus net monetary inflows. Notice that consumption of goods or services purchased outside the area would increase C and MO by equal amounts, so Y would not be changed when local residents spend outside the region.

Consumption

Consumption has two components. One component is independent of the level of income. Even if residents had no income, consumption might be financed from previous savings, for instance. But most consumption depends on the level of income. The marginal propensity to consume is a fraction of the increase in income that is spent. If the marginal propensity to consume is .80, then 80 cents of each dollar increase in income will be spent. Thus

$$C = A + bY, \qquad (6\text{-}3)$$

where

A = consumption that is unrelated to income
b = the marginal propensity to consume

Monetary Inflows

Proponents of the export-base theory argue that exports are the prime source of monetary inflow. Exports are determined by outside demand for goods and services produced in the region. Because the extent of outside demand is beyond the area's control, it is considered exogenous. (Some development officials attempt to increase the demand for products of a particular area. For instance, individuals may be encouraged to vacation in

New Orleans. Thus outside demand is not totally exogenous.) Accordingly, exports are the only source of monetary inflows. Therefore,

$$MI = E_0 \qquad (6\text{-}4)$$

where E_0 = exogenously determined export income.

Monetary Outflows

Monetary outflows are determined by the extent to which residents spend outside the area. As local incomes increase, spending outside the area will increase. Therefore, monetary outflows are determined by the level of local income. Purchases of goods and services from nonresidents, imports, are the primary source of monetary outflows. For simplicity's sake, assume that all monetary outflows are related to the level of income. Savings that are not reinvested in the local economy are another form of leakage. The greater the saving, the lower will be the marginal propensity to consume (b). However, to avoid complicating the model, the role of financial institutions in the recycling of savings is not addressed directly. Thus

$$MO = iY \qquad (6\text{-}5)$$

where i = the marginal propensity to import (create monetary outflows).

The Unified Model

Equations 6-3 through 6-5 can be inserted into Equation 6-2:

$$Y = A + bY + E_0 - iY \qquad (6\text{-}6)$$

or

$$Y = [1/(1 - b + i)] \times (A + E_0) . \qquad (6\text{-}7)$$

Based on Equation 6-7, the factors that determine regional income can be summarized. The first term represents the tendency for dollars to recirculate within the circular flow. The larger the marginal propensity to consume and the smaller the marginal propensity to import, the larger income will be. The second term represents autonomous spending—that is, spending unrelated to the level of regional income. A minimum level of consumption, A, and the level of exports, E_0, are not affected by income.

Changes in the variables of the model such as b, E_0, and A are determined by institutional, physical, and political factors beyond the scope of the export-base model. Therefore, according to the logic of the strict export-base model, income will increase only if exports, E_0, change. Setting ΔA to zero and allowing the change in exports to equal ΔE_0, the change in income is[3]

$$\Delta Y = 1/[1 - (b - i)] \times \Delta E_0 . \qquad (6\text{-}8)$$

Equation 6-8 indicates that a change in export income will change total income by $1/[1 - (b - i)] \times \Delta E_0$. Notice that $b - i$ is the marginal propensity to spend locally—the marginal propensity to consume minus the propensity to consume from outside the area. Thus the export base multiplier is conceptually similar to the Keynesian multiplier used in macroeconomic analysis. The multiplier effect occurs because the initial increase in export income is spent and respent, thus creating additional income. However, some of the additional spending "leaks" from the circular flow in the form of monetary outflow.

How to Operationalize the Export-Base Approach

Data on small areas are difficult to obtain, particularly information on marginal propensities to consume and marginal propensities to import. Surveys of local spending habits can be made to determine the propensity to spend locally, but such surveys are expensive and difficult to design as they would have to determine both consumer and business spending patterns to be considered a complete measure of import tendencies. To avoid the need for surveys, practitioners have developed a technique to estimate the local multiplier using readily available employment data. Employment is used as a proxy for income because of the lack of regional income data. Thus, whereas the formal model was concerned with income, employment is used to operationalize the model. On the basis of location quotients, surveys, or other techniques, local employment is split into the number of workers producing for export and the number producing for local consumption.

Two assumptions are useful in operationalizing the export base model. The first assumption is that income is proportional to employment. Therefore, nonbasic income as a proportion of total income will equal nonbasic employment divided by total employment. This assumption is important because it supports the use of employment changes as a measure of income changes. In the short run, it is likely that incomes could increase without employment increasing. In this case, per capita income would increase. However, it is reasonable to suppose that higher incomes would attract additional workers to the area. Hence the link between income and employment can be supported by the movement of labor from lower to higher wage areas. The second assumption is that the ratio of export employment to total employment is constant. Each new export job creates the same number of nonbasic jobs. This assumption implies that as the number of export workers (income) increases, the number of nonbasic employees (income) will increase in the same proportion as the existing export to total employment ratio. The assumption is important because when combined with the first assumption it allows the estimation of $b - i$. With reference to Equation 6-7, $b - i$ is the proportion of an income increase spent locally. Therefore, $b - i$ will be the same as the nonbasic employment to total employment ratio (the portion of total employment serving local residents). Accordingly, the export-base multiplier (Equation 6-1) can be expressed as

$$k = 1/[1 - (b - i)] = 1/[1 - (\text{NB}/T)] \qquad (6\text{-}9)$$
$$= 1/(B/T)$$
$$= T/B \, ,$$

where

T = total employment
B = export (or basic) employment
NB = nonbasic employment (serving the local market)

Therefore, Equation 6-1 may be expressed as

$$\Delta T = (T/B) \times \Delta B \, , \qquad (6\text{-}10)$$

where

ΔT = change in total employment

T = total employment
B = basic employment
ΔB = change in basic employment

Given an understanding of the theory that underlies the export-base approach, the multiplier can be easily calculated. If total employment is 2,000 and export employment is determined to be 1,000, then the employment multiplier would be 2.

Steps in an Export-Base Forecast

Export-base studies are used for a variety of purposes, and each study is normally tailored to specific circumstances. However, export-base studies tend to have similar structures. The structure of an export-base forecast may be summarized in five steps.

The first step is to determine the appropriate geographic area for study. The appropriate area is sometimes a compromise between the area relevant for the purpose of the study and the area for which data are available. A neighborhood or small town may be too small an area for a successful study because employment data on such areas are often not available. Furthermore, small neighborhoods or suburban communities have extremely high degrees of interdependence within the larger metropolitan economy. Such subareas do not have a sufficiently integrated internal circular flow, and the service workers are often not even local residents. The export-base concepts may have less meaning in such a very small area. Consequently, studies of very small areas are often undertaken in conjunction with larger studies of integrated areas. Although the appropriate area depends on the purpose of the study, cities, counties, or metropolitan statistical areas are generally chosen for analysis because such areas are integrated economies, export similar items, and are affected by the same trends.

The second step is to describe the local economy and determine the sources of export employment. This step sets the stage for deriving the multiplier. A table showing location quotients for each industry is useful for identifying export sectors. The methods shown in Chapter 5 are techniques that can be used to calculate export (basic) employment.

The third step is to determine k, the local multiplier. The question to be answered is, if basic employment increases by a given amount, how many additional jobs will be created in the region as a whole? As explained above, the multiplier may be expressed as total employment divided by export employment. Because export employment was estimated in Step 2 and total employment is readily available, this step can be less complicated.

The fourth step is to forecast exogenous changes in the local export sector. A frequently employed estimating technique is to apply national trends, appropriately modified to account for the local environment, to current employment levels so as to estimate the change in basic employment. Opinions of experts could be used to estimate possibilities of the development of new export sectors. This step can be quite complicated. However, the end result will be an estimate of the change in export employment (ΔB in Equation 6-1).

In the fifth step, once the export employment has been forecast, the multiplier can be used to determine total employment changes. For instance, if the multiplier is 2 and the export sector is estimated to increase by 75 jobs, then the total estimated increase in employment would be 150.

Because it was implicitly assumed that employment is proportional to income, the same multiplier can be used to estimate the change in total income given an initial change in export income.

The forecasting process need not stop at Step 5. In fact, the purpose of this section was to describe the bare bones of a typical study rather than to delve into the many complications that can arise in practice. The new level of employment may be used as information to forecast other variables such as income, population, housing demand, and traffic congestion.

Employment Impact Studies

Urban and regional economists are occasionally asked to estimate the impact of an event such as the opening of a new plant or the closing of a military base. The impacts of major changes may be wide-ranging, including those on local fiscal capacity and cultural opportunities. Employment impacts are a major focus of most economic impact studies. The export base methodology can be used to estimate the impact of a known or anticipated employment change. For instance, an analyst may be required to estimate the total impact on the economy if a local firm that exported its output and employed 200 people were to close. The initial change in export employment, −200, could be multiplied by the multiplier to estimate the total employment impact.

Of course, many of the techniques for estimating employment changes and for estimating the multiplier can be refined for an important forecast. The purpose of the above discussion was to present the essentials. Determining how to approach more complicated situations is a useful exercise.

Many observers are justifiably skeptical of employment impact studies because the authors or sponsors of the study often have an interest in exaggerating the size of the impact. For instance, the managers of a facility might hope to exaggerate its importance in the regional economy in order to increase their influence or to strengthen their ability to seek government assistance.

Local impacts of a plant opening or closing may be exaggerated by overestimating the size of the local multiplier or by exaggerating the size of the change in export employment. Small regions normally have significant monetary outflows, and, consequently, the local multipliers are usually between 1 and 2. However, in an effort to increase the size of the total employment impact, blatantly unrealistic multipliers have been used. Another way to exaggerate the local impact of an employer is to assume that all the employment in a particular facility is devoted to export. For instance, if a local university that employed 600 people were to close, an inaccurate analysis might assume that 600 jobs would be lost locally. In fact, some of the university students would probably transfer to another local university, junior college, or trade school, and as a result, other local institutions would increase their employment. Hence not all of the 600 jobs would be lost to the local economy.

⊠ Critique of the Export-Base Approach

The criticisms of the export-base approach suggest significant limitations. In general, objections can be divided into those that concern theory and those that concern technique when conducting an export-base forecast.

Primacy of Exports

Critics contend that the export-base theory places too much emphasis on exports and overlooks other important factors that can lead to growth. Regions may experience increases in income through increases in the productivity of resources, increases in investment from outside the region, or by substituting domestic production for goods and services that were previously imported.

"Reductionism" is an attempt to reduce a complex situation to one cause or to one explanation. The export-base approach is a reductionist analysis. Are exports the only source of monetary inflows? No.

Import Substitution

Import substitution is an alternative development strategy that some economic development officials have used to encourage growth without expanding exports. Rather than increasing exports it may be useful to produce locally what otherwise would have been imported. Such a strategy would result in fewer leakages; each dollar that enters the circular flow would create more income. A successful import substitution strategy would increase the multiplier.

An advantage of import substitution is that many products currently being imported into the area can be easily identified. If that product could be produced locally, it might have a cost advantage in the local market compared to similar imported products because the local product would probably require lower transportation costs compared to the imported product. Of course, import substitution may be more difficult than it first appears because the local community may not be able to produce many products economically. Raw materials may not be available, or the most economical scale of production may be too large to justify production for just the local market. In such cases, the imported items could still undersell the locally produced items in the local market.

Both Wilbur Thompson (1968) and Jane Jacobs (1969) emphasized the import replacement role in a region's evaluation (see Table 6.1). Persky, Ranney, and Wiewel (1993) have suggested that local development officials could implement an import substitution by examining the location quotients of industries that supply major businesses and by redirecting purchases of local governments to targeted industries.

Productivity

Improving labor productivity can also increase the level of income without increasing the level of exports. Suppose productivity increases in the nonbasic or service sector of the economy. The level of real income in the community could increase while the level of exports remained the same.

Productivity increases could also cause exports to increase if the improvement in productivity were in the export sector. In this instance, increased exports are associated with growth but the causation is not as implied by the export-base theory. The increased exports were not exogenous, such as an increase in outside demand. The increase in exports was caused by productivity-increasing forces inside the region, such as local research or education activities.

Exports Not Always Exogenous

The export-base theory includes the implicit assumption that the demand for exports originates outside the area. Several analysts believe that the ability to develop and produce exports may in fact rest with the quality of local services within the economy. Service firms play a role in building the export sector. A particular financial institution may provide capital needed to start an export business, a university may provide an idea that results in an innovation, or a land developer may create an attractive industrial park. Collectively, the service sector may provide an overall environment conducive to export development. Most large cities have development councils dedicated to encouraging economic growth. The most active members normally include bankers, real estate developers, brokers, university officials, and public utility planners. These individuals represent the service sector, but they play major roles in encouraging the location and growth of export firms.

In a related vein, Chinitz (1961) asked why some areas are able to rebound after losing their export base while other cities experience long periods of stagnation when they lose their base. He concluded that resilience depended on the structure of the local economy, especially the availability of intermediate services. Chinitz's analysis, which has been supported by Carlino (1980), contributed to the development of the supply-side approach discussed in the next section.

Small Versus Large Regions

The export-base theory may be more applicable to small regions, such as MSAs, than to large regions, such as state or multistate areas. As the size of the community increases, opportunities to increase income by internal developments increase. The world, a region in the cosmic scheme, has grown without exports. Clearly, the scope for growth through internal production is greater the larger the region. Thus the larger the region, the less important exports are and the less adequate the export-base theory is in describing growth.

Feedbacks

Feedbacks occur when one region's actions cause another region to increase its purchases from the subject region. Regional interdependence creates feedbacks. Actions of large regions may create feedback effects from other large regions. The extent of the feedback will depend on the strengths of the economic linkages between the regions. When a major region, such as the European Economic Community (EEC), experiences an increase in its purchases from the United States, incomes in the exporting region in the United States will increase. The United States may in turn increase its imports from the EEC, a major trading partner. Thus one reason for the EEC exports is the extent of their imports. Feedback effects are not accounted for in the simple export-base model. When the region is small or has weak linkages, these feedbacks can be ignored because income increases in a small region will have only negligible feedbacks. However, if the region is large, the feedbacks can be significant.

Automatic Inducement of Nonbasic Activities

The export-base multiplier is predicated on the assumption that when the export sector expands, the demand for local services increases and the increase in demand will be sufficient to bring forth an increase in supply of such services. However, some local services, such as those requiring large capital investment or highly skilled (or scarce) labor, may not be easily expanded. Therefore, nonbasic employment may remain constant for some time after a decrease in export employment. The increased demand for local services may not bring about an increase in supply. If exports increase (decrease) but the nonbasic sector does not increase (decrease), then the multiplier (total employment/basic employment) will not adequately reflect the impact of changes in exports.

Long-Run Instability of the Multiplier

In the long run, most of the "other things equal" assumptions that underlie most economic models will change. With regard to the export-base approach, changes in the fundamental economic relationships will alter the relationship between the export and nonbasic sectors. Hence the multiplier will change over time.

The marginal propensity to import and its multiplier is particularly sensitive to three variables: the size of the economy, per capita income, and the degree of spatial isolation. The smaller the economy of the region, the fewer the opportunities to purchase goods locally. For example, if you live in a small town and want a meal in a four-star restaurant, the service would have to be "imported," thus increasing the leakages. Higher-income individuals have greater propensity to purchase specialized goods that need to be imported. So, as per capita income increases, the marginal propensity to import increases. Finally, proximity to other communities will increase competition for local customers, and residents will have a greater tendency to shop outside the community. Thus areas within metropolitan areas will have smaller ratios of total employment to basic employment than isolated towns.

Excessive Aggregation

The assumption that the impact of all exports is the same is embedded in the use of the export-base multiplier. The likelihood that some types of exports may have a greater impact on the economy than other exports is ignored. In reality, some export businesses have many local suppliers and therefore have big multiplier affects. This contrasts with the impact of increased exports produced by a firm that imports all required intermediate inputs from nonlocal suppliers. In the latter instance, there may be no second-order consequences.

⌖ Supply-Side Approaches

Supply-side theories of economic development are partly an outgrowth of criticisms of demand-dominated approaches, such as the export-base theory. The heart of regional supply-side growth theories is the idea that regions grow because the supply of resources available within the area increases or because the existing resources are used more effectively.

Regional policymakers have done a better job developing hypotheses about what factors might affect the local supply of productive resources than they have in developing workable ways to stimulate the supply side. The current economic activities in an area may "explain" the supply of some factors of production. The current resources, in turn, shape the future businesses that will locate in the area. This circular explanation contains some truth but is not satisfying. A sketch of some potentially important determinants of supply would include intermediate inputs as well as the primary factors of production—land, labor, capital, and entrepreneurship.

Intermediate Inputs

The availability of intermediate inputs is an important supply factor. On the one hand, communities dominated by large, vertically integrated firms may have fewer intermediate inputs available to new businesses. On the other hand, new businesses in communities with many small interdependent firms may have access to a variety of intermediate inputs through other local firms. Consequently, it would be harder for a fledgling new business to obtain legal, trucking, and other services in a city like Pittsburgh than in a city like New York. In Pittsburgh, a high percentage of the trucking and legal services are inside large existing companies and thus are not available to small businesses.

Entrepreneurship

Almost every development economist has stressed the importance of the entrepreneur in risk taking and bringing factors of production together. Storey and Johnson (1987) attributed regional differences in rates of new business formation to differences in entrepreneurship. Booth (1986) attributed long waves of regional decline to the absence of entrepreneurial activity needed to stimulate employment growth. The founders of new firms are almost always local residents. There are few documented instances of entrepreneurs who relocate to a new community to start a business (Allen and Hayward, 1990, p. 56).

In spite of the generally recognized importance of entrepreneurship, economists know very little about factors that contribute to its development. The importance of risk taking and creativity and the presence of role models and family background are among the factors mentioned in the diverse and multidisciplinary literature that has attempted to understand entrepreneurship.

The interest in entrepreneurship has been spiked by findings that firms employing less than 20 people account for about half of all new jobs created. Small firms have more entrepreneurship per employee than large firms and are often associated with the early stage of a product's life cycle where percentage growth is rapid. Thus entrepreneurship has been seen as a key to developing fast-growth firms.

Capital

Capital is often considered the most mobile factor of production because of the existence of national and international capital markets. As a result, capital is available on roughly equal terms in different regions. For instance, an automobile loan may be secured in Chicago or Phoenix on approximately the same terms. Large corporations borrow in the national market, so the availability of capital to firms with access to national capital markets is not influenced by location. However, capital may not be equally available everywhere for small firms or for unique local purposes. In many instances, a business's location may affect capital cost or availability.

Individuals are important sources of capital, especially equity capital. Through various types of joint ventures, wealthy residents may provide funds for new enterprises. Venture capitalists specialize in identifying small, high-growth potential companies and providing them with funds for projects that commercial banks and other traditional lenders consider too risky or unorthodox. The venture capitalists normally take an equity position in the company (i.e., they will earn a share of the profits) and often provide business advice as well as money. Government and quasi-government agencies such as community development corporations have recognized the need that small firms have for capital obtained in a local capital market and have developed programs to increase the supply of funds to smaller companies.

Land

"Land" encompasses all naturally endowed factors of production. Location or ground or climate are part of land. They may be characterized as the most fundamental resources from a regional perspective as they are the only immobile factor of production. If nonland factors of production were perfectly mobile, land would be the only resource that would differentiate areas.

Resources such as mineral deposits, natural harbors, topography, and the agricultural fertility of the hinterland have played an important role in the historical development of cities. Although land is probably not now as significant an urban growth component as it was in the past, land continues to exert an influence on development. For example, processed food is an important part of the economic base of many midwestern cities, and the location of food processors is influenced by the production of agricultural land. Topography can affect building costs and hence growth prospects in specific parts of a metropolitan region.

In recent years, climate has been cited as an important determinant of urban growth. The rise of "sunbelt cities" and the amenity orientation of advanced technology firms have contributed to the perception that climate is an important growth determinant. Several econometric models have included variables such as average temperature and average number of days with sunshine as independent variables in employment growth models.

Labor

The size of the labor force is largely determined by population size. The quality of the labor force is more difficult to define than size, although quality is probably more important than size in determining an area's growth or revitalization prospects.

Past industrial activities help shape the skills of the current workforce. Not only are skills important but so are work habits and attitudes. The adaptability of the workforce is important to the ability of an area to generate new economic activities. Hence educational institutions have an important supply-side function.

⊠   Supply and Demand Approaches Compared

Economists recognize that both supply and demand are necessary to induce production. Thus neither the supply-side nor the demand-side approach should be rejected. There is, however, disagreement regarding which approach has the greatest predictive power under particular circumstances. On the one hand, if supply is very responsive to increases in demand (elastic supply), then demand-side approaches such as the export-base theory will have significant predictive power. On the other hand, if demand for the region's output is responsive to changes in local supply, then an increase in supply will quickly create a market for what was produced. In this case, supply-side theories will have good predictive power.

Implicit in the supply-side approach is the assumption that the demand for the region's output will be sufficient to employ any additional resources that may be created. Increases in supply will more easily translate into increases in output if resource prices are flexible downward. In this case, unemployed resources would cause resource prices to fall, the resources would be employed, and the resulting output could be sold at lower prices. Increases in the supply of resources will also tend to translate into increased output when there is increasing or unsatisfied outside demand for the region's products. Furthermore, the availability of many resources are important determinants of firm location. Firms create demand for additional local resources and often have established marketing contacts needed to sell what they produce. However, if a region already has unemployed resources, then increasing the quantity of the region's resources could aggravate the unemployment problem without causing output to increase.

⊠   **Summary**

In formulating an effective economic development strategy, it is helpful to understand where a community is in the development process and to have a theory about what drives a local economy. Stage theories describe the key stages that cities pass through as they develop. Thompson (1968) and Jacobs (1969) have similar theories of growth stages. Initially, a region may export one or only a few products. As regions develop, they achieve the ability to replace imports and generate new products for exports. Thompson's model emphasized the importance of industrial filtering. Jacobs emphasized the process of "adding new work to old" in the innovation process.

The circular flow model is a simplified model of how an economy operates. Five important subsectors of a local economy are the resource market, the local consumer market, interfirm sales, the local financial sector, and the import and export sector. The circular flow model can be used to illustrate equilibrium—when monetary inflows equal monetary outflows—and the local multiplier.

The export-base theory of growth is that exports are the dominant source of monetary inflows and hence the main source of growth. The export-base approach may be operationalized by assuming that income is proportional to employment and that the ratio of export employment to total employment is constant. Hence an export multiplier can be derived as the ratio of total employment to export employment. The export-base approach has straight-forward policy implications and is relatively easy to operationalize.

There are several criticisms of the export-base theory. First, it may place too much emphasis on exports. Import substitution is an alternative development strategy. Second, productivity improvement is another source of growth. Third, exports may not always be exogenous, particularly in the long run. Fourth, the theory may have more explanatory power for small regions than for large ones. Fifth, it ignores interregional feedback. Sixth, the export-base theory implies that additional local services will respond only to an increase in local demand. Seventh, the value of the export-base multiplier will change over time. Finally, the assumption that all exports affect the local economy alike is an oversimplification. In spite of numerous criticisms, the export-base theory remains a dominant theory of regional growth.

Supply-side theories emphasize the availability of inputs as principal growth determinants. The presence of intermediate inputs and the primary factors of production—land, labor, capital, and entrepreneurship—contribute to the ability of a region to produce. Supply-side factors may also account for the ability of a region to generate new sources of exports. Although demand- and supply-side approaches are sometimes presented as alternative theories, economists recognize that both supply and demand are necessary for profit- able production and economic growth.

Both supply of resources and export demand are potential constraints on growth. At any given time, one of the two factors may be a more important constraint. For instance, if a region has substantial unemployment, the con- straint on growth is likely to be demand. If the economy is at or near full employment, the constraint is likely to be supply.

⊠ Notes

1. The payments may accrue to household before the export sale or investment is actually made if business increases production in anticipation of export sales.

2. For reasons explained more thoroughly later, this figure was derived by using a multiplier of 1.43. This was derived as $1/[1 - (\text{marginal propensity to consume locally})] = 1/(1 - .3) = 1.43$. The initial \$100,000 of locally created income was multiplied by 1.43.

3. Let a new level of exports equal $(E_0 + \Delta E_0)$ and the resulting level of income equal $Y + \Delta Y$. Hence the new income level will be

$$Y + \Delta Y = [1/(1 - b + i)] \times (A + E_0 + \Delta E_0) .$$

Subtracting Equation 6-7 from the new income level results in Equation 6-8.

Additional Tools and
Perspectives on Economic Growth

The previous chapter provided an introduction to urban and regional growth emphasizing demand- and supply-side approaches. However, except for some very broad distinctions such as the basic-nonbasic categories or the various factors of production, Chapter 6 did not explore relationships among specific subcomponents of an area's economy. This chapter extends the analysis begun in Chapter 6 by presenting perspectives and tools that view local economies in a more disaggregated fashion.

⊠   Shift and Share Analysis

Shift and share analysis provides a retrospective view of the causes of growth. It is a technique for dividing an area's growth into three components. First, part of an area's growth can be attributed to national economic growth. Growth at the national average rate is termed the national growth component. If a locality grew at the national average, it would have maintained its share of national employment, hence the "share" term of shift and share analysis. Second, an area may grow faster (slower) than the national average if it has a disproportionate level of employment in industries that grew fast (slow) nationwide. For instance, financial services were a fast-growth activity during the 1980s. One would expect that if an area had a large employment base in financial services, it would have grown more rapidly than the national average. Growth that differs from the national average because of the initial employment composition of an area is termed the mix component. Third, an area may have a competitive advantage (disadvantage) compared to other areas because its environment is conducive (an impediment) to growth of particular industries. Growth differentials due to the nature of the local environment are termed the competitive component. The mix and competitive components account for regional growth that differs from the national level.

The formula for calculating the shift-share components for a single industry can be expressed as

$$\Delta e_i = e_i \left[(\mathrm{US}^*/\mathrm{US}) - 1\right] + e_i \left[(\mathrm{US}_i^*/\mathrm{US}_i) - (\mathrm{US}^*/\mathrm{US})\right] \tag{7-1}$$
$$+ e_i \left[(e_i^*/e_i) - (\mathrm{US}_i^*/\mathrm{US}_i)\right].$$

where

Δe_i = the change in local employment in industry i
e_i = local employment in industry i at the beginning of the period
e_i^* = local employment in industry i at the end of the period
US^* = total U.S. employment at the end of the period
US = total U.S. employment at the beginning of the period
$\quad\quad i$ as subscript indicates reference to industry i

The first term indicates growth that would occur if local industry i grew at the national average rate. The second term indicates extra (reduced) growth because a particular industry grew more (less) rapidly than the overall national average growth rate. The third term indicates that local industry grew more (less) rapidly than the national rate for industry i. The shift and share components for individual local industries can be summarized to provide an overall description of growth components. Table 7.1 shows the data and the results of a small shift and share analysis for a local economy.

An Application

How would an economic planner or analyst interpret the findings shown in Table 7.1? Star City (fictitious name) had a total employment increase of 100 workers during the 10-year period. If Star City had grown as rapidly as the nation as a whole, 123 jobs would have been added. Agriculture, manu-

TABLE 7.1 Shift-Share Analysis

a. Data

	Star City		United States (in millions)	
Sector	1970	1980	1970	1980
Agriculture	50	100	7	10.5
Manufacturing	125	175	4	5.6
Service	200	200	3	2.5
Total	375	475	14	18.6

b. Results[a]

		Components	
			Shift
Sector	Share (national)	Mix	Competitive
Agriculture	16	9	25
Manufacturing	41	9	0
Service	65	−99	34
Total	123	−81	59
Actual change = 100			

NOTE: a. Some columns may not add exactly due to rounding errors.

facturing, and services would have added 16, 41, and 65 jobs, respectively.[1] Therefore, there was a loss of 23 jobs in Star City's share of national employment. This negative shift of 23 jobs can be accounted for by the negative mix component. If Star City had an industrial base proportionate to the rest of the United States, the mix component would have been zero. In the example, agriculture and manufacturing grew faster than the United States' average and Star City had some employment in these nationally fast-growing industries. Thus the mix components for these sectors was positive. However, the service sector was a slow-growth industry nationwide and Star City had a strongly disproportionate concentration of employment in that sector. Therefore, the mix component for service was −99 and the overall mix effect for Star City was −82 jobs.

The actual shift was 23 jobs—Star City had 23 fewer jobs than "anticipated," based on overall national performance. The mix component by itself would have resulted in a shift of −81 jobs, but Star City appeared to be a particularly good environment for agriculture and services. Both activities grew more rapidly in Star City than they did nationwide. Manufacturing grew at the same rate in Star City as it did in the nation. Thus the region recorded a positive competitive component of 59.

The actual employment change was equal to the sum of the share (123), mix (−82), and competitive (59) components.

The positive competitive components in agriculture and services indicate a potential building block for future growth. For instance, a development official might try to determine exactly why local service firms maintained their employment levels while service employment declined nationwide. If one or two favorable aspects of the local environment could be identified, they could be used to help market the community to other service firms that might consider locating in the area. The shift-share approach can also be used to help spot weaknesses in the competitive environment that may require corrections.

Critique

Shift and share analysis has been widely used by planners and economic development officials to help them understand economic performance. It is relatively easy to use and understand. The data required to perform the analysis are readily available. However, the technique has some legitimate criticisms.

One criticism of shift-share analysis is that the components are frequently misinterpreted. Some critics have charged that shift and share analysis implies that industries should grow at the aggregate national rate. The national growth rate is used as a point of comparison, but there is no theoretical reason to believe that local employment growth should match the national rate. Likewise, the mix component should not be interpreted as implying that local industries "should" expand at the same rate as their nationwide counterparts. The national and mix component serve only as comparative benchmarks.

A second criticism is that the shift and share components may change depending on the level of industrial detail. For instance, if industries were greatly disaggregated so that, at the extreme, each plant constituted its own industry, the competitive component would be zero (the plant's growth would equal the national industry growth rate), and therefore the total shift should be attributable to the mix component. Defenders of shift and share analysis recognize this problem but reply that selecting the appropriate level of industrial detail is a problem common to most industry studies.

Third, although the competitive component may be useful in explaining what has happened, its ability to predict the future course of development has been questioned. The competitive component has been combined with national projections on the growth of a particular industry to improve forecasting. Using a "top down" forecasting technique for instance, a national forecast of growth in a particular industry could be adjusted up or down depending on an area's competitive component. However, critics of such forecasting techniques claim that the competitive component changes too frequently and rapidly in response to a variety of forces such as local taxes, resources availability, technology, and so forth. Therefore, a competitive component for one historical period may be a poor guide to future competitive components for the same sector.

Finally, critics have pointed out that although the competitive component can be an indicator of where to look for local strengths and weaknesses it does not identify *why* a particular sector may have a positive or negative competitive component. In fact, the competitive component is a residual and may not necessarily reflect what most of us envision when we talk of a good competitive environment. Thus analysts must go beyond the model to explain positive or negative competitive effects. For instance, suppose the steel industry in a particular region grew more rapidly than the industry did nationwide. A positive competitive component for that sector would result, but how would it be explained? Perhaps something about the local environment permitted lower-cost steel production and firms took advantage of the lower cost environment by expanding output. Alternatively, perhaps a steel executive made a *bad* decision to expand steel employment in that area. Both possibilities could explain a positive competitive component. More in-depth study would be required to distinguish between these and numerous other potential explanations of the competitive component.

⊠   Econometric and Simulation Models

Econometric models combine statistical techniques and economic theory to estimate relationships among variables. An econometric model might show that tax revenues increase by $100,000 for each 100-person increase in employment. Simulation models answer "what if" questions. For instance, a simulation model may be used to forecast the revenue impact if employment increased by 2,000 persons. A simulation model would allow a researcher to estimate the path of a community's development if current trends persist or if new trends develop. Both econometric and simulation models have a variety of uses, although this section focuses on how they are used to understand the growth process.

Econometric Models

Econometric models are perhaps the most widely used tool for analyzing regional growth. Econometric models normally combine both supply- and demand-side variables that may influence growth. Furthermore, although changes in production or employment are the primary outcomes of input-output forecasts, econometric models can include equations to estimate changes in other variables such as prices, tax revenues, fiscal impacts and other important urban or regional outcomes. A final advantage of econometric models is that they can be modified. If an unanticipated question arises, new equations may be added to the core model. For instance, if a city official wanted to know how a change in federal tax policies will affect the local economy, new equations could be estimated that feed into the core model.

Good econometric models are informed by economic theory. Theory normally specifies what variables are important and the causal relationship among them. Three major uses of econometric models are to test the validity of theoretical relationships, to specify the magnitude of relationships, and to assist forecasting. For instance, theory might indicate that migration into an area occurs when the local employment rate is less that the nation's. Statistical analysis might confirm the proposition and demonstrate that migration increases by, say, 3% a year for each percentage point difference between the national and local unemployment rate. A planner might then use the quantitative relationship between unemployment and migration to help forecast future population.

There are two important kinds of variables in econometric models. On the one hand, independent variables are not estimated by the model, they are taken as "given." On the other hand, the value of dependent variables can be predicted by the model. Often, independent variables can be thought of as a "cause" and dependent variables as the "effects." Parameters are a third important component of econometric models. They show the magnitude of the relationship between the dependent and independent variables. For instance, suppose a $120,00 increase (decrease) in regional exports resulted in an employment increase of 1 person. This relationship could be described by the equation

$$LE = 25,000 + 120E , \qquad (7\text{-}2)$$

where

    LE = local employment
    E = local exports in 1,000s

Econometric models may be estimated using cross-sectional data or time series data. Cross-sectional studies examine relationships that exist based on a variety of observations at a single time. Time series studies show relationships within a particular set of variables during various periods of time.

An Export-Base Example

Weiss and Gooding (1970) used an econometric equation to examine growth in the Portsmouth area. Although their study is dated, its simplicity and relationship to the export-base theory, described in the previous chapter, make it useful to study. Weiss and Gooding postulated that service employment should grow when export employment grows. However, one of the problems with the export-base approach is that it lumps together all export sectors, even though changes in some sectors may have a bigger impact than changes in others. Accordingly, a theoretical model was specified that divided the export sector into three categories reflecting the employment patterns in Portsmouth:

$$S = Q + b_1 X_1 + b_2 X_2 + b_3 X_3, \qquad (7\text{-}3)$$

where

    S = service employment
    X_1 = private export employment
    X_2 = civilian employment at Portsmouth shipyard
    X_3 = employment at Pease Air Force Base

Q and b_i are parameters that can be estimated statistically using multiple regression. A time series data set was collected for each of the independent variables and their relationship to service employment estimated. The statistical results yielded the following equation:

$$S = -12,905 + .78X_1 + .55X_2 + .35X_3 \qquad (7\text{-}4)$$
$$(t = 2.5) \ (t = 2.4) \ (t = 2.5)$$

$$R^2 = .78 \ .$$

Statistical tests were performed to provide a confidence level in the findings. The R^2 of .78 indicates the 78% of the variance in service employment (the dependent variable) was accounted for by the independent variables, X_1, X_2, and X_3. The t values indicate that the coefficients for each dependent variable are statistically different from zero.

The econometric findings can be used to simulate the impact of a change in employment in one of the three export sectors. Suppose, for example, that employment at Pease Air Force Base (X_3) was projected to increase during the next year by 100 persons. What would be the total impact on the economy? Assuming all other variables remained unchanged, the change in service employment would be

$$S = .35X_3 = .35(100) = 35 \ . \qquad (7\text{-}5)$$

Because the change in service employment is 35 and the change in export employment is 100, the total employment change due to the increase in export employment is 135. The multiplier for X_3 is 1.35 (135/100). For similar reasons, the multiplier for X_1 and X_2 equals 1.78 and 1.55, respectively.

The econometric model depends on the export-base theory. If, for instance, an observer believed that service employment significantly influenced private export employment, then causation runs both ways: S determines X_1 and X_1 determines S. In this case, a simultaneity bias would exist. Consequently, the estimate of b_1, the parameter that links service and private employment, may be inaccurate.

More Complicated Models

The model described had only one equation and there was only one "outcome"—service employment. Urban econometric models are usually much more complex. The ability to add additional equations to existing econometric models provides them with flexibility. Once a model is established, it may be extended or modified to address other questions. Suppose the developers of the model described above later wanted to estimate total regional income. Using similar econometric techniques, an additional equation could have been developed relating total income to employment in the service sectors and the three export sector. After estimating the parameters, the income equation might be

$$Y = a + 10,175S + 12,542X_1 + 17,159X_2 + 15,445X_3 . \qquad (7\text{-}6)$$

Notice how the outcome of the original model, service employment, feeds into the determination of total income. The model might be further expanded by including an equation relating both income and employment to changes in construction and another equation showing the link between the federal defense budget and employment in sectors X_2 and X_3. (Thus X_2 and X_3 will no longer be exogenous taken as a given to the econometric model, although they will still be independent variables in the local employment equation.)

Time lags could also be introduced so that the model's predictions for one period "feed back" and determine outcomes in later periods. For instance, a statistical relationship might be established between expenditures (E) in period t and taxes (T) in period $t + 1$; $T_{t+1} = a(E_T)$. By determining how key economic variables are linked theoretically and then using statistical techniques (primarily regressions) to quantify the relationships, large and complicated models containing hundreds of equations may be constructed (Rubin and Erickson, 1980).

Caveats

Econometric models are an established part of the regional economist's tool kit. However, anyone applying econometric findings to policy problems should be aware of two general types of limitations: measurement errors and specification errors. One measurement problem is that the values of parameters are based on past observations. Relationships among variables may change in such a way that the model that worked well in the past can no longer serve as a good predictor of the future. This is particularly likely to happen when large or abrupt changes occur. For instance, many economists believe that changes in financial markets that occurred in the 1980s rendered previously estimated relationships inaccurate. Most economic models are much better at "predicting" the past than the future. Some critics of econometric modeling would argue that in reality the "other things equal" assumptions needed to maintain stable relationships change too rapidly to allow good forecasts. In a related vein, Klaasen and Pawlowski (1982) pointed out that models that predict the future on the basis of current trends are bound to fail because current trends will change.

A second measurement problem involves data requirements. Even the best data collected from well-established sources (e.g., the Census Bureau) are subject to significant measurement errors. (Officials in many cities believe that the latest Census of Population has underestimated the number of city residents by failing to account for the homeless, families that were doubled up, the large portion of transients living in parts of major cities, and illegal immigrants. Because many intergovernmental funding programs are linked to population, the issue is vital to the size of urban grants.)

Many governmental statistics are published first as estimates and revised later for better accuracy. Consequently, model builders sometimes must choose between using the most recent data and using older but more accurate data. Furthermore, data for large, comprehensive econometric models are seldom available from published sources, so "proxy" variables are often required. The use of changes in employment to reflect changes in output is an example of the use of proxy variables. Sometimes, the use of proxy variables is benign, but sometimes, the practice can reduce the accuracy of the model.

Specification errors arise from theoretical misunderstandings or deliberate simplification. Suppose a regression model attempted to show that the local unemployment rate was a function of job growth. Because other factors that are practically impossible to measure, such as labor skills and migration patterns, are also important determinants of the unemployment rate, such a model is likely to exclude theoretically important variables and hence be misspecified. Often, models are knowingly misspecified, and sometimes, inaccurate theoretical understanding of the process being modeled results in misspecifications. Economists tend to assume that relationships among variables are linear or some other easy-to-model shape.

Both measurement and specification errors can be compounded when equations have multiplicative or exponential forms. If there were a $\pm 10\%$ error in measuring X, the problem would be greater if the equation to estimate Y were $Y = X^2$ than if the equation were $Y = 2X$ or $Y = 12 + X$. An additional type of error compounding can arise when long chains of logic are employed. If a logical chain has four steps from beginning to end (if A, then B, then C, then D) and if each step is 80% certain, then the certainty of the conclusion would be less than 50%. This type of problem arises when the results of one equation feed into another and is common to both econometric models and other models, such as input-output.

Local Leading Economic Indicators

Leading economic indicators are designed to anticipate turning points in economic activity rather than to forecast values of particular variables. The index of 12 leading economic indicators is a staple of national business cycle analysis. When the index of leading indicators declines for several periods in a row, a decline in output is normally anticipated. The longer and deeper the decline, the more likely a recession will occur. Regional economists have designed indexes of leading economic indicators similar to the national index. Although indexes of leading indicators are not strictly econometric models, econometric techniques are used in their development.

An index of leading economic indicators may be expressed as

$$I = \sum_{i=1}^{n} w_i X_i \qquad (7\text{-}7)$$

where

I = index value
w_i = the weight assigned to the ith indicator
X_i = the value of the ith time series indicator

The construction of an index requires both that the variables used in the index be identified and that an appropriate weight be assigned to each data series (Crane, 1993).

Kozlowski (1987) pointed out that regional economists have less choice in building an index of leading economic indicators than economists engaged in similar activity at the national level because they have fewer time series data sets to possibly incorporate into an index. In fact, the problem in constructing leading indicators at the national level is to filter out data series, whereas regional economists normally seek to expand the set of leading indicators. Table 7.2 shows the variables that compose the index of leading economic indicators for seven areas.

TABLE 7.2 Some Leading Economic Indicators

	Detroit	Wayne	Memphis	Nebraska	South Carolina	Texas	Toledo
Residential housing units authorized by building permit	x	x	x	x	x	x	x
Average weekly initial claims for unemployment insurance	x	x		x	x	x	x
Average workweek—manufacturing workers	x				x	x	x
Total deposits at financial institutions (deflated)	x	x				x	x
New business incorporations					x	x	
Change in credit outstanding							x
Average weekly earnings—manufacturing workers (deflated)			x	x			
Index of prices of farm products				x			
Ratio of coincident to lagging indexes			x				
Percentage industries reporting employment increases			x				
Nonfarm job openings—unfilled					x		
Unemployment rate					x		
Ratio—average weeks claimed to insured employment					x		
Unemployment insurance benefits (current dollars)					x		
Money stock—M2 (deflated)		x					
Standard & Poor's Index of 500 stock prices				x			
New car inventories—U.S. dealers' day's supply	x						
Index of consumer sentiment (University of Michigan)	x						
Number of components	6	4	4	5	8	5	5

SOURCE: Paul J. Kozlowski, "Regional Indexes of Leading Indicators: An Evaluation of Forecasting Performance," *Growth and Change*, Summer 1987, p. 65.

Kozlowski evaluated the accuracy of regional economic indicators. He found that they were accurate in forecasting peaks of economic activity. However, they were less reliable when used as independent variables in models that predicted levels of economic activity. Kozlowski's findings are not surprising because indicators normally require less data than econometric models and they reveal less about the nature of changes.

⊠   Importance-Strength Analysis

An importance-strength survey can be useful in assessing the attributes needed to foster growth of an industry in an area. It is intended to determine simultaneously how important locational attributes are and how the local environment compares to competitor environments. Because the importance of locational factors differ depending on the industry, the importance-strength analysis of locational environments should be industry specific rather than an amalgamation for all economic activities in general.

To conduct a survey that does not simply "average ignorance," it is necessary to seek the cooperation of individuals who have knowledge of the area's locational attributes, attributes of competitor regions, and the importance of locational attributes to the industry being studied. The best respondents are local executives in the industry under consideration. Local executives normally will have knowledge of both the industry and the local environment, regions that may compete with the locality for industry growth. The opinions of about 10 well-informed executives will probably be more useful than the opinions of hundreds of random citizens.

Once a group of local executives has agreed to participate, it should be asked to rank a list of locational attributes on two criteria: importance of the locational attribute and relative (compared to other areas) strength of the locational attribute in the community. Both importance and strength may be rated on a 1-10 scale.

The survey can be conducted either in a round table format or by a conversational-style telephone interview. By using an open-ended approach, the interviewer will gather unanticipated useful information. An additional advantage to using an interactive format is that the nature of locational factors or the reasons for the region's relative advantage or disadvantage can be better understood. Such information can be used to devise developmental strategies.

Table 7.3 illustrates how the data from an importance-strength survey can be organized. In this example, executives from automobile manufacturing were asked to answer the following questions:

"Rank the importance of the following locational factors on a scale of 0-10, with 0 indicating no importance and 10 indicating extreme importance."

"For each of the locational factors, indicate how competitive the Dayton region is relative to other regions, with 0 indicating not competitive and 10 indicating superior."

TABLE 7.3 Auto Components in Dayton, Ohio: Importance-Strength Matrix

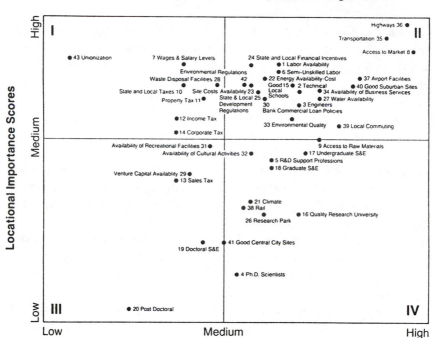

Characteristics in the upper-right-hand side of the matrix represent locational factors that are important and for which the region is strongly competitive. For Dayton, highways and market access are important strengths. Consequently, these locational factors could be promoted when trying to induce firms to expand, remain in the area, or establish a new facility locally. The upper-left-hand cell shows important locational characteristic for which the region is relatively weak. For instance, the high rates of unionization were seen as a locational weakness by automobile executives. If the region is to strengthen its appeal to firms in the automobile sector, it may be helpful to focus improvement efforts on these factors. However, some weaknesses may not be intractable. It is difficult to imagine politicians directly trying to reduce the extent of unions. However, local officials may address the perceived problem in other ways, such as improving labor/management relations.

A region may find that it is not competitive over a wide range of important locational factors. In such a case, it may be wise to focus development efforts

TABLE 7.4 Transaction Table (in dollars)

Sales From	Sales to			Final Demand		Total Gross Output
	Agriculture	Manufacturing	Service	Household	Exports	
Agriculture	300	350	300	1,000	700	2,650
Manufacturing	50	150	600	600	1,400	2,800
Service	500	800	800	700	1,050	3,850
Primary supply						
Households	1,100	300	100	30	20	2,450
Imports	700	1,200	115	120	0	3,170
Total	2,650	2,800	3,850	2,450	3,170	14,920

on other industries. Furthermore, if locational matrixes are developed for a variety of industries, then common strengths and weaknesses may be uncovered. Such commonalities may help local officials decide which improvements will enhance the locational environment for more that one industry. By finding locational commonalities, development officials may develop clusters of industries that may be a focus for development policies.

⊠ Input-Output Analysis

Input-output analysis is a versatile tool because it enables one to examine linkages among sectors. Input-output tables may be used to simply describe a regional economy or to analyze and forecast. This section first shows how input-output analysis can contribute to understanding interindustry linkages and regional structures and then discusses the model's usefulness in understanding the growth process.

The Transactions Table

The first step to understanding input-output analysis is to understand the transactions table. It shows sales and purchases for each sector in a regional economy during a year (see Table 7.4). The interpretation of the transactions table is straightforward. Reading across each row shows the annual dollar value of output that each sector listed along the left-hand column sold to each of the sectors shown on the top. For instance, Table 7.4 indicates that agriculture sold $300 of output to itself, $350 to firms in the manufacturing sector, $300 to firms in the service sector, $1,000 directly to local households, and $700 to businesses and households in the rest of the world as exports.

Reading down the columns shows where the sectors at the top purchased their inputs. In this example, local manufacturing firms purchased $350 from agriculture, $150 from each other, $800 from local service firms, $300 from local households (factors of production, especially labor), and $1,200 in the form of imports from individuals and businesses outside the area.

Besides the interindustry—what A, B, and C sell to each other—sectors, two final demand sectors are shown in Table 7.4. The household column reflects purchases of residents of the region and the export column reflects goods and services that are sold to nonresidents. Two primary supply sectors—household and imports—are also shown. Households provide labor, entrepreneurship, capital, and land as inputs, and the values in each cell of the "household" row reflect compensation for these services. The "import" row shows the dollar value of all commodities imported during the year. From Table 7.4 it can be seen that the manufacturing sector was the largest importer, importing $1,200 worth of goods from outside the region.

The basic transactions table provides detailed information about the local economic structure. However, the table can be rearranged to show the linkages between sectors more directly. A table of direct coefficients can be constructed to show the amount that each sector listed across the top will purchase from the sectors listed down the left per dollar of output of each sector listed across the top.

Table of Direct Coefficients

The table of direct coefficients is shown in Table 7.5. It was derived by dividing the amount that each sector purchased from each of the economy's subcomponents by the total gross output of each of the three producing sectors and the household sector. For instance, the manufacturing sector purchased $800 of inputs from the service sector in order to produce $2,800 of total gross output (see the transactions table in Table 7.4). Thus for each dollar of output the manufacturing firms purchased $.286 (800/2,800) from firms in the service sector. The direct coefficient for the manufacturing column and service row is the strongest linkage among the three industries in the model economy. Agriculture requires the most resources from local households: $.415 of household inputs is required for each dollar of agricultural output.

The table of direct coefficients implies a "fixed input production function." In other words, there is only one recipe for producing the output of each

TABLE 7.5 Table of Direct Coefficients (purchases per $ of output)

Sales From	Sales to			
	Agriculture	Manufacturing	Service	Households
Agriculture	.113	.125	.078	.408
Manufacturing	.019	.053	.156	.245
Service	.189	.286	.208	.286
Households	.415	.107	.259	.012
Imports	.264	.429	.299	.048

sector; inputs cannot be substituted. If the price of a commodity increased or decreased, the total amount spent on the commodity per dollar of output would remain constant. In reality, most production processes allow for some substitution, such as substituting capital for labor if the price of labor increases.

The table of direct coefficients illustrates interindustry linkage. For instance, if the agricultural sector were to produce an extra dollar of output, using the *same input proportions* that were used when the input-output table was constructed, it would need to purchase $.113 from other agriculture producers (i.e., when a hog producer purchases corn or feed), $.019 from the manufacturing sector, and $.189 from services. In addition, $.415 would go to households to pay for inputs, such as labor, and $.264 would be spent on imported inputs of all types. All manufacturing goods, services, agricultural products, and direct inputs from households that are purchased outside the region are included in the $.264 of imports.

Table of Direct and Indirect Coefficients

Regional multipliers can be obtained from the table of direct coefficients. This table shows only partial multipliers because they account for only first-round spending effects. Sectors providing inputs to manufacturing will require additional output from their suppliers, suppliers of suppliers will purchase more from their suppliers, and so forth. For instance, from Table 7.5 it can be seen that if the manufacturing sector increases its output by $1, $.125 of additional output will be required from the local agricultural sector. But if agriculture is to increase its output by $.125, agricultural firms must purchase $.0166(.1332 × $.1250) from other agricultural firms, $.0024(.0189 × $.1250) from manufacturing firms and $.0236(.1886 × $.1250) from service firms. Household income will increase by $.0134($.125 × .107) because of the

TABLE 7.6 Table of Direct and Indirect Coefficients

	Agriculture	Manufacturing	Service	Household
Agriculture	1.570	0.373	0.255	0.815
Manufacturing	0.342	1.250	0.298	0.538
Service	0.757	0.651	1.490	0.907
Households	0.717	0.310	0.179	1.440

primary factors of production needed to produce the extra output required by manufacturing. But household income will also increase because of the increases in agricultural and service output created by the initial increase in manufacturing output. The household income will be spent according to the coefficients in the "household" column of Table 7.5 if consumption patterns remain constant. Obviously, one can only scratch the surface of the various feedbacks before the calculations become very awkward.

In theory, these ripples would continue forever. However, each round of spending results in successively smaller amounts of induced output. The cumulative size of the various rounds of spending can be calculated mathematically.[2] The results are shown in Table 7.6. It shows the dollar amount of output that would be required from each sector listed on the left to accommodate $1's increase in output from each sector listed at the top. In other words, if manufacturing increased its output by $1, the total effect on the agricultural sector would be to increase output by $.5354. The total effect is the sum of the following:

Direct effects: The first-round increase shown in the table of direct coefficients

Indirect effects: The interindustry effects as local industries purchase from one another

Induced effects: The additional increases in output due to household spending and the indirect effects of household responding

Uses of Input-Output Tables for Growth Analysis

Both the tables of direct coefficients (Table 7.5) and direct and indirect coefficients (Table 7.3) have many uses in growth analysis and economic development policy. This section shows how input-output tables can be used to

- assess local economic structure
- estimate imports
- inform locational decisions and industrial targeting

- forecast and determine economic impacts
- simulate technological change

Assessing Regional Structure

Comparing one region's direct and indirect coefficients with those of another area can provide a useful perspective on its internal structure. Underdeveloped regions normally have few internal interindustry linkages because they lack an integrated economic structure. The lack of internal linkages can be an impediment to development because if a firm increases its output few of the benefits will ripple through the rest of the economy; the local multiplier will be smaller. Likewise, small regions will have fewer internal linkages than larger regions because small regions are more likely to import required inputs. Interindustry linkages will be larger for a nation as a whole than for a region because a smaller portion of a nation's input requirements are imported, whereas imports for a region include goods purchased from other regions.

Suppose regions A and B are similar in size, produce a similar output, and use identical production techniques. Therefore, the input requirements of the regions are the same. However, suppose region A is well integrated internally and region B has only a few significant interindustry linkages. There would be many more gaps—$0s or very low transaction amounts—in region B's input-output table, implying that its economy is less integrated. Consequently, intermediate inputs would have to be imported into the region. When an industry expands, it will have a bigger impact on other industries in region A because of strong linkages.

Estimating Imports

It is also useful to compare local input-output coefficients with national coefficients to estimate imports. Suppose that nationally the electrical machinery sector sells .10 cents to the motor vehicles sector per dollar of motor vehicle output. Furthermore, suppose the corresponding coefficient for a locality is .04 cents as indicated by a local table of direct coefficients. Also, assume that the national economy is closed, so there is no international trade, and that the level of production technology locally is the same as the national level's. The difference in coefficients implies that for every dollar of output by the regional motor vehicles sector, .06 cents worth of electrical machinery is imported. If the motor vehicles sector is large, the dollar value of imported electronic equipment may be large. The total value of the imports of electrical machinery for motor vehicles could be calculated by multiplying .06 times the value of automobile output. Consequently, a development planner may wish to determine whether there was potential for growth in the electrical machinery sector based on the potential for import substitution through sales to motor vehicle establishments. Of course, there are other locational requirements besides the presence of a buyer that a community must satisfy if an area is to attract electrical machinery producers. However, the structural perspective given by comparing the national and local table of direct coefficients can be a useful starting point for analysis.

Informing Locational and Targeting Decisions

The identification of imports from comparing national and regional coefficients can assist in locational decisions. A firm may wish to locate near potential customers. A firm located near its customers may be able to undersell competitors because of lower transportation costs, provide better service, or cultivate contacts that could enhance future sales. Hence some firms may chose to seek locations where imports of their product are substantial.

Urban and regional planners may also use input-output analysis to help target the types of industries they would like to attract. Development officials may wish to recruit industries that strengthen interindustry linkages so as to build a more substantial agglomeration in a particular industrial cluster. For instance, a food processing plant might be attracted to an area that produces a type of agricultural product. This strategy may involve attempting to attract buyers of products already produced in the region or sellers of products that other industries purchase. Another development strategy might be to target high-value-added industries, activities that purchase a large portion of inputs directly from households.

Economic development officials might reasonably believe that local subsidies are easier to justify if the benefits flow to a large portion of the economy, help clusters they wish to nurture, or require large inputs from households, thus creating household income. Because input-output tables indicate how each sector affects every other sector and households, they can be very useful in industrial targeting.

Conducting Impact Studies

The multipliers can be used to make forecasts and to perform impact analysis. An input-output forecast would normally first require an estimate of final demand (export levels) for each sector. Because final demand is exogenous, estimates of final demand must come from outside the input-output model. The endogenous sectors could then be confronted with the set of final demands, and the output of each industry as well as its transactions with every other industry could be calculated. When exports are known, total output of each sector can be calculated. When the total output of each sector is known, the value of interindustry transactions can be determined. Essentially, a new transactions table could be created reflecting alternative levels of exports.

Impact analysis is similar to other projections except that the impacts are usually special events rather than a general change in export demand. The impact of closing a university, for example, could be simulated using input-output analysis. In this case, the external demand for services (or education, if a very detailed model were being used) would decrease by the amount of outside funds going to the university (state and federal funds plus tuition paid by nonresident students). The direct, indirect, and induced declines in output due to the university closing would constitute the impact. In all probability, all of the sectors in the input-output model would be affected, although some would be affected more than others.

Examining Technological Change

Input-output analysis has also been used to simulate technological change. Suppose a panel of engineering experts reported that new technology would reduce the dependence of manufacturing on the agricultural sector by 10%. In economic terms, the impact could be expressed as follows: For each dollar of manufacturing productions, manufacturing firms will purchase 10% less from agriculture. But if less per dollar of output is spent on agriculture, another sector's sales to manufacturing will have to increase because the value of total output must equal the value of the inputs. Perhaps the household sector would "sell" more entrepreneurial services to manufacturing on the assumptions that the lower agricultural requirement would flow to households in the form of higher profits. Alternatively, perhaps service firms will replace the agricultural input. Perhaps the savings from lower agricultural requirements will be distributed evenly among the other sectors. In any event, a new set of direct input requirements reflecting the most likely repercussions of technological change can be developed.

To simulate the impact of the technological change, the exiting set of final demand requirements can be applied to the (assumed) new set of direct requirements. A new set of outputs for the local sectors could be derived. As a result of the simulation, the level of total output and the distributions of output among the sectors can be calculated.

⊗ Summary

Several important empirical tools are used to understand the process of local economic development. Practitioners should understand the strengths and weaknesses of these tools. Shift/share analysis is a technique for dividing an area's growth into three components. First, the share component of growth is equal to the national average growth rate. Second, an area may grow differently from the national average due to its mix of industries. Third, an area may have a favorable or unfavorable growth environment. Shift and share analysis has been criticized because the components are frequently misinterpreted and because the competitive component is a residual that can be attributed to a variety of other factors.

Economic models use statistical techniques and economic theory to estimate relationships among variables. Good econometric models are informed by economic theory. The export-base model can serve as the theoretical foundation for an econometric model, with changes in export employment serving as the independent variable. Nonbasis or service employment would be a dependent variable. Econometric models have important weaknesses: Relationships among variables may change so that models that worked well in the past might not do so in the future, and variable data are often lacking. Simulation models answer "what if" questions, such as how key social indicators would change if a particular theory were implemented. Many simulation theories use econometric techniques, such as regression, to establish relationships among variables.

Leading economic indicators are designed to anticipate turning points in economic activity. Housing permits are an example of a leading indicator. A sharp increase in housing permits suggests an increase in economic activity several months in the future.

An importance-strength analysis allows policymakers to identify local attributes on two scales simultaneously: importance and the locality's strength in terms of the attribute. Policies may be developed to strengthen important yet weak attributes. Important attributes in which the area exhibits strengths can be promoted.

Input-output analysis can be used to determine the impact that an increase in the output of one sector will have on other sectors of the economy. The total impact is the result of direct, indirect, and induced effects. Input-output analysis has several uses, including assessing regional structure, estimating imports, assisting in targeting decisions, conducting impact studies, and examining structural change. One of the major advantages of input-output analysis is that the results provide substantial industrial detail. The most noticeable difficulties in using the input-output approach are the high cost of data collection and the static nature of the model.

⊠ Notes

1. These figures were obtained by multiplying the national average growth rate of 32% by the initial year employment in each section. Notice a slight rounding error, as the employment increase in the individual sectors sum to only 122.

2. The table of direct and indirect coefficients is the $(I - A)^{-1}$, where A is the matrix of direct coefficients and I is an identity matrix of equal dimensions.

Issues in Economic
Development Practice

Previous chapters described theories and tools that help analyze local development. Economic development officials must use theories and empirical evidence to formulate action plans. This chapter examines issues that local development planners confront when developing and implementing policies. Many of the issues discussed in this chapter are presented as either/or cases for purposes of exposition. In practice, economic development officials should recognize truth in both extremes and construct economic development strategies accordingly.

⊠ External Benefits From Economic Development

The external benefits that local residents receive from new economic activity are the major incentive for local development programs. When economic growth occurs, a wide variety of individuals benefit both directly and indirectly. Although the objectives of economic development programs are not always explicitly stated, most communities have three objectives: job and income creation, fiscal improvement, and physical improvements. Although local workers are usually the most direct beneficiaries of the external benefits from development, property owners may also realize gains through higher property values and rents. Others may benefit from lower taxes because of a larger tax base. Besides public objectives, public officials and private investors engaged in economic development efforts have their own aspirations for success, recognition, and wealth.

Job and Income Creation

Communities with loose labor markets are characterized by high unemployment, low wages, discouraged workers, and underemployment. Many of these communities have experienced painful plant shutdown and declines in the number of available jobs. Currently, many individuals are "piecing together" a living with several part-time jobs. Individuals in loose labor markets often must leave the area to find work. Programs to encourage more local jobs include public employment and private sector job development. However, private sector job creation efforts account for many more new jobs than direct public job efforts.

Most economists regard job creation as a primary purpose of local economic development strategies. Many state and federal grant programs employ job creation as an explicit program goal along with other important grant selection criteria. Indicators of labor market problems are also criteria in state and federal project selection so that monies will tend to flow to areas with employment problems. Job creation is closely associated with improvements in real incomes. However, planners must distinguish between per capita income growth, which will benefit current residents, and increases in total incomes which could occur primarily because new residents moved to the area to secure existing jobs.

Fiscal Improvement

Many municipalities encourage economic development in the expectation that new businesses will contribute more in tax revenues than any extra municipal services will cost. Generally, land uses devoted to commerce and manufacturing generate net revenues for the city, whereas middle- and lower-income residential property tend to cause public service costs to increase by more than the tax revenues generated. Thus communities seeking to strengthen their fiscal positions will usually attempt to attract either upper-income residential housing or businesses.

Fiscal objectives often result in competition among localities within a metropolitan region. Unless tax sharing agreements among neighboring communities exist, only the locality where a business actually locates will receive increased property tax revenues. (Some areas that have local income taxes may benefit if residents receive jobs in businesses located in nearby communities.) The job creation benefits of a new or expanded business will be more diffused throughout the metropolitan area than the fiscal benefits. New jobs may be obtained by residents throughout a metropolitan area regardless of whether or not they live in the municipality in which the business located.

Physical Improvements

Finally, many urban officials view economic development as a way to achieve physical improvements in their community. For instance, public officials may want to attract a new business to a particular corner of the downtown area so as to remove an existing eyesore or because too much vacant land in the downtown area creates an image of lack of progress. This motive is a remnant of the urban renewal period of economic development when physical change was the principal criterion used to evaluate the success of economic development predictions. Today, many neighborhood economic development efforts emphasize physical improvements.

⊠   Who Benefits From Growth?

The formal goals of economic development should not mask the fact that there are often some groups that will benefits from growth more than others. Although the beneficiaries of growth vary dramatically depending on the type of growth, some generalizations are possible.

Demand for output of the export sector is not likely to be altered by growth of the local economy because demand for exports is determined outside the area. However, local growth will increase the demand for products and services that are normally considered part of the nonbasic sector serving the local population, such as brokerage services, grocers, retail activities, and newspapers. Increased demand for local services will in turn tend to increase the price and wage of resources, including labor used to produce nonbasic goods. Hence owners of resources that produce for local consumption may experience increases in income as the result of regional growth.

The permanence of the gains from growth depends on how quickly resources move into the sectors experiencing an increase in demand. If resources from elsewhere move quickly into an expanding sector, resource

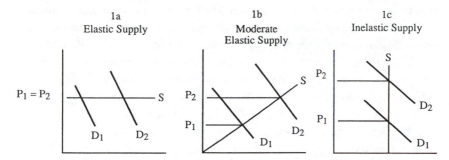

Figure 8.1. The elasticity of supply determines the extent that the price of a resource will increase due to a demand increase. The more inelastic the supply, the higher the price increase will be. The same logic applies in reverse when demand falls.

supplies will tend to be elastic and the benefits for the original resource owners will be short-lived. The increase in demand will translate into higher factor prices only briefly. The elasticity of resource supply will depend on how easily additional resources can be brought into the area and the ability of resources to shift from other local sectors to the sector experiencing a demand increase. The longer the time period, the greater the likelihood that resources can be brought from outside the area. Therefore, the size of the annual benefits from growth will probably diminish in the long run for owners of resources with elastic supplies.

Figure 8.1 illustrates three possible resource supply situations. In the first case (1a), the supply of the resources to the local economy is perfectly elastic. Thus an increase in demand for the resource will not cause the price of the resource to increase. This case may approximate the actual situation for many factors of production in the long run or for regionally mobile factors of production even in the short run. The second case (1b) represents a situation where some new resources enter the area but not enough to bring the price down to the original level. The third case (1c) illustrates a perfectly inelastic supply. The total impact of the demand increase is absorbed in the form of a higher price. Figure 8.1c could represent a resource for which increased compensation does not bring forth greater resource supply.

Characteristics of Resource Supply

The supply of money capital to most sectors of local economies is very elastic. If the expected rate of return on newly invested capital increases, investment from outside will very quickly flow into the area, thus reducing the interest disparity. Banks and other financial institutions are connected to national and international money markets. However, owners of capital embodied in real assets invested prior to local economic growth may earn above normal rates of return, at least on a temporary basis, depending on where their capital was invested. Individuals who purchased buildings may find that their rents increased due to local growth. Therefore, the rate of return on real assets may be greater than would have been anticipated. Similarly, owners of local service businesses may experience increased rates of return. The ability to maintain above-normal rates will depend on the speed with which new competitors enter the industry.

Some members of the labor force may also earn above-normal income due to local growth. Imagine an automobile salesperson whose income increased because of larger sales attributed to the stronger local economy. Thus the salesperson could be a beneficiary of local growth. However, the salesperson's increased compensation is likely to be only temporary. The owner of the dealership may realize that the income of the sales staff has increased and cut commission rates accordingly, or other dealerships may enter the area, thus reducing sales at the original dealership. In general, the mobility of labor will cause some gains due to growth to dissipate over time. However, even temporary gains are beneficial, and "temporary" may be several years in some cases.

Unemployed workers have opportunities to benefit from the increased jobs associated with growth. In fact, an expanding facility is likely to directly and indirectly create jobs that will be filled by unemployed residents. Those unemployed who capture new jobs may benefit in both the short and long run. However, in the long run, growth may attract unemployed workers from elsewhere into the local area and the previous unemployment rate may be reestablished. Some of the original residents may have obtained permanent employment as the economy grew. Similar benefits may accrue to underemployed residents who secure better jobs during the transition. Bartik (1991) estimated that 80% of jobs created in a metropolitan area are likely to go to in-migrants in the long run of 5 years or more.

Owners of local monopoly resources are likely to benefit from growth, even in the long run. Landowners do not have to worry about an increased supply of land coming into the area. Since the supply of land is fixed and each site has slight monopoly power, landowners will maintain benefits from growth even in the long run. It is not surprising that individuals involved in land development are usually prominent pro-growth advocates. Similarly, some franchise owners may have been granted licenses to serve a region and can maintain that "monopoly" as the region grows.

The lumpy nature of much economic activity can contribute to the perpetuation of monopolies. Suppose a shoe repair shop requires a population of at least 10,000 to provide sufficient demand to earn normal profits. If an area grows from 10,000 to 15,000 people, the owner of the shoe repair store could earn above-normal profits because of the 50% increase in the market size. Yet there would not be room for another competitor. A second shop would face the possibility of splitting a 15,000-person market. (A new store might not even be able to capture half the market.) Therefore, a population of 15,000 would not be large enough to support two stores.

New firms may enter a region that has experienced a demand increase only after substantial time lags. Even after a new enterprise enters an area, it may take a long time for it to get established to the point where it is a strong competitor with existing businesses. The original enterprises will have established customers, locations, and reputations that can provide an advantage for generations. The lumpy nature of economic activity and the time lags that characterize new business formation help explain why small retailers tend to be pro-growth advocates.

Many individuals will benefit from the increased amenities, shopping choices, and other opportunities that become available as their community grows. Hence not all of the indirect effects of growth are monetary.

In general, money capital is highly elastic. Labor resources tend to be elastic, especially for labor resources that move easily from one community to another. Real-property owners, including owners of land, will benefit from growth because most real-property resources are somewhat or highly inelastic, especially in the short run. Lumpiness in the size of demand needed to support an additional resource contributes to inelasticity in business. Franchise owners and other holders of monopoly resources will benefit from growth in the long run.

Opponents of Growth

The benefits discussed above were primarily concerned with household income. Growth may also affect an area negatively. Many individuals oppose growth because they believe it makes their area less attractive. Higher prices, particularly in resource inelastic sectors, are a cost of growth that may be imposed on many residents. For instance, growth will probably affect housing rents. An individual living on a fixed income may be disadvantaged due to higher prices that may accompany growth. Furthermore, additional production tends to be associated with more pollution, and population growth is associated with greater congestion. Individuals who do not receive substantial growth benefits may feel they are losers from growth. The extent of negative growth spillovers and the inability of everyone to share fully in the benefits of growth explain why some communities have instituted "no growth" campaigns.

States and regions are much more receptive to growth than they were in the late 1960s when the slow-/no-growth advocates had substantial influence. Most regional communities realize that some economic growth is necessary to provide jobs for current residents and their children. If no new jobs are being created, some out-migration will occur simply due to natural population increases.

The strongest antigrowth coalitions tend to be within suburbs or neighborhoods of metropolitan areas. Many individuals seek to protect their immediate neighborhood from negative growth consequences (the NIMBY, or "Not In My Backyard," phenomenon) while benefiting from growth in other parts of the metropolitan area. The prevalence of such attitudes often brings suburbs in conflict with each other and hinders metropolitan cooperation.

⊠ Problems With Local Competition for Economic Development

As cities have increased their efforts to attract businesses or to encourage expansion, they have become competitors in a "market for jobs" (Blair, Fichtenbaum, and Swaney, 1984). City officials essentially attempt to purchase jobs and the related benefits associated with economic growth by offering businesses a wide variety of subsidies. The market for jobs seldom operates so explicitly that a community would, say, offer $10,000 per job created. Rather, communities offer indirect inducements in an almost endless combination of direct and indirect forms. Table 8.1 lists many of the subsidy techniques used by local communities. An important skill of an economic development official is to combine these subsidies into a package that will appeal to businesses without costing the community too much.

The purpose of this section is to discuss some of the problems and issues that occur as communities attempt to use public funds to encourage economic development.

TABLE 8.1 Common Direct Economic Development Subsidies

Type of Subsidy	*Comment*
Tax abatements	A reduction of tax liability either permanently or for a period of time. Most types of taxes can be abated.
Low interest loans	Can help reduce costs as well as provide seed money to help start-up companies that may be high risk.
Infrastructure and site assistance	These subsidies include providing land at reduced costs, construction of buildings, and providing public infrastructure such as roads and sewers. "Incubation" programs include site assistance.
Labor force training	Communities may finance the training of workers, including selection. Wage subsidies may be included.
Regulatory relief	Firms may be exempted from environmental, safety, or other state and local regulations. Can be part of "cutting red tape."
Sale-lease backs	A firm may sell its build to a community and lease it back at a nominal rate, thus providing an infusion of capital.
Technical assistance	Economic development agencies may provide a variety of technical assistance in areas of finance, marketing exporting, technology transfer, and so forth.

Is Local Economic Development a Zero-Sum Game?

One of the criticisms of local economic development activities is that cities compete with each other without increasing the number of jobs available. Consequently, whatever one community gains, another community loses. An example of a zero-sum game occurs when a company announces that it will establish a facility in one of three or four cities and suggests that the ultimate site will depend heavily on the size of the local incentive package. Zero-sum games are particularly likely to occur when communities within a particular metropolitan area compete for jobs because the firm has probably already decided to locate somewhere in the area. The 1988 *President's National Urban Policy Report* expressed concern over the zero-sum game aspect of economic development:

> At the federal level place specific economic development policies often do nothing more than tax one place to improve conditions in another. The wealth of both places is not greater and may actually be less than it might have been. (U.S. Department of Housing and Urban Development, 1988, p. II-2)

Although economic development efforts can result in zero and even negative sum outcomes, they need not necessarily do so. Three examples of economic development activities that result in positive sum benefits may guide local efforts in the "market for jobs." First, the economic development incentives offered by localities may have greater value to businesses than they cost local governments. For instance, a city may build an industrial park costing $1 million. If it provides benefits to existing and potential firms of $2 million, the value creation constitutes a positive sum outcome. Because of the quasi-public-goods characteristics of many economic development projects (one project benefits many firms simultaneously), the value of a single project may exceed the costs.

Second, economic development efforts may cause a firm to locate in an area of high external benefits rather than in an area of low external benefits. For instance, assume that City A has full employment and possibly heavy congestion. Perhaps individuals would have to move into the area, thus expending resources in relocation if the firm were to locate there. Consequently, current residents would receive few external benefits from new economic development activity. Suppose, however, that there is significant unemployment and unused infrastructure in City B. The external benefits from job growth are significant. If economic development efforts encourage job creation in City B rather than City A, the country as a whole will experience positive gains. Even though the level of economic activity would be the same if the firm located in A or B, the benefits are greater at B. Thus redistributing a fixed level of economic activity can increase benefits from economic development.

Third, local economic development efforts can help create jobs. Imagine a firm that could generate significant external benefits to the community if it started operations. However, the expected profits are not quite large enough to justify opening. In this case, a small economic development subsidy would make the firm profitable. If the economic development incentive was less than the value of the external benefits the subsidy made possible, a positive sum-game would result.

Inefficiency and Oversubsidization

The existence of potential gains from local jobs is a necessary, although not sufficient, condition for efficient local job creation programs. If economic development officials knew better the nature of the community benefits their community might receive from particular types of economic development they would be better able to operate efficiently in the job creation process. If officials in a community offered the firm more than the minimum subsidy necessary to attract it or to induce it to expand, oversubsidization would occur. There are at least five important reasons why the market for jobs tends to be inefficient:

- Practical problems of collective action
- Information asymmetry
- Unspecified property rights
- The operation of federal economic development programs
- Differences in the cost and value of subsidies

Collective Action

The ability of local governments to operate efficient incentive programs depends on how well the political process operates to reflect the interest of citizens. There are two potential problems here: First, a small group of highly interested persons can influence government more than a large group of moderately interested persons because the small group has an incentive to bear the costs of influencing governmental action, and second, it is less costly for individuals represented by existing organizations to influence policy than it is for unorganized individuals.

A consequence of political action characteristics is that cities are more likely to enter the market when new jobs offer external benefits to existing, influential groups than when the benefits flow to politically unorganized groups. Thus redevelopment projects that enhance the interests of major property owners and retail businesses are more likely to receive assistance than projects lacking influential beneficiaries. Also, existing establishments that threaten to reduce their workforce are in a strong position to mobilize political support to secure a public grant. In contrast, small firms are less likely to muster the support needed to receive a special incentive.

The economic development incentives are also likely to be affected by the strength or weakness of local politicians. Because the costs of an industrial location are generally paid in the politically distant future, a weak officeholder may have an incentive to overpay for a major industrial location. In their case study of a nearly $200 million locational subsidy package to General Motors, Jones and Bachelor (1984) reported that GM had an advantage negotiating subsidies with Detroit officials because local economic problems made state and local elected officials anxious to secure the plant. In this case, even a fairly popular mayor was unable to resist pressures to provide huge locational incentives.

Information Asymmetry

Information asymmetry arises when the circumstances surrounding a transaction are better known by one party than by the other participating parties. Such a situation can arise when one party deliberately provides distorted information to other parties.

Typically, private parties involved in economic development negotiations have incentives to provide selective or distorted information. For example, a firm trying to make a plant-closing decision may be forced to choose between two locations. The firm has information regarding the decision that it does not have to disclose to the cities offering to subsidize operations. This advantage provides the firm with bargaining power.

Vaguely Defined Product

A third deterrent to efficient market operations is the poorly defined nature of the good (a "job") or poorly defined property rights. Although most negotiations over industrial location include corporate estimates of the number of jobs that will be created, firms do not guarantee specific numbers of job characteristics in exchange for locational grants. Often, temporary (i.e., construction) employment is included in the job estimates, and seasonal low-paying jobs are not distinguished from better jobs. Most observers believe that grantees tend to overstate the number of jobs that would be created by businesses by as much as 30%. Cities seldom attempt to elicit guarantees that a particular number of jobs will be provided for current residents, partly because job creation is difficult to forecast. However, many communities are inserting "clawback" clauses when they provide economic development incentives. The clause requires firms to repay part of the benefits they received if jobs or other external benefits fall below a certain level.

Federal Subsidies

A fourth factor that may reduce efficiency is federal assistance that encourages cities to offer more for jobs than the benefits received or that subsidizes cities competing against each other for the same jobs. Of course, federal assistance is appropriate when the federal interest in job creation transcends local interests, perhaps because of externalities received by other local areas in addition to the area that captures the firm. But to be efficient, the federal programs must be carefully structured to avoid situations in which one city bids against another in a zero-sum game with federal dollars.

Subsidy Cost Versus Value

How much of a subsidy actually reaches the intended party compared to the taxpayers' cost? Two types of problems can cause the value of economic development incentives to the firm to be less than the cost to taxpayers:

1. The subsidy program may provide costly goods and services that are not highly valued by the locating firm (similar to a gift that is expensive but not appreciated by the receiver).
2. Unintended parties may capture some of the benefits.

The most obvious instance of a poorly targeted subsidy is when a local community provides a service or infrastructure improvements that cost taxpayers more than they are valued by the firm the community is trying to attract. For example, suppose a region spends millions of dollars to beautify an industrial park. The better looks undoubtedly would be a plus in attracting firms and jobs, but would firms value the beautification efforts enough to warrant the community's cost? (Of course, beautification programs provide benefits to residents as well, so one could argue that the marginal benefits to the community outweigh the cost.) However, if the community has a narrow goal of attracting a particular firm, the more directly the benefits are tailored to the firm, the greater the firm is likely to value the benefits.

Suppose a property owner had a parcel of land that he wished to develop as an industrial park and he convinced the city council that a tax abatement would be necessary to attract firms. Consequently, the city agreed to provide a tax abatement for any employer building a new facility in the industrial park. Prior to the availability of the tax abatement, the landowner might have asked $10,000 an acre. Because of the availability of the abatement, the demand for the land in the industrial park will increase. The owner may raise the price of the land to $15,000. Thus the landowner may capture part or all of the value of the tax abatement. In this case, the landowner will capture $5,000 of the development incentive. Not all of the abatement's value will accrue to the industrial firm that locates in the area.

Subsidy programs have been compared to carrying water in a leaky bucket. Some of the water will leak out on the way from the well to the destination just as some of the subsidy often goes to unintended parties.

What does a job cost? One indication of an inefficient market is the presence of large variations in the product's price. Of course, the price of a job could vary even in an efficient market, owing to variations in job quality and externalities associated with jobs. Nevertheless, the cost of a job varies so much even within a local area that there can be little doubt that the market is inefficient.

Data on the cost of a job are fragmented and difficult to obtain. Lack of cost data is itself an indication of an imperfect market because well-functioning markets are characterized by buyers and sellers who know the prevailing price. However, the scattered evidence from major federal programs shows that cost per job created ranges from over $300,000 to as little as $5,000. (The cost of a job is the subsidy per job, not the capital-labor ratio.) The conclusion that there are wide cost variations is clear. The variation in the cost of jobs is accentuated because jobs created in small retail and service establishments receive no direct subsidy. Hence the cost of an unsubsidized job is zero.

Discretionary Versus Entitlement Subsidies

Discretionary policies provide local development officials with choices regarding the type or size of an incentive they may wish to extend to a particular business. Benefits from entitlement programs are due to any firm that meets a set of stipulated requirements.

The advantage of discretionary programs is that governments may avoid paying unnecessary subsidies or tax expenditures. The disadvantage of discretionary programs is that government officials must make decisions regarding business potential of firms seeking subsidies. Can the firm succeed? How much of a subsidy is necessary? Government bureaucrats may not be able to make such decisions accurately. Entitlement programs create a business climate that all qualifying businesses can potentially exploit. Once the framework is established, government officials need not be directly involved in business decisions.

Cost Minimization Versus Human Capital Strategies

The majority of economic development tools are designed to reduce business costs and hence attract new industries to an area. Business cost-reduction approaches have been criticized for three reasons. First, cost minimization approaches may tend to attract branch plants of mature industries, yet most growth is generated internally to local businesses. Unfortunately, existing businesses often pay (either directly or indirectly) for subsidies given to attract new firms. Second, it is extremely difficult for most regions in advanced countries to compete with locations in less developed countries on the basis of cost. Large multiplant companies are in a position to consider locations throughout the world. Third, local economic development strategies should attempt to increase local living standards, not just increase the number of jobs. A cost minimization strategy might actually lead to lower per capita incomes for residents if low-paying jobs are created.

The human capital strategy attempts to provide businesses with a high-quality labor force. The labor force will appeal to activities that perform nonroutine operations such as corporate headquarter work, skilled operations, and technologically oriented activities. Advocates of the human capital approach contend that local residents will be better served by stimulating growth in these better-paying occupations. However, there is a danger that low-skilled populations could be left out of a development plan that values only high-paying, high-skill jobs.

Warner (1989) conducted an empirical test to determine whether improvement in variables associated with cost minimization or variables associated with human capital improvement best explained changes in per capita income among urban regions between 1977 and 1984. He concluded that the human capital approach is more effective in increasing average incomes. Although the specifics of Warner's empirical tests may be questioned, they indicate that regional development officials should not overemphasize cost reduction programs at the expense of the human capital strategy.

The major problem with labor force development programs is that there are insufficient jobs for all individuals qualified to be trained after training programs are successful in placing their students, but they may simply bump someone with equal or superior skills. Thus a particular program may seem to be successful from the perspective of the persons in the program, but from the perspective of the larger community it is a zero-sum game. Job training works best in a job-growth environment or when an employer needs workers with skills that are not available among other unemployed persons in the community. In an atmosphere of slow growth and high local unemployment, training programs may have difficulty placing clients or simply affect who is hired.

⊠   Cumulative Causation

Cumulative causation refers to the process in which a change in one direction may reinforce other tendencies for change in the same direction. Myrdal (1957) believed that disequilibrium growth development paths were common:

> In the normal case, there is no tendency towards automatic self-stabilization in the social system. The system is not by itself moving towards any sort of balance between forces, but is constantly on the move away from such a situation. In the normal case, a change does not call forth countervailing changes, but, instead, supporting changes which move the system in the same direction as the first change but much further. Because of such circular causation, a social process tends to become cumulative and often to gather speed at an accelerating rate. (p. 13)

Although Myrdal was primarily considering underdeveloped regions when he discussed the process of circular causation, the concept has been applied to urban systems. The selective nature of outmigration can contribute to cumulative decline. For instance, in a metropolitan environment, higher-income families tend to move into the suburbs. As the affluent families leave the central city, families with greater public service needs and lower capacities to pay taxes are left behind. The resulting fiscal mix increases the tax burden of remaining high-income families and reinforces the tendency toward outmigration of even more upper-income families. The decline may be reinforced because the outmigration that results in lower income and lower fiscal capacity may, in turn, contribute to other types of deterioration such as crime, urban ugliness, and fewer amenities. The population-income decline may also contribute to the movement of retail and other service jobs to the suburbs. The job shift will be particularly significant to the extent that higher-income families (which account for a disproportionate amount of spending) lead the exodus.

Similarly, when an area starts to prosper, self-reinforcing factors may tend to cause cumulative growth. Higher incomes allow for more amenities, attract businesses, and increase agglomeration economies. An area that has a growth reputation may attract additional investment that will, in turn, contribute to growth.

Of course, a new equilibrium will ultimately be established. A city will not increase or decline forever because countervailing forces such as higher or lower land prices eventually will become increasingly powerful. In this sense, most phenomena are equilibrating in the long run. But the disequilibrium models have the advantage of highlighting the potential for cumulative change that may occur over some portion of a community's adjustment path.

Economic development officials should be particularly concerned about threats that could place the community on a downward spiral. Determining when a community may be near such a tipping point requires substantial judgment, but the loss of a major employer, the technological trends that threaten to render some local process uneconomical, or increasing bad reputations for crime or poor education could be catalysts for cumulative decline. Conversely, development officials should be aware of potential opportunities that could place the community on an upward growth path.

Baumol (1963; Oates, Howrey, and Baumol, 1971) developed a mathematical model that illustrates how a negative (positive) change could institute a cumulative downward (upward) growth path. The Baumol model employs an abstract concept called "deterioration," which represents a variety of urban problems such as crime, poverty, congestion and so forth. His model is based on two relationships:

1. The higher the level of deterioration in any given year, the lower the regional income in succeeding years.
2. Slow or negative income growth increases deterioration.

Under these conditions, it is possible for deterioration to real growth to lead to more deterioration and cumulative decline.

Bradford and Kelejian (1973) provided empirical evidence that urban decline can be cumulative over a significant range. Specifically, they found that middle-class families were more likely to reside in suburbs, hence the higher the percentage of poor persons residing in central cities and the lower the fiscal spillovers for middle-class suburban residents. Thus a city with a high proportion of poor residents and associated poverty programs could experience further declines in the middle-class population.

Policies that change the relationship between income and the rate of deterioration are critical given the cumulative decline model. A policy that directly increases income for only one period may be unsuccessful because the decline may not be stopped permanently. Thus the income increase will be temporary only. A marketing campaign that convinces people of the advantages of urban living, metropolitan government, or better urban design that reduces the annoyances of high-density population are examples of actions that could permanently increase equilibrium incomes by altering the relationship between deterioration and income.

⊠   Targeting Development Efforts

In Rubin's (1988) analysis of attitudes of local economic development officials, he suggested that they "shoot any thing that flies and claim anything that falls" (p. 236). Rubin's analysis highlights an important tendency. Officials often fail to target activities and, therefore, perform their duties without a strong strategic framework. Many development officials are now attempting to target their economic development efforts so as to focus on only certain types of activities. Advantages of targeting include better resource use and a better chance to build an economic agglomeration that will set the stage for cumulative growth. A principal disadvantage of targeting is that opportunities that are not within the community targets may be overlooked. Another problem is that community officials may not have sufficient knowledge to select an appropriate target.

Most communities target particular industries. However, it has been suggested that focusing on industries only may not be a detailed enough target because within any industry there are many functions and a type of local environment that is best for each function. For instance, within the automobile industry there are research, sales, accounting, human resources management, and numerous functions. A "crosshair" targeting has been suggested whereby policymakers target particular functions within a closely related group of industries. Thus there are two targets: industry and activity.

Thompson and Thompson (1987) suggested five types of activities that communities may use in targeting economic development efforts: routine operations, precision operations, research and development, central administration, and entrepreneurship. Each of these "paths" requires different locational attributes. A development officials may wish to analyze which type of activity fits the community's existing resource base and its aspirations. These paths are not mutually exclusive. They are sometimes substitutive, often representing a sequential development path.

- *Routine Operations.* In mature industrial areas, routine operations are hampered by high local wages, fringe benefits, and unionization rates. Therefore, firms that perform routine operations would not be attracted to many declining industrial areas. If a declining industrial area sought to focus efforts in attracting this type of employment, the authors suggest wage cuts, investment in education, outmigration assistance, or import substitution.

- *Precision Operations.* Firms engaged in precision operations require a work-force skilled in technology. However, mature regions tend to have a less mobile workforce, many of whom are near retirement age. So these areas are in danger of losing their competitive edge in skilled labor. The public policy directive should encourage young, skilled individuals to stay in the area by providing the environment that appeals to them.

- *Research and Development.* Because this activity has received substantial press recently, the research and development path tends to be the one most often desired by development officials. To evaluate the area's potential, the authors assess doctorates in science and engineering and total funds allocated to university research and development as the primary criteria.

- *Central Administration.* According to Thompson and Thompson (1987), one of the marks of advanced local economic development is an important role in central administration. To measure this, a "count" is taken of the *Fortune* first and second 500 firms located in the region. If there is an adequate number, then others will take advantage of the tertiary services provided within the region. One disadvantage of "heavy industry towns," however, is their bad track record for hiring women and minorities. If these opportunities are missing, the region will not be attractive to two-wage-earner couples who are mobile, highly educated, and pursuing specialized careers.

- *Entrepreneurship.* To cultivate entrepreneurship, the environment must be fertile for cultivating new businesses. The environment must foster innovation, creativity, and risk taking and have a source of capital. The critical question becomes whether the costs of restructuring the local culture to stimulate entrepreneurship is justified based on the likely benefits. Many communities will find it difficult or impossible to create an entrepreneurial climate.

Finally, choosing regional development paths should be likened to state public policy. The state affects economic development when it allocates funds for university research, higher education, transportation, infrastructure repair, airports, and so forth. Although the economic development impacts are often unintentional, they can affect the state settlement patterns for years to come.

⊠ Policy and Complex Systems

Cities have been described as many complex systems so that a single policy change will affect numerous, often unpredictable, consequences. Furthermore, the system is built on many feedback loops. A feedback loop works to keep a complex system in equilibrium. For instance, an increase in incomes will make an area attractive, drawing new residents. The new residents will tend to lower average incomes. Similarly, programs to help the poor will attract more poor families from outside the city and make poverty more attractive for families that would otherwise work to stay above the poverty line, according to this perspective.

Forrester (1969) developed a complex, simulating model of an urban system. Later work has refined his approach (Van de Berg, 1986). Forrester's model led to the following generalizations:

1. *Counterintuitive.* The outcomes from a particular intervention is often the opposite of what would be expected. Attempts to reduce poverty may attract more poor to the city from the limitless environment, thus increasing the rate of poverty, for example. Since urban policies normally have intuitive appeal for political reasons, policies are likely to fail (see Point 3).

2. *Insensitive to parameter changes.* Sensitivity analysis (changing the assumed value of parameters) indicated that major changes in many parameters did not significantly change the equilibrium outcome in the long run.

3. *Resistent to policy change.* This conclusion is implied by the first two points and is partly the result of the free migration from the "rest of the world." For instance, suppose the local government transfers a given amount of money from rich to poor. The initial impact will be to increase incomes of lower-income households, but other low-income families will move into the area to take advantage of the program. As the number of recipients increases, benefits diminish until equilibrium is reestablished. In equilibrium, the poor in the city would have incomes equal to households with similar skills in the "rest of the world."

4. *Containing influential pressure points.* In spite of Point 3, changes at critical pressure points can result in major changes in outcome, but such pressure points are not easily determined. In fact, they are also often counterintuitive. Thus simulation models can be useful policy tools by helping determine what changes will result in desired outcomes. For instance, in the *Urban Dynamics* model, a reduction in worker-housing would decrease the underemployed population and increase the managerial population and new business.

5. *Differing in short- and long-run consequences.* Short-run reactions to a policy change are often what one would intuitively expect, but in the long run, the reactions will be the opposite. For instance, the simulation of the effects of an employment and training program first reduced the number of unemployed but later resulted in slightly higher levels of unemployment than otherwise would have occurred.

Obviously, the model is not optimistic regarding policy effectiveness. Many economists have criticized the *Urban Dynamics* approach, claiming that the conclusions follow from the structure of the model. The serious problems of most large-scale urban models limit their usefulness. However, the view of cities as complex systems with feedback mechanisms is a lesson that policymakers must look beyond the direct impacts of programs and consider many likely repercussions.

⊠ Summary

Most economic development projects have a combination of goals: job creation, fiscal improvement, and physical improvement. This chapter examined several issues that must be grappled with in pursuit of these objectives. Although some of the issues are described as polar cases, in practice local officials must balance the advantages and disadvantages of various approaches.

Although economic development promises substantial benefits to communities, the benefits are seldom distributed evenly across the population. When the local economy expands, the demand for exports likely will be unaffected because it is determined predominantly by forces outside the area. However, demand for nonbasic goods and services will increase. Hence demand for some local resources will increase. The permanence of the increase in the value of local resources will depend on the elasticity of supply. However, growth may also harm some individuals. Higher prices, congestion, and other quality-of-life issues underlie many antigrowth coalitions.

As communities compete with one another in a "market for jobs," economic development officials should be aware of the potential for zero-sum outcomes—either one city may gain at the others' loss or the benefits from growth may be taken from taxpayers and given to businesses. Whether a zero-sum outcome occurs or not depends, in part, on the external benefits that may be generated.

Although local competition for jobs may be beneficial, it can be inefficient, and businesses may receive excessive subsidies. There are at least five important reasons why the market for jobs tends to be inefficient: problems of collective action, information asymmetry, poorly defined property rights or outcomes, operations of federal programs, and cost/value differences. These problems can be minimized by well-designed economic development programs.

There is disagreement regarding whether economic development strategies should emphasize discretionary or entitlement subsidies. Discretionary programs rely on skills of economic development officials to avoid oversubsidization. There is also disagreement regarding whether development strategies should focus predominantly on cutting business costs through subsidies and tax cuts or should emphasize investment in human capital through education and training.

Cumulative causation refers to a situation in which a change in one direction reinforces other changes in the same direction. Economic development officials should be particularly alert to avoid downward-spiral situations.

There are pressures on local economic development officials to explore all possible opportunities. Yet such a shotgun approach may waste resources. Targeting economic development toward highly promising opportunities, or "crosshair" targeting, focuses on resources but could result in overlooked opportunities.

Because local economies are complex systems, a single change can have numerous feedbacks and unintended consequences. Therefore, development planners should examine programs carefully to minimize unintended negative consequences.

9

Resource and Commodity Flows

Local economies operate in an increasingly open environment in which most resources and commodities may move to other areas if rewards are sufficient. The attraction of resources into the area is often a critical part of the development process. The importance of resource flows has increased with the globalization of the economy and the emergence of multinational economic institutions. Resources are likely to shift among nations as well as regions within a nation. In practice, the distinction between regions within a country and nations has faded as groups of nations have formed multinational economic units. Urban policymakers recognize that local economies can be influenced significantly by trade patterns and resources flows. This chapter seeks to explain influences on the flow of economic resources that can be critical to local economic development efforts.

⊠ Models of Trade and Resource Flows

Two simple models of regional interaction are developed in this section. The first assumes that resources cannot move from region to region but that commodities can. The movement of commodities will equalize wages. The second model is built on the assumption of perfect resource mobility. In this case, worker mobility will equalize wages.

Comparative Advantage

The theory of comparative advantage was developed to show that countries can benefit from trade. The principle of comparative advantage states

189

that if factors of production cannot move between areas, then residents should specialize in commodities they can make relatively cheaply compared to other countries. Relative cost is determined in terms of opportunity cost—the number of units of a commodity (or service) that must be foregone to produce another product. If countries produce goods and services in which they have a comparative or relative advantage and then trade with other countries for other goods, the specialization and trade can potentially benefit both countries. The theory of comparative advantage is the basic reason why United States policy seeks to expand free trade and why we have sought to reduce trade barriers through agreements such as the North American Free Trade Agreement.

Heckscher-Ohlin Theorem

Heckscher (1919) and Ohlin (1933) hypothesized that if a country had a relative abundance of a particular factor of production, it would have a comparative advantage in the production of goods that require large amounts of the abundant factor. For instance, a region with abundant topsoil and rain could be expected to have a comparative advantage in agriculture products, which could be exported. Thus, although factors of production may be immobile, Heckscher and Ohlin envisioned a mechanism whereby the abundant factor of production would be mobilized as they become embodied in the dominant exports.

The commodity flows will affect not only commodity prices but also resource prices. A country with abundant labor will tend to have low wages (relative to the rest of the world) prior to trade. Export of labor-intensive products will increase the demand for labor and hence the wage. Labor-short countries will import labor-intensive products, thus taking pressure off labor demand, which in turn tends to lower wages for their workers. One reason why labor unions favor some tariffs on goods from labor abundant countries is that domestic wages and employment can suffer from the inflow of cheaper products. In a world of perfect knowledge and commodity mobility, the Heckscher-Ohlin theorem leads to the conclusion that commodity movements will result in equalization of factor prices. In this sense, commodity movements can be a substitute for resource movements.

Comparative Advantage Reconsidered

The theory of comparative advantage and its complement, the Heckscher-Ohlin theorem, have been challenged on four grounds. First, empirical studies to determine whether countries export products that require a large portion of abundant inputs and import products that require resources that are scarce locally have not found the expected pattern of trade (Bowen, Leamer, and Sveikauskas, 1987). Second, areas may not specialize in their comparative advantage because the mechanisms and institutions necessary for specialization may not exist. Third, comparative advantage is a static theory. Some analysts believe that nations should produce goods and services in which they may have a comparative cost disadvantage in the short run in order to develop a comparative advantage. Finally, while free trade may potentially enrich both trading blocks, it may not enrich everyone within both nations. For instance, trade with low-wage countries may depress wages among certain groups of wage earners in the United States. Consequently, free trade raises issues of equity.

Resource Mobility

The theory of comparative advantage was developed on the assumption that resources were immobile. Whereas some resources may be regionally immobile, urban economists consider most resources to be fairly mobile among regions. Certainly, there are fewer impediments to the movement of labor and capital between regions in the same country than to factor movement between countries. In a world of perfect information and no relocation costs, factors of production would move to the region where compensation is highest. Figure 9.1 can be used to analyze resource mobility. Assume there are two regions and that compensation for labor (or any other) resources is initially $2 per unit greater in region J than in region I. The differential would induce migration from region I to region J. As labor leaves I, the supply of labor will decrease and wages will increase; as the supply of labor increases, wages will fall. When the compensation of the factor of production is equal for the two regions, migration will stop.

Next, consider how relocation costs will affect adjustment. A move would be worthwhile if the present value of future earnings in the destination region minus the relocation costs exceeds the present value of future earnings in the region of original residence. To provide a sufficient incentive to relocate, relocation costs must be less than the present value of future extra returns that the factor could earn in J compared to I.

Figure 9.1 shows the labor supply curves shifting so as to eventually equalize factor prices because of the assumption of costless mobility. If resources relocation were costly, then the present value of the difference in

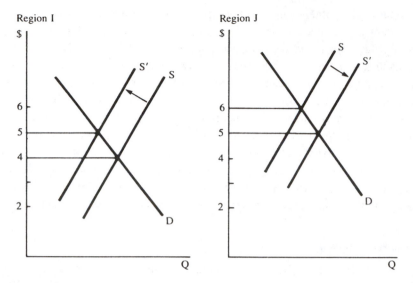

Figure 9.1. A model of resource mobility. The resources in Region I are initially priced below the same resource in Region J. Therefore, resources move from Region I to J, decreasing supply and increasing the price in Region I. The supply increases and the price falls in Region J.

compensation over the life of the factor of production would equal the relocation costs in equilibrium.

The adjustment process is not instantaneous and may slow as the wage gap in the two areas narrows.

The model represented by Figure 9.1 does not show a demand response. In reality, a low resource price in one region could induce users of the low-cost resource to move into the area. Hence movements in demand may also help eliminate price differentials. For example, suppose labor and capital are the principal factors of production. Labor may relocate from a low-wage to a high-wage region, but simultaneously, capital may flow to the low-wage region to take advantage of the low-cost complementary input.

Evidence of factor mobility raises an interesting question for manpower and development officials. Efforts to increase wages for local residents by increasing labor demands could be futile if, when local wages increased, other workers moved into the area, tending to reduce wages to the level of nearby regions. Even if wages did not fall, new entrants could capture some of the jobs. Consequently, many local officials have decided it is preferable to spend economic development dollars to train current residents so that they can command higher wages due to unusual skills.

⊠ Economics of Migration

When development officials consider migration in and out of an area, they may wish to understand the causes of population and labor movements. Economic models provide some important insights that planners may find useful. In general, migration is the result of push factors in the region of origin and pull factors in the destination area.

Figure 9.1 illustrates migration based solely on wage differentials. When the two markets were in equilibrium, the migration would stop according to the model.

Migration can occur even when regional factor markets are in equilibrium. Lifestyle changes at key periods of life—at graduation, at marriage, before and after military service, after the birth of children, at retirement, and after the death of a spouse—are not always motivated by wages. At each of these "passages," the motive for relocating may be quite different.

Nonwage Factors

Most empirical studies indicate that labor tends to migrate to high-wage or employment-growth areas, but nonwage factors also help explain migration. First, fringe benefits as well as the basic wage rate should be recognized. Many migrants are interested in the total compensation package, not just wages. Second, cost of living might have to be accounted for to reflect the fact that individuals desire a higher real compensation, not just a higher money wage. Both fringe benefits and differences in costs of living are relatively concrete concepts. More complex factors must also be considered, such as the quality of life, future pay and promotion prospects, and so forth.

"Equalizing differentials" refers to compensation differentials that will persist over time even if labor were perfectly mobile. For instance, an individual may be willing to accept 25 cents per hour less in pay to enjoy the climate, quality of life, and future opportunities in a locality.

The costs of relocation also enter the individual migrant's decision in a way that is more complicated than may appear. In a simple model, the relocation costs might simply be the cost of transporting one's possessions from one place to another. However, other monetary costs include the cost of selling a house and transaction costs of closing accounts, purchasing new license plates, and so forth. Nonmonetary costs include hassles, loss of proximity to friends and relatives, taking the children out of school, and lifestyle changes. In many cases, these factors may be more important than monetary costs. Uncertain prospects are another type of cost likely to be considered very significant by risk-adverse individuals.

Harris-Todaro Model

Harris and Todaro (1970) developed a model that explains why migration tends to be toward cities in spite of some high urban unemployment rates. It also explains the tendency of wage differentials to persist in spite of migration. They postulated that migration occurs when the actual wage in the area of origin is less than the *expected* wage in the area of destination. The expected wage is the actual wage times the probability of being unemployed. Assume new residents believe they have the same probability of employment as current residents. If the wage rate were $10,000 annually and the unemployment rate were 20%, the expected wage would be $8,000 ($10,000 × .20).

To understand the Harris-Todaro model, assume a high-wage and a low-wage area. Also assume that wages in the high-wage city are institutionally fixed by law, union, or custom. Thus wages will not decline in the face of substantial unemployment. If there were full employment initially in both regions, workers would migrate to the high-wage area. If the number of jobs in the high-wage area remained the same, unemployment would increase because migrants are willing to trade off the risk of unemployment against the potential for higher wages. Because of the higher unemployment due to migration, national product would fall. Workers would become unemployed rather than be employed in low-wage (low-productivity) jobs. Nevertheless, the migration would be in the self-interest of the migrants, given their assumption about the probability of employment.

Three important implications of the Harris-Todaro model are as follows:

- Migration to the high-wage city may fail to lead rapidly to wage equalization.
- Both wage rate and the level of unemployment may increase with city size.
- It may be difficult to prevent unemployment from rising in high-wage areas open to migration.

The Harris-Todaro model helps explain why some low-income persons may prefer to seek employment in large cities with high wages and high unemployment rates rather than seeking work in towns with lower levels of unemployment.

Gravity Models

Migration flows are frequently estimated with a gravity model. Gravity models assume that migration between two regions increases in relation to the population of the region and decreases with distance between them. In the basic model, population represents the likelihood of a random individual leaving or migrating to an area. Distance is the main impediment. The following is an example of a simple gravity model:

$$M_{ab} = P_a \times P_b / (D_{ab}^2),$$
(9-1)

where

M_{ab} = migration from A to B
P_a, P_b = population in A and B, respectively
D_{ab} = distance between A and B

The most obvious problem with the simple gravity model is that migration between the places would always net to zero. To avoid this outcome, other variables have been included to reflect opportunity differences. Differences in wage, income, and unemployment rates have been the most frequently used measures of opportunity differentials.

Another criticism of gravity models is that they are poorly specified because distance does not adequately measure difficulty of journey, particularly in an era of modern transportation. To address this problem, travel time has been substituted for distance in some models. Social and political barriers, as well as uncertainty, are more important barriers. These factors are poorly correlated with distance. For instance, it is probably easier for a Texan to migrate to Oregon than to Mexico. So, although gravity models are used as empirical shortcuts, they do not reflect important theoretical factors that reflect opportunities and difficulty of journey.

Beaten-Path Effect and Intervening Opportunities

One reason why gravity models are sometimes inaccurate is due to the beaten-path effect. The beaten-path effect refers to the observed tendency of individuals from a particular area of origin to select the same destination. Often, a few "pioneers" from an area will migrate first. Later, others, often relatives, will follow. Most migrants do not consider a shopping list of destinations. They do not ask "Where among all possible places will I move?" Usually, they consider only one destination—often where their friends or relatives can provide job, housing information, or other help. Previously settled friends and relatives often also help support new migrants if necessary. Thus, by following a beaten path, migrants can lower money, uncertainty, and the social costs of relocating. A recent migration path between retired migrants from the Panama Canal Zone and Dothan, Alabama, illustrates a beaten path. The beaten-path effect helps explain the concentrations of particular ethnic groups in particular cities. The concentrations of Poles in Milwaukee, Irish in Boston, or Cubans in Miami can be attributed to the beaten path.

Besides lowering migration costs, the beaten-path effect has two other important implications for economic development officials. First, the flow of migrants may become self-perpetuating as migration costs fall and additional migration is stimulated. Second, the beaten path can be traveled both ways, so there is often a noticeable return migration. If economic prospects dim in the destination area or if migrants otherwise become disenchanted, large numbers may return to the place of origin.

Net and Gross Migration

When economists first collected and analyzed data on migration, they were mainly concerned with net migration, the difference between in- and out-migration. However, net migration patterns mask substantial differences in the level of gross migration because some individuals move into an area at the same time others move out.

Table 9.1 illustrates four different gross migration patterns:

1. High mobility/high in- and out-migration
2. High in-migration/low out-migration
3. Low in-migration/high out-migration
4. Low in-migration/low out-migration

TABLE 9.1 Gross and Net Migration Flows and Local Economic Conditions

		Out-Migration	
		High	*Low*
In-Migration	High	Low net migration (i.e., footloose population, college or military)	High net migration (i.e., area of expanding opportunities)
	Low	Negative net migration (i.e., area of declining opportunity)	Low net migration (i.e., stable job base, few new opportunities)

Both the case of high in-migration/high out-migration and low in-migration/low out-migration could result in low net migration but for very different reasons. The former instance may indicate a very dynamic economy attracting a highly mobile, opportunity-seeking population. The latter case is characteristic of a stagnate community with an older, less mobile population.

Retiree-Migrant Development Strategy

Fagan and Longino (1993) have suggested that migrating retirees may form a solid basis for building an economic development strategy. They point out that retirees are mobile and many have substantial incomes. They compared the economic impact of a new manufacturing plant employing 100 persons to 100 in-migrant retiree households. They concluded that the economic impact of the retirees would be nearly four times that of the manufacturing employees.

Retirees tend to be either amenity seeking or dependency seeking. Amenity-seeking migrants are oriented toward natural environments, among other things, whereas dependency migrants move to be near a caregiver. The beaten-path effect also influences retiree migrants. A community seeking a retirement development path should probably attempt to establish an amenity-rich environment with good health care facilities. Rural areas near areas with metropolitan amenities and medical facilities may be an excellent setting for planners to develop a retirement-oriented development path. Even if development officials do not find it advisable to attempt to attract retirees from elsewhere, an economy may receive a substantial benefit by *retaining* retirees who might otherwise live elsewhere.

⊠   Mobility of Capital

Discussions of capital flows are often confused by the various meanings of "capital." In everyday use, capital often means money and assets that can be converted into money, but economists define capital as produced goods that can be inputs into further production. Accordingly, capital includes physical inputs into the production process, such as buildings, machinery, and also human capital. The amount of physical capital is usually expressed in monetary terms ("The machine is worth $100,000") because money is a measure of value. So the distinction between money and real capital is easily blurred. The value of human capital can be expressed in terms of the increased value of increased earning power. For an individual, the distinction between money and physical capital may not always be important because an individual can convert some types of real capital into money by selling assets. However, a society as a whole cannot convert between capital and money.

Money capital is generally considered to be highly mobile among regions. Individuals and corporations can move accounts and transfer funds from financial institutions in one region to financial institutions in another region in a matter of minutes. Differences of fractions of percentage points trigger massive money capital flows from one region to another.

Economists are generally as concerned with real capital as they are with money accounts because real capital is one of the basic factors of production. Real capital used in production is much less mobile than money. Buildings and some heavy machinery are almost place-bound, once created.

In spite of the limited mobility of some real capital, an individual may sell such an asset and transfer the proceeds to another region. So capital may be spatially mobile from the perspective of an individual even if the physical asset is immobile. Furthermore, since real capital is *valued* in money, the amount of capital invested in a region can shift quickly even when the real capital does move. For example, a facility that is operating efficiently may have high value based on the income stream it generates. But if the owner decides to abandon operations because the local environment is no longer suitable, the value of the physical assets could quickly drop to zero. Abandoned facilities may even have negative value if demolition and clean-up costs are significant. Of course, if an alternative use for an abandoned facility were found, its value could be supported, but experience indicates that alternative uses often cannot be found.

In light of the various definitions of capital, three types of capital mobility can be identified. First, money capital can be transferred from one region to another either in exchange for goods and services or to finance real investment. Second, physical assets can be transported from one place to another, although the mobility of many physical assets is limited. Finally, the value of physical capital may change, reflecting changes in the economic environment.

Many development officials seek to increase capital available for investment in their area. Although pure theory leads to the conclusion that capital will be employed where it earns the highest return, this is not always the case. Investors often fail to identify excellent investment opportunities in part because of lack of knowledge. Development officials can play a role in informing investors of opportunities they might otherwise overlook.

The following are hypotheses about factors that limit the flow of capital to its area of highest return:

- Lenders may be reluctant to extend loans to businesses located in the central city because they incorrectly perceive high risks of central-city investments. Racial bias against Blacks and other minorities is considered to be linked with the failure of institutions to invest in minority-dominated sections of the central city.
- Rural areas may fail to attract capital because they are underserved by financial institutions. Hence it is more difficult for businesses to develop in rural areas. Special government programs have been developed to stimulate the supply of capital to rural areas.
- Firms may have a preference for reinvesting profits internally rather than investing outside the company. The preference for internal investment may be due to better knowledge about in-house opportunities or a psychological preference for control. Hence distressed cities with few profitable firms have less access to this source of funds.
- Investors with small amounts of money have difficulty directly lending in distant regions because of high transactions costs. Investors need to be able to assess risks and may therefore avoid making loans to less-known companies when they cannot obtain adequate knowledge of the company. Such investors may participate in nationally marketed securities, or they may limit their investments to the particular regions they know. This point is reflected in the belief that venture capital is not equally available in all regions. Local officials may seek to increase the inflow of capital into a region by programs to inform investors of opportunities or by programs to provide investors with higher returns for making investments in perceived high-risk areas.

⊠ Innovations and Ideas

Ideas and new ways of doing things are a major source of economic growth. Economic development officials traditionally have been more concerned about innovations than inventions. Innovation is the economic application of a new idea, although the distinction may become blurred when the same person is both the inventor and the innovator. Not only are innovations important to economic growth, but the rate at which innovations are copied, modified, and spread to other sectors of the economy influences economic progress.

At first glance, it may seem reasonable to assume that innovations would spread quickly and uniformly. After all, ideas are weightless, so it is easy to assume they are costless to transport. As Borts and Stein (1964) said, "A new manufacturing process or a new machine is, under competition, available to all" (p. 81). However, numerous empirical studies have indicated resistance to innovation. The length of time between an invention and its commercial application can span decades, and gaps of several years are common. More important for our purposes, there is a spatial pattern to the spread of ideas and innovations.

Spatial Diffusion

Innovations tend to originate in large metropolitan areas. The spread of innovations can be complex and differs, depending on the production process or the product being developed. In general, innovations tend to spread from metropolitan areas along a variety of paths.

Metropolitan Origination

There are many related explanations for the dominance of metropolitan areas in the development of new ideas, products, and production processes. Pred (1966), in a historical study of the spread of industrial innovations, used a supply and demand framework to explain the predominance of the metropolis in the innovative process. The quantity of innovations is greater in urban areas because both the supply of and demand for innovations are greater.

On the demand side, urban areas provide greater economic rewards for innovation because markets for new products and processes are more readily available. New products may capture only a small market share initially, so a large local market may be critical to achieving an adequate initial sales level. The demand for process innovation in metropolitan areas is due to the larger agglomeration of producers. A new production process may have applications in a variety of industries.

On the supply side, metropolitan areas have a greater variety of support activities needed for innovations. Skilled engineering consultants, marketing firms, lawyers, intermediate manufacturers, venture capitalists, and other important contributors to the innovative process are all more readily available in metropolitan areas. Urban areas may also be the workplace of innovative elites and other individuals in key national information loops. Recently, policymakers in many urban areas have been deliberately perusing strategies to enhance the supply of local innovations by encouraging incubators, inventors, entrepreneurial networks, and research parks.

Diffusion

New products and processes spread from the point of innovation in three distinct ways. First, there is a tendency for consumer-oriented innovations to spread in a radial pattern from the source of the innovation outward. Movement of an idea from the central city to suburban areas is an example of the radial diffusion pattern. Innovations that depend on personal, nonbusiness contacts are likely to have a strong tendency to spread in a radial manner.

Second, innovations move among cities of roughly equal size. For instance, an innovation may appear in Houston and Chicago at similar times. The similarity of environments including similar supporting services to those that stimulated original initial innovations in metropolitan areas make replication in similar metropolitan areas more likely.

Third, the diffusion of innovations from major metropolitan areas to smaller places in the major area's sphere of influence can be explained by business organization patterns. Thus the corporate headquarters will tend to be the location of a company's first fax machine. If the innovation is successful, it may filter down to regional offices and later to local offices. Distribution channels for consumer products and information channels may also follow business organizations.

Implications for Regional Development

The diffusion process from metropolitan areas to smaller places, coupled with the tendency for products to grow rapidly in the early stages of their life cycle, has been termed industrial filtering. Figure 9.2 illustrates the time path of employment growth in a typical industry. The explanation for the shape of the industrial growth curve centers on the fact that early in an industry's development any absolute increase in output or employment will be a larger percentage increase. Furthermore, sales in the early stages include both new

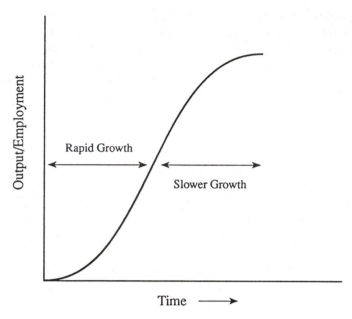

Figure 9.2. Employment growth over industrial life cycle. More rapid growth occurs during the early stages of an industry's life cycle. As the industry ages, growth slows.

purchases and replacements, whereas in later stages only replacement production is needed.

Metropolitan areas tend to be the site of production early in the life cycle of a product or process. After a process is better understood and is broken into routine steps or after a market has been established for a product, a shift in the site of production to smaller towns often occurs. Firms may relocate to take advantage of lower costs in smaller, less urban places. The large metropolitan areas have a higher proportion of fast-growth activities, but those activities spin off to smaller places. Accordingly, metropolitan areas will tend to lose a portion of their economic base to lower-cost cities.

Large cities may require a more highly skilled labor force because products in the early stages of development involve nonroutine production. The different skill requirements may account for the persistence of higher incomes in urban areas. Strategic investments in education, training, and quality environment may help metropolitan areas attract and develop the skilled labor force needed for nonroutine operations. Larger cities may also explore ways to maintain activities that originate there and hence slow the filtering process. Conversely, smaller cities may consider how to speed up the filtering process so they can capture industries early in the product life cycle.

Recently, some policy analysts have questioned whether major urban areas can maintain their leadership in innovation if the site of production becomes too remote. Underlying this issue is the concern that, if research becomes too distant from the shop floor, researchers will lose their sense of purpose. Giese and Testa (1988) examined Chicago area research and development firms. They concluded that metropolitan regions can retain their eminence as industrial research and development centers even as the manufacturing activities decline.

⊠ Mobility and Development Policy

Many policy areas involve mobility issues. Economists generally believe that the economy operates more efficiently when resources are mobile, so removing unnecessary barriers to mobility is often viewed as a way to improve performance.

Jobs to People Versus People to Jobs

One of the perennial regional development issues is whether government policy should encourage job creation in high unemployment areas or whether individuals should be encouraged to move to where jobs already exist. Both moving jobs to people and moving people to jobs have been suggested as partial solutions to the problem of poverty. The issue presupposes the existence of a geographic mismatch between available jobs and workers. Table 9.2 provides a comparison of the two approaches.

Supporters of the jobs-to-people approach generally believe that people are so reluctant to move that the inducements—both carrot and stick—would have to be substantial before they would move. They also point out that push factors, such as high unemployment rates and low incomes are poor predictors of out-migration. Therefore, "natural" market forces will not necessarily result in the efficient movement of people to jobs. Jobs-to-people advocates also contend that job-creating activities can be induced to locate to areas of high unemployment at a low cost or with little or no loss of aggregate national output. Clark (1983) argued that only a jobs-to-people approach can support the stable communities and the social relationships that "community" implies.

TABLE 9.2 The People Versus Places Controversy

Issue	People Prosperity	Places Prosperity
Rationale	Only individuals matter. Individual welfare is relatively independent of place condition.	Places also matter. The welfare of individuals is relatively dependent on place condition.
Presumed efficiency	Not certain. Might increase GNP by improving labor force quality nationally.	Inefficient. Lowers GNP effects if orthodox view is correct.
Effects on interarea migration	Probably accelerates it.	Retards it.
Strategy	Bottom up. May take a "worst-case-first" approach.	Too down. May focus on places with most development potential (within eligible area).
Benefits to the nonpoor	Undoubtedly some. Probably not as many as in other cases.	Clear and substantial benefits to the nonpoor cases.
Most obvious drawback	Does little to mitigate the social and psychological costs of economically forced migration. May do little to aid the survival of dying places.	As a strategy to aid the long-term poor, it is at least partly defeated by labor force mobility and elasticity.
Political support	Relatively weak, particularly if programs bypass local political structure.	Very strong support from the political establishment of eligible areas.
Relation to recent locational trends	No necessary conflict.	Definitely swimming against the tide.

SOURCE: John M. Levy, *Urban and Metropolitan Economics* (New York: McGraw-Hill, 1985), p. 150.

The jobs-to-people approach has been criticized because it appears to place the welfare of places over the welfare of people. "We must do something to help Dallas," an advocate of place prosperity might say. However, jobs-to-people strategies are really designed to help people where they live, not places per se.

The people-to-jobs approach assumes that the market allocates investments efficiently among cities and regions, so the government should not attempt to alter the pattern. Individuals are assumed to be highly mobile, and jobs are not easily transferred from one region to another. Furthermore, advocates of the people-to-jobs approach suggest that even if the government attempted to stimulate development in declining regions the efforts would probably fail because the governmental resources available for regional development are small compared to private investment.

Immigration and Urban Development

Urban development officials often find it difficult to address the issue of immigration because of conflicting domestic interests. A simple supply and demand model of immigration can clarify conflicting interests regarding the migration issue. Suppose U.S. residents were divided into capital owners and laborers. As additional foreign workers enter the country, labor compensation would drop due to the increased labor supply. Because of the potential for lowering the wage rate of current workers, labor representatives tend to favor restrictive immigration policies. The competition between low-skilled native and foreign workers often results in conflict, particularly when economic competition is mixed with cultural or racial differences. Bloomberg and Sandoval (1982) contrasted the tensions along the California-Mexico border with the border shared by Detroit and Windsor, Ontario. Whereas the potential for conflict has led to strains and racial divisions in California, the commonality of interests and/or cultures has resulted in economic integration between Detroit and Windsor "almost as fully as if they were the same nation" (p. 20).

If capital and labor are complementary inputs (i.e., increased labor enhances capital productivity), then capital owners would welcome additional immigrant labor because the larger quantity of workers would tend to enhance the productivity of capital and depress wages. Undoubtedly, many employers recognize that they benefit from an increase in labor supply. The simple model helps explain why some employers and trade associations favor allowing large numbers of migrants into the United States and oppose sanctions on employers who hire illegal aliens. Many industries in the Southwest and the Farm Belt and some unorganized urban manufacturers are dependent on labor from abroad.

Complications

There are several complications that limit the simple labor supply and demand approach. First, consumers may also benefit from high levels of immigration, particularly consumers of products where immigrant labor tends to cluster. The lower wage rates may translate into lower prices. Since workers are also consumers, it is necessary to balance these two effects to determine net benefits from migration for a particular labor group.

Second, labor is not homogeneous. As there are, in fact, many types of labor, the impact of immigration on wages and employment depends on the type of labor that enters the country and on whether labor markets are linked or segmented. If labor markets are linked, wages of employees in sectors with few immigrant workers may be depressed because of the possibility of substitution among types of labor. However, many economists believe that labor markets are segmented. If labor markets were completely segmented, each market segment would be unaffected by events in other markets. In this case, only the domestic workers who competed directly with immigrant workers would be adversely affected by immigration. Borjas (1987) presented empirical evidence indicating that immigrants are a substitute for some types of U.S. labor but a complement to other types. Consequently, the overall effect of immigrant labor on earnings of the native-born worker is small.

Evidence indicates that even if markets are segmented, the skills of migrants are so varied that few labor markets are unaffected by migration. About 40% of legal migrants are managerial or professional workers, and about 30% are operators, fabricators, and laborers. Consequently, there are no major labor groups protected from competition due to migration. However, the immigration mix is changing. The portion of unskilled and semiskilled immigrants is increasing. If illegal immigrants were included in the statistical estimates, the number of unskilled laborers would increase significantly.

Even if most immigrants were initially low-skilled workers, the longer they are in the country the more likely they will be to acquire the skills necessary to qualify for higher-skilled jobs. Therefore, skilled workers will not necessarily be protected from competition from initially unskilled immigrants in the long run. (The potential for skill changes is even greater from an intergenerational perspective.)

Finally, not all migrants are poor or unskilled. Many bring substantial capital and skills into the country when they migrate. In fact, most countries have immigration policies that make it much easier to gain entrance if the applicants have assets. British Columbia has experienced an economic development boom due to the relocation of wealthy Chinese from Hong Kong. Thus the stereotype of the impoverished immigrant with no way to earn a living but by selling labor is not always accurate. It may describe illegal migrants but does not fit the case of most legal migrants. In the United States migration is selective, so migrants generally have a means of earning a living.

Foreign Ownership

Tolchin and Tolchin (1987) suggested that foreign ownership of key industrial sectors threatens to dilute U.S. political sovereignty. Foreign ownership, they contended, may undermine the ability of the United States to control its own fate and defend its status as an economic power. Other observers have expressed the fear that the situation will degenerate to a point where important economic decisions are made abroad and U.S. workers become relegated to low-paying, routine jobs. However, most economic development planners view foreign investment as an opportunity.

Foreign investment has contributed to the economies in many regions. For instance, many areas in California have greatly benefited from Asian investments. South-central Ohio has developed based on Japanese automobile investment. Not only have the Japanese helped create jobs, but they have undoubtedly contributed to the improvement of new management and production techniques on the part of domestic producers. The total quality management (TQM) movement was based on principles first employed in Japanese firms.

Local economic development officials are increasingly seeking to attract foreign investors because they believe the benefits in terms of local economic expansion far outweigh the costs. States are organizing overseas trips for local officials in an effort to encourage foreign investment and to open export markets for local goods. Because the Japanese have been major investors in recent years, many analysts have questioned whether locational factors that are important for American companies are important to Japanese "transplants." Doeringer and Terkla (1992) and Blair and Premus (1987) found that Japanese firms place a high value on the following:

- Governmental cooperations
- The prospects of forming reciprocal relationships between the company and the local community
- Flexible labor environments including flexible work rules
- Proximity to Japanese cultural events
- Good international communications and transportation facilities
- Personal relationships built over years

⊠ Summary

Local economic development efforts take place in an increasingly open economy. Polar theoretical models provided the initial perspective. On the one hand, if resources are immobile but commodities are mobile, then regions will benefit by producing and exporting the product in which they have a comparative advantage. Commodity trade can be a substitute for factor mobility; regions will export products that require a high proportion of the abundant factor of production. On the other hand, if resources are perfectly mobile, they will tend to flow from the low-return to the high-return area. If compensation reflects productivity, then the resource flow will increase total output in the combined regions.

Migration is the result of push factors in the place of origin and pull factors in the destination area. Most empirical studies indicate that labor tends to migrate to high-wage areas, but wages alone are inadequate to explain migration determinants. Migration will tend to equalize wages unless there are equalizing differences.

The Harris-Todaro model described the tendency for workers to move to high-wage/high-unemployment areas. The higher wage offset the probability of unemployment.

Gravity models assume that migration between two regions increases in relation to population and decreases with distance between places. A major criticism of gravity models is that they are poorly specified because they fail to reflect all of the factors that contribute to migration. The beaten-path effect illustrates how knowing individuals who have already migrated to an area may encourage additional migration.

Many communities have successfully implemented retiree-migration strategies. Such a strategy offers promise for amenity-rich areas in particular.

Capital is generally considered a mobile factor of production, although there are numerous obstacles to capital movement. In light of various definitions of capital, three types of mobility can be identified. First, money capital can be transferred. Second, physical assets can be moved. Third, the value of physical capital may change.

Patterns to the movement of innovations and ideas also affect economic development. Innovations tend to originate in metropolitan areas. The spread of innovations occur across and down the hierarchy and away from the innovative center in a radial pattern.

Interregional resource flows play an important role in policy questions. The issue of whether jobs should move to high-unemployment areas or whether people should move to where the jobs are may hinge on the relative mobility of labor and capital. Immigration policy is aimed at restricting international labor mobility without imposing an undue burden.

10

Land Use

Economic development officials are often concerned with land use within a metropolitan area. Economic development decisions frequently include alterations in land use. Officials should, therefore, understand the economics of real estate development decisions. Furthermore, land use patterns contribute to the desirability and productivity of a city. The ability to influence land use decisions is an important economic development lever.

⊠ What Gives Land Value?

Technically, "land" is a natural factor of production, and therefore the supply of land is unaffected by price. Real estate analysts are careful to distinguish between land and property. A property is land and improvements, such as buildings. This section starts by examining land in the absence of capital improvements so as to understand what kinds of capital or structures are combined with land.

Land Rents and Value

Rent generated by land can be thought of as a flow of income. The value of that income flow should equal the value of the land. However, because dollars received today are worth more to investors than dollars received in the future, in 10 years for example, future dollars must be discounted to reflect the value differences of dollars received in different time periods. The sum of the discounted present value of the future rents equals the land value. In a perfectly functioning economy (where, among other things, investors had perfect information), the present value of future returns would also equal the sale price of the land.

If land were expected to provide a constant return in perpetuity, the formula for determining value would be

$$V = R/d,\qquad\qquad\qquad(10\text{-}1)$$

where

  V = land value

  R = the periodic return (net of other costs such as property taxes)

  d = appropriate discount rate. The discount rate is similar to an interest rate and will rise and fall depending on the conditions of the economy.

The logic of Equation 10-1 is that, if the value of the land were taken in cash and invested in a comparable investment, it could command an interest rate of d. Thus $V \times d = R$, the cash value of the land if placed in an equally risky investment (V) should earn an annual cash return (R) equal to the return from the land.

Equation 10-1 has two limitations. First, it applies only to assets that generate a return in perpetuity. In practice, even agricultural land will not generate a constant return forever. Most agricultural land benefits from numerous capital improvements that have a limited life. For instance, the soil can be depleted. Second, the assumption of a constant return year after year is unrealistic. Equation 10-2, developed later in this chapter, addresses these two problems in a more flexible but complicated model.

The Nature of Rent

The return to land is a residual—what is left after all other resources have been paid their market-determined price. Because labor, capital, and entrepreneurship can move to where their compensation is highest, these factors must be paid competitive rates. Whatever is left after paying the mobile factors of production is the residual to land—rent.

Ricardo (1911) concluded that sites receive different rents because of varying productivity. Productivity of land was attributed to its fertility and its proximity to markets. For instance, suppose the most productive use of site 1 is to produce $3,000 of corn at a cost of $2,500 for nonland inputs. The return to land would be $500. Thus $500 would equal the rent. If another site could be used in such a way as to generate a larger difference between the value of the output and the input costs, the return to land would increase. Accordingly, the return to land was a residual, and the more productive the site the greater the residual.

Ricardo's analysis also showed that the more productive land would be used more intensively. For instance, fertile land might be worked by four employees, whereas low-productivity land might be worked by one person. In general, valuable resources tend to be used more intensively.

Ricardo's analysis was expressed in the context of agricultural land where fertility was the dominant factor in determining productivity. In an urban setting, access to urban "goods" and protection from urban "bads" are the most important factors in determining productivity. Of course, the valuable features of access differ for varying types of land use. For instance, a fast-food restaurant would value access to mealtime traffic, a law firm its access to courts and documents, and households their access to good schools or protection from crime.

To understand the relationship between productivity and access, imagine a site that provides the best access combination for a retail clothing store. Other uses would generate a smaller residual to land. Due to its location, the clothing store could earn gross revenues of, say, $300 per period. Suppose that after deducting capital costs (including construction of the store), labor, and normal profits, $180 would be left. Competition among other clothing retailers or potential clothing retailers would drive rents to $180.

Proximity and access are not the same thing. Often, access is limited by social, political, and geographical barriers, not just distance. For example, in most suburban areas, it is the school districts that create access. Political access explains why property values jump thousands of dollars from one side of a street to the other.

Time and convenience are important determinants of access. Modern transportation networks have made access as much a function of urban infrastructure—type of roads, availability of mass transportation, and so forth—as of simple physical distance. There are also social dimensions to the accessibility concept. Fear of crime, for example, has caused many individuals to feel that areas in the central city were not accessible to them.

Highest and Best Use

One of the first questions developers raise is "What is the most profitable use of a site?" The most profitable, legal use of land is called the highest and best use (HBU). The most profitable use will also be the use that provides the greatest residual to land. Clearly, the residual to land depends on how it is used. The residual to land will differ if the site is used as a parking lot or a grocery store.

The HBU is not necessarily the most socially desirable use because land uses have considerable positive and negative spillovers. Construction of a supermarket in the middle of a rare downtown open space may be the most profitable legal use, but some might argue that it is not "best" in an social or ethical sense. Therefore, development officials should be aware of third parties who may be helped or harmed when making zoning or other land-use decisions. However, there is a link between the most profitable use and the most socially beneficial use. The profitability of a particular land use is usually due to the fact that consumers are willing and able to pay for location in the form of higher prices for the goods sold at that location. Therefore, the market for land usually reflects societal demand for products at particular places.

The most profitable use of land is seldom the most intensive or most highly developed use. For instance, a high-rise apartment (land and capital) is usually more valuable than a single-family house, but it will not necessarily be more profitable to construct high-rises rather than single-family houses on vacant land. Low-density housing is built in many areas because the cost of construction for a high-rise is also greater than for single-family construction and rents per unit may have to fall to ensure adequate occupancy. The key question in HBU determination is *what use will provide the greatest return to land (residual) after construction and operating costs have been subtracted?*

Table 10.1 shows a hypothetical relationship between intensity of development cost and the return to land. Keep in mind that the values shown as "present value of income" are the discounted value of the gross revenues generated by the property minus operating costs. The economies of vertical construction are illustrated by the lower per-story cost of the second level. However, construction costs per story start to increase after the second level, because it is increasingly expensive to construct additional stories. At the same time, the present value of the property increases at a decreasing rate reflecting the fact that per-unit property rents might fall due to increased vacancies or the need to lower rents to avoid increased vacancies. The combined result of these forces causes the present value of the land's residual

TABLE 10.1 Highest and Best Use Determination (in dollars)

Intensity of Use (number of stories)	Present Value of Income	Present Value of Nonland Cost	Value Residual to Land
1	200,000	100,000	100,000
2	400,000	175,000	225,000
3	575,000	300,000	275,000
4	750,000	525,000	225,000
5	900,000	775,000	125,000
6	1,000,000	1,250,000	−250,000

to fall after the third floor. The present value of the return to the land is maximized at three stories. Hence a building of three stories is the highest and best use.

Table 10.1 illustrates the HBU principle by examining different heights of a residential building. In all cases, the land use was residential. However, the same method applies to the choice among types of uses. For example, to determine whether a bakery or a three-story apartment would be the highest and best use, a similar calculation of the residual to land could be made.

Market Mechanisms

Market processes reinforce the tendency of land to be put to its highest and best use. For example, suppose an individual owns a parcel of land for which the most profitable use requires construction of a three-story apartment building (use 3 in Table 10.1). However, the owner of the property intends to build a one-story building (use 1 in Table 10.1). Perhaps the owner doesn't know a multistory structure is the highest and best use, or perhaps the owner lacks the financial or other technical skills necessary to develop a three-story apartment. The land would probably still be developed according to its highest and best use. Another developer might notice the vacant parcel (developers actively seek out such properties) and after analysis determine that a three-story apartment would be optimal. The developer could offer to buy the land for a maximum of $275,000. Because the residual to land is only $100,000 as a single-story building, there is ample bargaining range in which the two parties may reach a mutually satisfactory deal. Perhaps the original owner will sell the land and use the proceeds to purchase a property elsewhere on which a one-story building would be the highest and best use. If the owner knows

TABLE 10.2 Highest and Best Use of a Developed Property (in dollars)

Land Use Conversion	Present Value of Income Change	Conversion Costs	Residual to Existing Property
Gas station (existing use)	0	0	0
Body shop	52,500	20,000	32,500
Gas/grocery	10,000	15,000	−5,000

the initial market value of the property, he would find it more profitable to sell the land and buy another lot rather than develop it as a one-story building.

If the real estate market were operating with perfect knowledge, there would be many potential buyers willing to pay a maximum of $275,000. Thus competition would drive the price to exactly $275,000.

Existing Structures

The HBU discussion has been about use of land prior to development, but the HBU principle also applies to changing preexisting structures. The use that will provide the greatest residual after additional capital costs such as remodeling or demolition have been subtracted from the total value of the renovated property is the highest and best use. This approach implicitly assumes that existing construction costs ("sunk" costs) must be paid even if the building is demolished. Like land, the preexisting structure is immobile and hence is treated like land. Now the residual is attributed to land and preexisting buildings. Table 10.2 illustrates how the owner of a gas station should analyze the modification of his property to either add a convenience grocery store or to convert it into a body shop. The addition of a convenience store would cost more than the increase in the present value of the income generated by the improvements. Consequently, the gas station/grocery store would not be a profitable land use change. The conversion to a body shop is feasible because the present value of the increased income is greater than the cost of the improvements.

⊠ The Land Development Process

This section builds upon land use theory by showing the type of analysis that land developers use to determine HBU in a world where information is

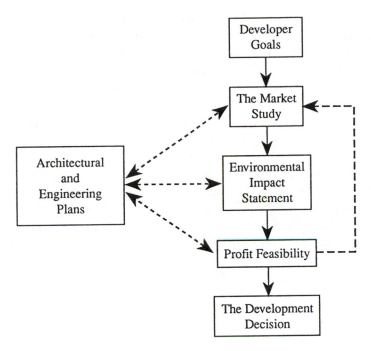

Figure 10.1. The land development process. The process starts with developers' goals and proceeds to increasingly complex stages. There is interaction between financial and engineering analysis.

costly and imperfect. It indicates how the hypothetical figures in Tables 10.1 and 10.2 can be derived.

The amount of effort that goes into a land-use study depends on the scope of the project and the value of the land. It would not be cost-effective to evaluate every possible land use for a particular site. Some decisions are based only on hunch. For instance, a retailer may open a store simply because it is believed to be a good area and space is available. However, major decisions are usually based on careful analysis. Figure 10.1 summarizes the steps in a typical land use study.

Developer Goals

The developer normally initiates the land development process. The developer's objective may be approximated by the desire to maximize profits, but routes to profit maximization include maximizing current cash flow, sheltering income from taxes, appreciation, personal use, or other factors. Income generation might be the goal of a retired investor, whereas a younger person might want to emphasize appreciation. Thus developers normally determine their appropriate mix of objectives before focusing on particular real estate investments. During the early planning stages, a developer may have a site and wish to determine a use for it or have a general development concept, such as a motel on the east side of a city, and be seeking an appropriate site.

The initial concept should fit the developer's goals. For instance, construction of a new apartment complex may have good appreciation and tax shelter potential, but it may not generate short-term cash flow. The development concept might simply be a rough idea that an apartment complex or an office tower would be profitable in a particular area. Preliminary architectural sketches may be drawn to illustrate the proposed concept, but the ideas are very tentative at this stage.

The Market Study

After a development concept has been tentatively identified, the analysis proceeds to the market study phase. The market study will help determine whether there is a market for the space under consideration, the likely income generation, and what potential impediments exist. The market study may also help the developer secure a loan, attract investors, or argue for public support, such as zoning changes or development incentives.

Suppose the general development concept is for an office building. The current and future market for the office space will be examined. The land development researcher will usually develop a grid showing characteristics of existing offices in the area including rents, occupancy rates, location, and amenities. This information will give the developer an idea of whether there is a current demand for additional space, the rental range that can be expected, and what features the project should include. Future employment will be forecast to determine whether the demand for office space will continue. Building permits will be examined to assess future increases in the quantity of space available. (Often a tight real estate market is accompanied by numerous construction plans by developers planning to take advantage of the high rents and low vacancies. Because of time lags in construction, a tight market could become a glut if many new projects are completed at the same time.)

The concepts of supply and demand are useful in market analysis even though supply and demand curves are seldom estimated. On the demand side, researchers normally assume that existing rents for similar projects, perhaps adjusted for inflation, will reflect rents on the proposed project. Market growth is also examined to provide an indication of how the demand will change. Population growth is a good indicator of demand increases for residential and retail commercial properties. Demand for industrial and office space is harder to forecast because these land uses depend on employment growth in specific industries. A target rental range for the proposed project is based on the prevailing and future market conditions.

Supply-side factors include planned new developments that may be indicated by building permits and other current building activities. Current occupancy rates are used to determined whether there is an under- or oversupply at current rents. An estimated occupancy rate for the proposed development will be established based on rent levels and the prevailing market conditions. If occupancy rates were generally low in the area, few developers would anticipate a change in market conditions because such a market situation is likely to be temporary. The low occupancy rates will tend to depress rents. In this case, rents may be projected to grow slowly or fall.

Environmental Impact Concerns

Environmental impact statements (EIS) are required by both state and federal governments. Most large development projects require a careful analysis of the project to ensure that a variety of direct and indirect impacts of a project are examined. EIS focus directly on social and ecological community impacts or spillover effects. Thus a project's impact on crime, poverty, and employment should be as much a part of the EIS as the effect on birds and water quality.

There is no formula for constructing an EIS. The nature of the project should dictate the questions that require attention. However, several steps characterize many environmental impact statements (Council on Environmental Quality, 1972).

1. Describe the *present conditions*. Includes physical, social, and aesthetic features of the area. Those features to be discussed later in the report and that may be controversial should receive the most attention.
2. Describe the *proposed project*. Maps showing the project's relationship to the community and the region are normally included.

3. Discuss *impacts of the proposed action.* The Department of Housing and Urban Development has suggested 14 areas that ought to be included: geology, soils, special land features, water, biota, climate and air, energy, services, safety, physiological well-being, sense of community, psychological well-being, visual quality, and historic and cultural resources.

4. Consider probable *adverse environmental impacts* that cannot be avoided or that would be adverse to the environmental goals of the nation or community. This step requires a value judgment concerning what impacts are adverse and distinctions between significant and insignificant adverse effects. Urban real estate projects should be particularly sensitive to social impacts, such as congestion, and solid and liquid waste disposal issues.

5. The review of *alternatives* to the proposed project may require consideration of appropriate alternatives to proposed actions that may have a less adverse environmental impact. Alternative land use proposals include adjusting the size of the project and varying the mix of units (to decrease density), building designs, and landscape possibilities.

6. Distinguish between the *short-term and long-term impacts.* The time dimensions vary from very-short-term construction disruption, to short-term effects (such as temporarily increased erosion), to permanent changes in the natural or social environment. The long-term impact forces policymakers to think beyond the projected economic life of a project.

7. Discuss *irreversible impacts and irretrievable resource losses.* Agricultural topsoil that is destroyed is an irretrievable loss; the commitment of public resources to support a development—police, roads, and so forth—is, for the most practical purposes, an irreversible commitment. This section should not simply reiterate impacts discussed in previous sections. Rather, the focus should be on resource use.

8. Discuss *potential problems and objections* raised by other governmental agencies as well as private organizations.

Profit Feasibility

The market study and EIS should help the developer decide whether a project can be sold or rented within the target price range and whether it is environmentally and politically workable. It does not, however, assess whether the project will be profitable. This will be done in the profit feasibility study. To determine profitability, the present value of returns must be compared to the present value of the costs. The returns will normally be spread over the economic life of the property, say, 20 years. Most of the costs will be incurred in the year of construction, although maintenance and utilities, taxes, and possibly financing charges will be future costs. Income tax factors may also be incorporated in the feasibility analysis.

The general formula for estimating the value of property with a limited economic life and fluctuating returns is

$$V = NOI_0 + NOI_{1(1 + d)} + NOI_{2(1 + d)^2} + \ldots + NOI_{n(1 + d)^n}, \qquad (10\text{-}2)$$

where

V = property value
d = appropriate discount rate
NOI_i = net operating income in year i

Subscripts indicate years in the future, with 0 indicating now.

Net operating income is income after subtracting operating expenses. Operating expenses for a typical urban property include utilities, property taxes, management fees, maintenance, insurance, and so forth. Clearly, the higher the net operating income, the greater the value of the property. Thus, if future or expected rents from a property increase while expenses remain constant, its value will increase assuming everything else remains the same.

There are complicated controversies surrounding the way the discount rate should be calculated. For our purposes, d can be considered as representing the return to capital such as an interest rate plus a rate to account for the return of capital. For instance, if the interest rate on comparably risky investments is 10% annually and the rate to account for the return of capital is 2% annually, then d would equal 12%. By application of Equation 10-2, you can see that the higher the discount rate the lower the value of the property will be, other things equal.

Equation 10-2 is important because when development projects are being considered, estimates of future net operating income are combined with the discount rate to determine the value of the proposed property. The estimated value can be compared to the project's construction costs as a guide to the type of development that should occur. If the construction costs were subtracted from the estimated value of the property, the value of land would be reflected.

As a general rule, if the present value of the project discounted at the appropriate rate is greater than the costs of the development (including land and capital costs), the project is feasible. If the present value is less than the construction costs, the project is not feasible because the developer cannot earn the required rate of return. Why is there less real estate development when interest rates are highest? The higher discount rates make for lower property value of proposed projects.

In applying Equation 10-2 to the case of, say, a new downtown office building, NOI would be the rents minus the operating costs, such as management, labor, property taxes, and so forth. NOI_n might include a liquidation value. The discount rate, d, might also be adjusted to reflect costs other than the interest rate and the return of capital, such as extra risk, management effort, and so forth.

Although the formula for converting future returns to present value is straightforward, the application is often difficult and can seldom be applied mechanically. It is difficult to determine the appropriate discount rate and forecasts of future rents are subject to error. Nevertheless, valuation concepts expressed in Equation 10-2 are important in determining how a particular site will be used.

Usually, the initial economic analysis will be based on "quick and dirty" assumptions. A pro forma statement, for instance, may show a static picture with NOI and reflecting a "typical" year. The static picture ignores variations in cost and revenue patterns that may occur over time. If initial pro forma calculations indicate the project could be profitable, more thorough analysis will be undertaken. The final cash flow analysis will account for the timing of cash expenditures and receipts during construction and throughout the project's life as well as possible lower rents during the start-up phase.

Suppose at some stage the feasibility study indicated that the project was not profitable? Rather than immediately abandoning the idea, the developer might redesign architectural features to reduce costs. Perhaps some features of the project could be cut—the number of rest rooms in an office complex could be decreased or gingerbread removed from a facade. Attempts to raise revenues will also be explored. Perhaps space could be rearranged to provide more rentable areas. Interaction between the architectural and economic aspects of the plan will continue until a decision is made to abort or proceed with the project.

If the present value of the returns is equal to or greater than the present value of the construction and operating costs, the developer will earn or exceed the rate of return given by the discount or target rate and the project will continue toward development. Table 10.3 is a simplified cash flow analysis of a project based on equation 10-2. Although many of the details of a large-scale model are missing, the basic elements are present. It is based on the assumption that the project is built in Year 0 at a cost of $1.3 million. The immediate costs include land ($300,000) and building ($1,000,000). Income

TABLE 10.3 A Simple Cash Flow Analysis (in dollars)

		Year		
Step	1	2	...	20
1 Income	300,000	312,000	...	632,055
2 − Operating expenses	135,000	140,400	...	284,425
3 = Net operating income	165,000	171,600	...	347,630
4 − Cost recovery	50,000	50,000	...	50,000
5 = Taxable income	115,000	121,600	...	297,630
6 Change in taxes	34,500	36,480	...	89,289
7 Cash flow after taxes	130,500	135,120	...	258,341
8 Present value cash flow after taxes	118,636	111,669	...	38,401
9 Sum present value on investment	118,636	230,306	...	1,425,738

Explanations by line:
1   Increasing at 4% per year
2   Equal to 45% of line 1
3   Line 1 minus line 2
4   Depreciation at $50,000 annually
5   Net operating income less cost recovery
6   Taxable income × .30
7   Line 3 less increases in taxes
8   Line 7 discounted at 10%
9   Running total of line 9

in the first year is projected to be $300,000, and property rents are assumed to increase 4% annually throughout the 20-year life of the project. Expenses are 45% of rents, so expenses also increase with inflation. Line 3 is the net operating income discussed in conjunction with Equation 10-2. Although property taxes have been deducted from gross income to calculate NOI, additional calculations are necessary to account for income tax factors. Depreciation, an important tax shelter item, is $50,000 annually. The developer is in a 30% marginal tax bracket, so after-tax income will differ from the before-tax income. Line 7 shows the present value of future after-tax income.

The discounted value of the income flow is shown on line 8. The investor's discount rate or target rate is 10%. Accordingly, the present value of the $130,500 after-tax income in Year 1 is $118,636($130,500/1.10) and in Year 2 is $111,669[$135,120/(1.10^2)]. Line 9 is simply the sum of the present values for the current year and succeeding years.

After 20 years, the sum of the present value of income is $1,425,738 which is greater than the $1,300,000 construction cost. (The initial construction cost was not discounted as it occurred in the first year. A more complete analysis could show monthly expenses appropriately discounted.) The present value of the future net income discounted at 10% is greater than the project cost, which was assumed to be $1.3 million, so the project would be profitable. If the discount rate were to increase to 15%, the present value of the project's net would be insufficient to justify the project.

The value of land is the residual value after accounting for other, mobile factors of production used in the construction of the project. Because capital costs were assumed to be $1 million, the residual to land suggests a land value of $425,738, the original $300,000 paid for the site plus the $125,738 excess. Alternatively, land value may be calculated as the value of the project ($1,425,738) less the capital costs ($1 million). If the developer purchased the land for $300,000, as was initially assumed, he or she would have gotten a good deal. If other developers recognized that the present value of the returns indicated that substantial profits were attainable, they might have been interested in the site, driving the price up, decreasing above-normal profits. If, however, preliminary feasibility analysis indicated that the present value of the returns were less than the present value of the costs (including estimated land costs), the developer would be in a strong position to negotiate the land price downward. Assuming the land market functioned well and assuming the developer had in fact identified most profitable land use, the property owner would have no better offers.

The Development Decision

After examining the market and profit feasibility analysis, the developer will be in a position to determine how to proceed. If it is decided to go forward with the project, the market and profit feasibility study may serve as a basis for securing a loan or attracting other equity investors. On the other hand, the investor may determine that the project is not feasible and profitable and abort the development. Other options include waiting until market conditions change or selling the plans to a developer who is interested in proceeding with the project.

Implications for Development Officials

Development officials are frequently asked to provide assistance to developers who want to build projects. Developers often argue that some type of public assistance is necessary because the project would not be profitable otherwise. For instance, a developer might agree to build housing downtown if a special low-interest loan were provided. Suppose also that public officials believed that downtown housing was a community priority because it would help revitalize the central business district. Thus development officials would have to consider whether it was advisable to provide the developer with a subsidy and, if so, how much of a subsidy.

In considering whether some public assistance might be necessary, a public official should examine the projected cash flow statement. If the analysis showed that the project would be profitable without public assistance, the case for a public subsidy would be weakened greatly. Even if the developer's data indicated the project would not be profitable without public support, public officials would be wise to examine the model's assumptions carefully. The developer may have underestimated profitability so as to pressure the public officials into giving a large subsidy. In other cases, some developers might be overly optimistic, asking for a smaller subsidy than might really be necessary. Thus public officials might be led to contribute to a project that was likely to fail, leaving the downtown with another empty building. Even publicly built projects, such as parking garages, convention centers, and sports facilities, should be subject to a cash flow analysis to determine whether the project will infuse money into the public treasury or be a resource drain.

Key questions in analyzing a profit feasibility statement are the following: Are the revenue estimates realistic? Has the market been properly identified? Are there any hidden costs or unanticipated problems? Is the discount rate appropriate? Because of the discounting process, errors in early year revenue and cost projections will have a much bigger impact on the present value than errors that occur in outlying years. For instance, with a discount rate of 12%, an error of $100 today would result in a $100 error in the final present value estimate. If the same $100 error occurred in the 20th year, NOI estimated, it would cause only a small percentage change in the estimated present value. So more attention should be given to early year estimates.

Land Use Patterns

The activity with a residual sufficient to pay the highest price for a site will determine the land use. This section shows how competition among various activities results in systematic land use patterns. This section first describes the "monocentric city model." Patterns of land use are based on the assumptions that the central business district is the point of maximum access and that transportation costs increase moving from the central business district (CBD) in all directions. Later, assumptions are relaxed and more complicated patterns of land use are described. However, two key principles are always evident: Activities seek access to urban goods, and the activity willing and able to pay the highest rent for a site determines its use.

The Monocentric City Model

The concentric circle model is predicated on the assumption that land in the center of the metropolis is the most valuable because it provides firms located there with maximum access to urban goods, such as customers, supplies, and so forth. Thus the CBD is the site where the firms would be willing to pay maximum land rent. The level of land rent the firm would be willing and able to pay will decline at locations increasingly distant from the CBD. Activities have "rent bid" functions that show the amount that firms in an industry would pay for land at various distances from the center. Firms in most activities would have greatest demand at the metropolitan center, and demand would decrease at more distant locations. Each industry would have a different rent bid curve, depending on the maximum amount that firms in that industry would bid for the land (the residual to land). However, because most businesses desire access to similar urban goods, the rent bid curves will generally tend to be highest at the CBD and decline from that point. Figure 10.2 illustrates a pair of rent bid curves suggested by the concentric circle model and shows the land use pattern that would result.

Why do some activities have higher rent bid curves at the CBD? First, activities that have a strong need for access will tend to outbid other activities for prime CBD land. Second, activities that cannot substitute other inputs for access afforded by central locations will tend to dominate CBD locations.

In urban areas, the most valuable property is dominated by financial, legal, and central administrative functions. The need by individuals in these activities for a central location is due primarily to the importance of face-to-face contact among executives. Individuals in these activities require frequent, often short-notice meetings. Because the time of lawyers, financiers, and executives is valuable, their transportation costs are high. Individuals are expensive to transport, particularly highly paid executives. Economic development officials often seek to improve the CBD as part of an effort to encourage administrative and financial activities to locate in their area.

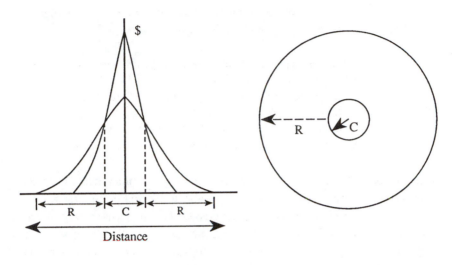

C = Commercial Use
R = Residential Use

Figure 10.2. Rent bid curves and the concentric circle model. Competition among various activities may result in a concentric circle pattern of land use under certain theoretical assumptions.

Retail activities also value proximity to CBD locations because of their centrality to customers. Industrial activities historically have been attracted to near-CBD locations due to access to ports, railheads, and roads. However, these ties have diminished since World War II. Today, new industrial facilities are oriented toward highway access points. Furthermore, zoning regulations have tended to exclude many industrial activities from near-CBD sites.

The value placed on CBD land for residential use is not as high as for financial and administrative uses. A few households are willing and able to pay a sufficient amount for near-CBD sites, so some high-rise residential buildings exist near the CBD. However, most households appear to value CBD access less than other activities. Consequently, many types of households have located varying distances from the CBD.

CBD land is not only the most valuable but also the most intensively used. It is no coincidence. Valuable resources tend to be used intensively. This explains why CBD land usually has the dense day-time population and the tallest buildings.

Larger cities have higher CBD densities than smaller places. If population is held constant, four factors normally affect CBD density:

- Newer cities developed around the automobile tend to use central locations less intensively than older "trolley car" cities.
- Higher-income groups are more likely to decentralize. Thus cities with high-income populations will have less concentrated densities.
- Low-quality central city housing leads to lower intensity in the core of the city.
- Low manufacturing employment contributes to lower CBD densities.

American central cities have lower population densities than their European counterparts for many of the reasons given above, especially the first point.

Most observers believe that the predicted land use patterns of the concentric circle model are inaccurate. The inaccuracies are due to the restrictive assumptions that ignore variations in transportation costs and resources within a metropolitan area. More realistic land use patterns result from more realistic assumptions. Yet the principles of access and HBU remain important elements in all land use models.

Roads and Axial Development

The recognition of highway systems requires modification of the concentric circle model to reflect lower transportation costs along main arteries. A site near a main road may be further from the CBD than other sites and yet have better access. Developers will be willing to increase the amount of rents they will pay to be near a road. Figure 10.3a is a land use pattern that might exist if the assumption of equal transportation costs in all directions were dropped from the concentric circle approach. Rivers and other natural services could be incorporated to show how other variations in transportation costs affect land use.

The doughnut city may be an emerging land use form. As beltways around cities provide good access to the entire metropolitan areas and as the areas just a few blocks from the CBD are increasingly associated with urban "bads," new development is becoming highly centered near the beltways; with the possible exception of the CBD, many central cities have experienced little development. Thus large parts of the central city may become the hole in the beltway development's doughnut.

The introduction of roads into the model also helps explain commercial strip development—commercial strips that dominate the row of buildings on

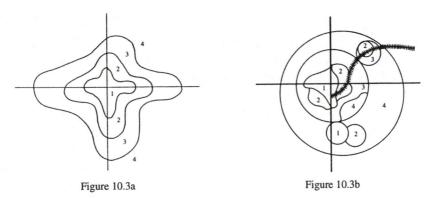

Figure 10.3a   Figure 10.3b

Key: 1 = Commercial/financial
     2 = Industrial
     3 = Residential
     4 = Agricultural
     ▦▦▦ Rail
     —— Roads

Figure 10.3. Additional land use models.

either side of major roads. This pattern is often called "ribbon development," and it reflects the desire of many businesses for access to a stream of customers rather that a stationary customer base.

Agglomeration and the Multiple Nuclear City

The multiple nuclear city is perhaps the most sophisticated model of the modern metropolis because it recognizes that land use clumps appear because of agglomerations economies within a single organization and among establishments. Intraurban agglomeration is an important aspect of the CBD's attractions, and the same set of forces can cause subcenters to develop beyond the CBD. A medical complex encompassing several blocks is an example of a specialized cluster. It would be ludicrous for a hospital complex to occupy a narrow concentric circle around the CBD, as would be suggested by a literal interpretation of the concentric zone model. Agglomeration economics also encourages clustering of groups of firms. Perhaps firms needing access to a railhead (and firms needing access to firms that locate near a railhead) will form a cluster, and across town another cluster of manufacturing firms may form. Figure 10.3b illustrates the multiple nuclear city.

Outlying retail clusters are an important element of the multiple nuclear city. As cities grow, access to the CBD becomes more difficult for families living near the periphery. Retail centers develop to serve the increasingly large suburban markets. Additional activity, such as offices, entertainment, and residencies, may unfold around regional shopping malls, particularly if the transportation system is oriented toward the subcenter. As the metropolitan area expands, previously isolated communities may be brought into the metropolitan network. The enveloped communities will experience land use changes, and they develop into subcenters within the metropolitan system.

Subcenters vary in size, ranging from small breaks in general decline in density to those that dominate the land use for miles around and rival the CBD in many aspects.

Speculation

Large tracts of land are often maintained in low-density uses, such as parking lots or agriculture, while intensive development occurs nearby. The owners may be speculating that the land will be suitable for a different use in the future and therefore land values will increase faster than the current discount rate. For instance, residential use may prevail in an area where unimproved lots sell for $20,000 per acre. An owner may believe that if the land is not developed now it will be worth more per acre than $20,000, plus the accrued interest, in the future if it could be sold as part of a major subcenter.

Speculation usually involves differences of opinion about the future. If a current landowner was prepared to develop housing on that land, it might be sold to a speculator who believes a shopping center would be feasible in the future. Therefore, the land's value would rise more rapidly than the current interest rate and more rapidly than the current owner anticipates. Causes of differing opinions involve such factors as anticipated public improvements, the path of development, and the general state of the economy. The imperfect nature of the real estate market also contributes to speculative holdings. Consequently, land use development is not smooth or incremental as implied by the model of axial growth. "Leapfrog" development will be observed.

⊠ Change and Growth

The urban landscape changes slowly. Two major reasons for inertia are the long physical life of buildings and interdependence of land use. Most structures could last for hundreds of years. Locational interdependence among land uses and coevolutionary development of urban infrastructure creates a situation where one business may be reluctant to relocate unless many other activities in the neighborhood also relocate. As important as inertia is, our understanding of land use patterns will be inaccurate if viewed as static.

The Spreading of the Metropolis

The CBD is declining in relative importance. Metropolitan areas are growing outward faster than they are growing upward. The CBD's share of retail trade has dropped significantly in almost all cities. Accompanying the spreading out of the metropolis has been a decline in the relative importance of the central city in terms of population and economic activity compared with the suburbs. Factors contributing to metropolitan spread include urban growth, declining transportation costs, new production techniques, values, and income growth.

Growth

Growth tends to be on the urban fringe. As the city grows, natural boundaries such as rivers or lakes may weaken the role of the CBD as the maximum access point. Congestion and low-income zones of transition often separate the CBD from important suburban markets and sources of labor. Hence growth tends to increase demand for land throughout the urban region but the increases are greater at the periphery and near the subcenters than near the CBD.

Transportation Costs

Transportation cost declines have decreased the cost of access to the CBD for firms and households located in outlying areas. The preferences of firms and households that were initially indifferent between a nearer-CBD/higher-rent site and a more distant/lower-rent location have tilted toward more distant location. Thus lower transportation costs will contribute to metropolitan spread. Commuter-oriented highways and beltways have provided important transportation cost advantages to suburban areas.

Production Techniques

Technologies that reduce the need for CBD access or increase the need for land have contributed to urban spread. Cheap electric power and the development of the electric motor have tended to encourage horizontal, assembly-line production rather than production in a multistory plant. Thus new facilities have required more land, which in turn has shifted their orientation toward outlying areas.

Many observers believe that computers will allow individuals to work at home rather than in an office. There will probably still be a need for face-to-face communication and a social need for contact with individuals at work. Nevertheless, there is little doubt that the telecommunication and computer technologies have decreased the importance of CBD access.

New technologies are decreasing the need for clerical, typing, and related functions to be located near corporate-level decision makers. When information was kept on paper and transferred by hand, a decision maker had to be near the paper as did the clerks and typists. Many firms are now finding it more efficient to relegate many "back office" functions to locations in the suburbs. Land is cheaper, and a suburban workforce has developed that is difficult to attract to the city. The corporate headquarters is still tied to the CBD because executives and other officials still require face-to-face contact with each other and with other businesses, but even the tie of corporate headquarters is declining.

Values and Image

The values placed on access to the CBD and the goods available in the central city have changed. Families increasingly prefer single-family detached housing and the set of values associated with a suburban lifestyle. As households move away from the CBD, some businesses will follow markets and sources of labor. Some businesses may be affected by the same set of values as households. There is an as yet unresolved debate in the urban literature regarding whether jobs follow households to the suburbs or whether people follow jobs. Although one factor may eventually be shown to be more important than the other, both undoubtedly are operating in the city today and weakening the relative importance of the central city.

Because values have tended to favor outlying locations, the popular image of the central city has deteriorated. In most metropolitan areas, the CBD is no longer seen as the urban apex. It is viewed as a place of abandoned buildings and home of the indigent, porno stores, and criminals. To alleviate the problem, some communities have tried to separate the CBD from the nearby zones of transition, but the "enclave" strategy has not been a complete success.

Incomes

As incomes increase, families tend to spend an increasing proportion of their income on housing. They also may want to alter the kind of shelter from multifamily housing, which is land intensive to detached single-family housing, which is land extensive. The best buys on single-family housing with large lots are distant from the CBD. In fact, such properties are rare in central cities. Thus increased incomes are associated with the spreading out of the city.

Evaluating Metropolitan Spread

The desirability of recent changes in metropolitan form has been questioned by many planners, and many economic development officials work to maintain the economic viability of the CBD. Observers at various times have argued that metropolitan spread is bad environmental management, bad economics, and bad aesthetics. Sprawl increases the need to travel and therefore contributes to environmental pollution and excessive energy use. It also reduces agricultural land and wildlife habitats. Critics also argue that the easier it is for the city to grow outward, the greater the rate of wasteful abandonment of intercity properties. Sprawl requires construction of costly new infrastructure as well as new housing and retail space. Critics of suburbanization and urbanization also argue that too much agriculture land and green space is lost. Another criticism is that sprawl contributes to an ugly urban environment with "ticky-tacky" suburban housing in contrast to a more interesting urban landscape that characterizes more densely built European cities.

Sprawl also results in political fragmentation, which lessens the control that the central city has over its metropolitan environment. As a result of political fragmentation, several authors have contended that weak central cities reduce the economic prospects of the entire metropolitan area (Rusk, 1993; Voith, 1992).

Defenders of metropolitan spread contend that location is a matter of personal preference and market economics. If individuals believe that suburban life is better and they are willing and able to pay for the extra land and related costs, then land should be put in its highest and best economic use, according to some economic development officials. Similarly, if businesses find decentralized locations better suited to their needs, than they should be allowed to compete with other activities for the land. If the process results in the decline of the central city, then consumer and individuals obviously did not value central-city locations. The market will allow land to be put in its most valued use. Furthermore, space for agricultural use can be "made" through irrigation, forest conversion, and so forth, as agricultural land will not diminish.

The issue of urban sprawl is a question of balance rather than total cessation of outward urban growth or continued rapid outward growth. However, it does lead one to question political regulation of land use.

⊠   Land Use and Economic Development Tools

A variety of distinct rights are associated with a particular property. Lawyers use the analogy that the multitude of rights are like a bundle of sticks, each stick representing a right. The government has taken the sticks called police power, taxation, eminent domain, and escheat, the first three of which are important economic development tools:

- *Police power* is the authority of government to regulate use to enhance or preserve health, safety, and the general welfare. Zoning and building codes are the most important police powers.
- *Taxation* affects both the return that property generates and local revenues. Property taxes can affect land use because they lower the return on a real estate investment. Some states allow agricultural land to be taxed at a lower rate than improved property. This differential discourages development and encourages urban sprawl.
- *Eminent domain* is the right of government to purchase property if its use is needed for a public purpose such as a road or a park. What constitutes "public purpose" has been a source of land use debate.
- *Escheat* is government's right to all land for which there is no private owner. For instance, if someone dies without heirs, the deceased's property will be claimed by the government.

Zoning and Its Critics

Zoning is probably the most significant determinant of land use among the government sticks. The need for zoning is widely accepted, but zoning is not without its critics. Bernard Siegan (1970) suggested that zoning is an unnecessary encumbrance on the operation of the free market. He contended that Houston, Texas, is an example of a city that developed with limited zoning laws. Yet Houston is pleasant, and the location of residential areas next to commercial property has not resulted in "incompatible" land use. As in most cities, industries in Houston locate near the major highway and railways and do not "invade" residential areas. In Houston, however, these locational patterns are more the result of market economies than zoning regulation (although there were other land use controls available to public planners). In place of zoning, developers of large tracks of land sold property but restricted the deed of sale. They required all future owners to restrict the use to functions compatible with the rest of the subdivision. The deed restrictions made it easier to sell the sites initially and improved resale value.

The argument that private contracts could replace or at least reduce the need for land use regulations would not be particularly appealing if individuals were satisfied with zoning regulations. However, there are at least five specific ways that zoning may hinder economic development:

1. Changing land use becomes difficult. Zoning often prevents redevelopment of an area when, for example, a change from residential to commercial land use is needed. Mills (1989) showed that zoning encourages land owners to attempt to have their property zoned in socially inefficient ways and suppress potential net social gains because it is often difficult to rezone a property.

2. Zoning may inflate land costs. Zoning restricts the amount of land available for certain industrial, commercial, and multifamily use. This limits the supply of land for such purposes and artificially raises land price.

3. There are aesthetic and social shortcomings of zoning. Architectural critics sometimes claim that zoning (and building codes) detract from an area's quality of life.

4. Public planners make mistakes. The free market will occasionally err. The result will be an inefficient or socially harmful land use. Even the officials who plan, often with the aid of "market signals," make mistakes. Critics of zoning argue that public officials may be more likely to misallocate land than developers. Furthermore, the government planners' mistakes may be quite harmful because they are large-scale mistakes.

5. Exclusionary and fiscal zoning occur. Many communities attempted to zone out the poor by prohibiting all but very expensive housing. Other communities allow only such construction that will generate more tax revenues than it will cost to service the property. Hence apartments with three or more bedrooms are unpopular in many communities because such apartments will generate less in revenues than a single-family house, but the large number of bedrooms implies that the tenants will have school-aged children. Families with children tend to be high-cost residents particularly because of the associated educational

expenses. Such practices may enhance the economies of some areas, but they may create problems for central cities that often bear a heavier cost of providing services for low- and moderate-income families.

Related Economic Development Tools

Using the basic governmental rights in property, local officials have developed ways to use land use powers to serve development needs.

Directed Development

Community planners use zoning and extension of public services to direct economic development into areas that may provide agglomeration economies. If officials sought to develop an area as industrial, they might extend infrastructure such as roads and parking areas that would accommodate large trucks. Zoning would be coordinated with infrastructure construction to avoid incompatible land uses. The combination of zoning and infrastructure policy are intended to attract industries. Encouragement of a retail area or a "theater district" could be encouraged by other types of infrastructure, such as lighting, privacy landscaping, and parking. Building codes and related regulations can be used to create an architectural look that may contribute to the economic development aims.

Infrastructure extensions and zoning may also be coordinated to limit growth or sprawl. By refusing to extend some public services and appropriate zoning to areas, development costs can be reduced and economies from urban density may be achieved.

Linkage

Linkage programs have carried a step further the idea that current city residents should receive compensation for the costs of development. Linkage programs are attempts to require developers to provide support for unrelated development as a condition for permission to develop their original project. The logic of linkage programs is that land in certain areas of a city, such as the CBD, are desirable development sites. However, residents living in other parts of the region, such as city residential neighborhoods, will not benefit from the development. Hence permission to develop in some areas must be linked to projects that can benefit residents living elsewhere. It has also been argued that new downtown development causes indirect negative consequences (congestion, pollution) for current residents, and linkage programs can help compensate for these adverse impacts.

Under linkages programs, a developer may be required to commit to employment guarantees, high-quality building design, residential housing projects, transportation services or other activities that may be unrelated to the project under consideration before construction is approved.

Flexibility

There has been a trend toward providing developers more flexibility in meeting legal requirements and avoiding overly homogeneous development. Public land planners are currently modifying the way they regulate to give private developers and market forces more leeway while maintaining some control over externalities. The expectation is that the flexibility will encourage economic development.

Transferable development rights is one technique that has been used to avoid congestion. Traditionally, land use planners have specified the maximum number of apartment units that each proposed building may have. A developer could apply for a zoning change, and each permit was then determined on a case-by-case basis. The transferable development rights technique provides a way of regulating density in an area but also allows greater scope for market forces. Community officials may simply rule that within a particular district the number of units (or number of floors) may be no more than N. The rights to build apartment units will be distributed among landowners according to an equitable formula. Perhaps each acre could be assigned the right to 10 residential units. If a landowner wants to build a project with more units than he was originally assigned, the extra development rights could be purchased from another landowner. Thus the overall density of an area may be controlled consistent with the available city infrastructure. Yet rigid zoning is avoided.

Planned unit developments (PUDs) allow developers to propose a comprehensive plan for an area that may mix single-family housing, multiple-family housing, commercial land use, and even industrial use in a single development. "New town" developments are large-scale applications of PUDs.

Floor area ratio is a technique that limits the ratio of total floor area to the area of the lot. If an area was regulated with a floor area ratio of 1, an individual may construct a one-story unit on the whole lot, a two-story unit on half the lot, a four-story unit on one fourth of the lot, and so forth. Density is controlled, yet private developers have more flexibility than they would have with many zoning laws.

⋈ Summary

This chapter surveyed land use. An efficient distribution of land uses contributes to local economic development prospects. The return to land is based on productivity. In the case of urban land, productivity is a function of access to goods in the environment. Land value equals the return to land (rent) divided by the discount rate. Rent is the residual to land after the other factors of production have been compensated. Land is fixed in supply, not created by the efforts of man, so some economists have maintained that the return to landowners is unearned.

The highest and best use of land is the most profitable use, subject to legal restrictions. Access is an important determinant of highest and best use. Market processes reinforce the tendency of land to be placed in its highest and best use.

A land use study is frequently conducted to determine the appropriate use of a site. Developer goals are set; market, environmental impacts, and profit studies are undertaken; and finally, a decision is made. The critical step in a land use study is a cash flow analysis to determine the present value of the future returns from a project. If the discounted present value of future returns is greater than the project's cost, the project is likely to be undertaken. Public officials and private developers often use cash flow analysis in their negotiations.

The combination of individual development decisions results in land use patterns. The simplest model of a metropolis is the concentric circle model. More complicated models can be developed by introducing roads, agglomeration economies, and speculation. However, all land use models of urban development are based on the idea that firms bid against each other for land and the highest bidder (subject to legal restrictions) determines land use. In the theoretical models, rents will be greatest at the point of maximum access, the center of the metropolis, and declines at points of less desirable access. However, the multiple nuclear model allows for subcenters of activity and density.

Land use patterns are changing in response to such factors as urban growth, changes in transportation costs, production technology, values, and incomes. Currently, the outward spread of the metropolis is a major land use trend.

Political factors also influence land use. Zoning is the primary tool used to regulate land use, but it is not the only tool. Zoning is intended to reduce land use spillovers. However, zoning has been criticized for being both ineffective and inefficient. The current trend is to allow developers more flexibility. Infrastructure placement can be a tool to direct development to particular areas. Attempts to ensure that benefits from central business district locations spill over into neighborhoods are termed linkage.

11

Housing and Neighborhood Development

This chapter focuses on housing, the land use that most directly affects the welfare of families. The National Housing Act of 1949 declared that "the general welfare and security of the Nation and the health and living standards of its people require a decent home and suitable living environment for every American Family." Economic development officials are concerned about housing because it directly affects community welfare, is a basic building block of neighborhoods, generates local tax resources, and affects the quality of life in the entire community.

⊠ Fundamentals of Housing Economics

Supply and demand analysis is useful in understanding forces that affect the housing market. Figure 11.1a illustrates a traditional academic supply and demand model for housing. The equilibrium price and quantity of housing are determined by the intersection of the supply and demand curves.

Ceteris paribus, or "other things being equal," assumptions are necessary to allow the assumption that the equilibrium price and quantity remain stationary. Supply and demand curves represent the behavior of producers and consumers. However, their behavior is stable with respect to price and quantity only when all relevant variables other than price and quantity are held constant. The most common factors that must be assumed constant in supply and demand analysis of housing are shown in Table 11.1.

238

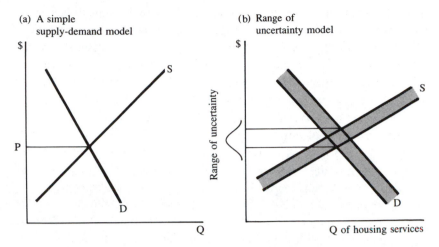

Figure 11.1. Two models of the housing market. The traditional supply and demand presentation implies that a single, observable price will emerge. In reality "fuzzy" supply and demand curves might be used to illustrate the range of uncertainty.

TABLE 11.1 Important Ceteris Paribus Assumptions

General	Specific Real Estate Example
Demand	
Price of other goods	Price of home fuel
Consumers' tastes and preferences	Recent importance of family rooms
Size of the market factory	Number of families in a city due to factory relocation
Incomes of consumers	Incomes in a city or employment
Expectations	Inflation changes beliefs about future housing prices
Supply	
Price of inputs	Price of lumber, tools, etc.
Number of producer	Number of building contractors
Conditions of technology	Advances in factory fabrication of homes or plastic plumbing (where legal)

The ceteris paribus assumptions are not strictly met in reality, but that does not diminish the usefulness of supply and demand analysis. Paradoxically, it is the violation of the assumptions that makes the model useful. When any of the factors assumed to be constant change, the relevant supply or demand curves will shift. Thus it is changes in the ceteris paribus assumptions that give predictive power to economic models. For instance, if an increase in income was anticipated while other important factors remained relatively stable, housing prices could be projected to increase.

The horizontal axis traditionally measures the quantity of a homogeneous product per period of time. Yet houses are very dissimilar. To finesse the problem of what is being measured on the quantity axis, economists have assumed that housing can be defined in terms of "units of housing services." A mansion might contain five units of housing services, whereas a small apartment might contain only half a unit. The level of housing services contained in a dwelling unit can vary with design, location, and other features. The neighborhood environment and local public services that residents may receive can also be considered part of housing services. Although the method of measuring the units of housing services is complex and has been widely criticized, it is conceptually sound (Bartik, 1988).

Price is also a slightly more complicated concept when applied to housing because some housing is purchased and some is rented. However, conversion between rent and sales price is straightforward. The value of a house is the discounted present value of the rents. In a well-functioning market, value will equal sales price. Therefore, it is conceptually easy to move between rent and sales price. If rents rise, sales prices rise (assuming factors such as maintenance cost and expected life of the property do not change). If housing prices rise, monthly payments increase. The relationship between the flow of income and sales price may be expressed using the same formula that was used previously to estimate property values:

$$SP = R_0 + \frac{R_1}{(1 + r)} + \frac{R_2}{(1 + r)^2} + \ldots + \frac{R_n}{(1 + r)^n}, \qquad (11\text{-}1)$$

where

SP = sales price (assumed to equal value)

R_i = net rent (excluding associated expenses) the property could command in year i; R_n includes liquidation price and R_0 is rent due now

r = Applicable discount rate

n = holding period

Variations of Equation 11-1 are used by real estate appraisers in determining the value of income-producing properties. In the case of owner-occupied properties, it is necessary to estimate the rental value of the housing service. The imputed rent is the monetary value of the periodic flow of benefits from the property that could be attained if rented.

Hedonic Pricing[1]

Hedonic pricing models segment the housing services bundle into detailed components and use statistical techniques, such as regression, to determine the marginal value of each component. The value of the entire housing bundle can then be determined by aggregating the value of various components. This section is intended to provide an overview of hedonic pricing, not to show the detailed statistical mechanics of the approach. (An appendix to this chapter shows hedonic pricing applied to aspects of a quality-of-life index.)

The essence of hedonic pricing models can be summarized in Equation 11-2, which states that price is a function of housing characteristics:

$$P = f(C_i), \tag{11-2}$$

where P is price and C_i is the ith characteristic (i.e., size, access, number of baths, etc.). Equation 11-2 is a general functional form. When the function is specified, the coefficients associated with each variable express the value of that characteristic, holding all other characteristics constant.

For instance, if value were determined only by the square footage of the apartment and the number of bedrooms, the hedonic equation might be

$$PR = a + b_1(\text{sq. ft.}) + b_2(\text{bedrooms}), \tag{11-3}$$

where

PR = property rent per month
a = intercept term
b_1 = number of square feet of space
b_2 = number of bedrooms

Using regression techniques, the value of a_1, b_1, and b_2 could be determined. Suppose the regression technique resulted in the following equation:

$$PR = 75 + .40(sq. ft.) + 2.0(bedrooms). \qquad (11-4)$$

Then, a 3-bedroom, 1,000-square-foot apartment would be expected to rent for $481[75 + ($.40)(1,000) + ($2)(3)]. The model not only provides information on the components. For instance, an extra bedroom adds $2 per month to the rent, holding the apartment size and all other factors constant.

Actual-price models are much more complex than the simple, linear, two-independent-variable model illustrated by Equation 11-2. However, a study by Guntermann and Norrbin (1987) provides a more realistic example. They used a hedonic pricing model to estimate apartment rents for private development in the Phoenix, Arizona, metropolitan area. Their model contained over 20 independent variables, such as amenities, age, whether children were allowed, and so forth. Their model explained 81% of the variance in rents.

The market comparison approach has long been used by real estate practitioners to estimate value. Although this approach lacks the statistical rigor of the hedonic price model, it is based on the same concept—housing is a bundled good.

There are four steps in the market comparison approach. First, examine the subject property for which price is to be estimated. Second, collect data for three or more similar properties that have been sold and have known sales prices. Third, adjust the sales prices of the comparables to reflect the price they would have sold for if they had the characteristics of the subject property. If a comparable property is better than the subject property in some respect, then the sale price of the comparable should be decreased. If a comparable property is worse than the subject on a particular feature, then the comparable's price is adjusted upward. Usually, judgment and experience are used in making adjustments. Finally, the values of the comparable properties are averaged to provide an estimate of value of the subject property. Table 11.2 summarizes this process.

Uncertainty, Market Imperfections, and Competition

In perfectly competitive markets, such as the New York Stock Exchange or commodity exchanges, prices are set by impersonal market forces. Every buyer or seller is a price taker. Real estate transactions are fundamentally different from the competitive markets in that buyers and sellers can only guess the price for which a particular property will sell. Another important difference between real estate and competitive markets is that while there are

TABLE 11.2 Market Comparison Approach to Value: Grid Analysis

Improvements	Comp A	Comp B	Comp C	Subject Property
Sale price	$56,000	$53,500	$48,000	?
Time of sale	Recent 0	1 year ago +2,700	18 months ago +3,500	Now
Location and neighbor- hood conditions	(Better) −$5,000	(Worse) +$5,000	Worse +$3,000	Average
Architectural style	Worse +$500	Better −$1,000	Worse +$250	Good
Total square feet	2,500 sq ft −$7,000	Same 0	Same 0	2,300 sq ft
Kitchen size and design	Better −$500	Same 0	Same 0	Average
Heating and air conditioning	Same	Same	Same	Electric
Number of rooms	(8) 0	(7) +$3,000	Equal 0	8
Number of baths	(2) 0	1-1/2 +$1,300	2 0	2
Type of construction	Better −$1,200	Better −$700	Better −$1,500	Poor
Physical condition	Same 0	Better −$1,000	Worse +$1,200	Average
Garage and other outbuildings	Same	Same	Same	1-1/2 car
Lot value difference	+500	Equal	Equal	Average
Indicated value	$56,000	$59,700	Overall rating $54,450	
Correlated value of subject property	($56,500 + $59,200 + $54,450) ÷ $56,883			

generally hundreds of buyers and sellers in any real estate market at any given time, there may be only one or two sellers and only a few buyers for any particular property. Thus each participant in a real estate market has some ability to affect price.

Because of the nature of real estate markets, price is seldom known before an actual sale has been made. The equilibrium price for a particular class of property in a given area may be better visualized as a range rather than as an exact point. Figure 11.1b shows a modified supply and demand graph for a select type of real estate such as a three-bedroom, one-and-a-half-bath ranch house in the Saville subdivision.

The supply and demand curves in Figure 11.1b are fuzzy and a range of uncertainty is indicated because any one individual who decides to sell will affect supply, and there is no way to be certain ahead of time exactly how many similarly priced properties will be for sale. Likewise, demand for narrowly defined types of property can be affected by the behavior of any single purchaser.

⊠   Residential Location and Neighborhood Change

The choice of where to live is an individual decision shaped by larger social forces. Individual decisions have the cumulative effect of forming recognizable neighborhoods. This section describes the processes that result in the social and economic similarity of neighborhood residents. The models discussed suggest levers that local development officials may employ to affect change.

The Filtering-Down Theory

The filtering-down theory explains how different socioeconomic groups come to occupy particular neighborhoods. The theory was originally put forward by Burgess (1952) to explain his observations about Chicago, where higher-income households moved farther from the city center and slightly-lower-income groups occupied the vacated housing.

As incomes among a high-income group rise, demand for housing increases. Some individuals will be able to satisfy their increased demand for housing by buying newly constructed houses. The newly constructed house will likely be located further from the heart of the city where vacant land is available. It is usually cheaper to build on vacant land than to bear the opportunity cost (i.e., the remaining value), demolition, and clearance expenses of building on a site with existing buildings. Furthermore, inner-city lots are generally too small to accommodate the preferences of upper-income households.

The filtering process depends on what happens to the houses vacated by the families that purchased newly constructed homes. There are three likely possibilities:

- *No filtering.* Families of similar economic backgrounds might purchase the vacated houses. In this case, there would be no change in the economic status of the neighborhood. The filtering process will not be effective in increasing the supply of housing to lower-income groups.

- *Complete filtering.* Suppose that families of comparable incomes were not interested in moving into the vacated properties at the price the initial occupants paid, although the quality of the housing unit had not deteriorated. In this case, the price of housing in the neighborhood would fall and the house would be affordable to lower-income households. The house could be described as filtering down to lower-income families. This second case is the clearest example of how poor families may benefit from the filtering process.

- *Filtering and adaptation.* Houses will often undergo some adaptive change when they filter to a lower-income group. One important reason for the change in the housing stock is that lower-income groups may be unable to afford the same levels of maintenance as the previous higher-income group. Also, lower-income groups may wish to divide the house to accommodate more people than previously. In physical terms, the lower maintenance levels might be reflected in houses that were in need of paint, had cracked windows, and so forth. Some adaptation will result in lower-quality housing services, although the quantity of housing services provided in a neighborhood may increase if properties are used more intensively. In this case, the housing units in the neighborhood filtered to a lower-income group, but whether the housing services increased would depend on the extent of the adaptive adjustment. If the decline in housing quality is slight, the adaptive filtering will probably lead to better housing for the lower-income group.

The three possibilities could describe what might happen to an individual house. If the focus of analysis is on the neighborhood, possibilities 2 and 3 will change the socioeconomic composition. To the extend that adaptation occurs, the physical characteristics of the neighborhood will also change.

The filtering theory does not necessarily require a growth pattern in which lower-income groups move outward from the central city. For instance, the filtering process could operate equally well if we assumed that new houses were being built along major urban corridors or radiating outward from more than one urban subcenter. Furthermore, the filtering process need not start at the top of the income scale. If middle-income families move into newly constructed housing, the filtering process could start with the income group just below the movers.

Initiating and Perpetuating the Process

Why do higher-income groups move from the neighborhood in the first place? What initiates the filtering process and keeps it going? Most filtering models assume that the process is initiated by individuals moving outward from the center of the city as their incomes increase. This process is part of the trade-off model described below. Little (1980) suggested that the filtering process may be touched off by "mobile externalities," such as congestion, noise, or fear of crime, that move outward from the urban core. These externalities may trigger the relocation process. Low-income and minority populations may be viewed as a negative externality by many upper-income families. As the supply of low-income housing in the inner city is diminished through deterioration and demolition or as additional low-income families move into the urban area, pressures to move outward increase.

After a certain concentration of a group has moved into a neighborhood, the filtering process may quicken. Racial transition of neighborhoods is sometimes characterized by a tipping point. Evidence indicates that when a neighborhood reaches a point where between 20% and 30% of the population is Black, the neighborhood becomes stigmatized as a Black area and the speed of racial change accelerates. The same concept probably applies to neighborhood transition in general. For instance, once a neighborhood becomes identified as working-class rather than middle-class in the minds of buyers and sellers, the transition may accelerate.

Blockbusting and redlining are two other responses that may initiate or perpetuate the process of neighborhood transition. Blockbusting refers to real estate activity whereby brokers encourage Whites to sell at a low price by preying on fears that Blacks are taking over their neighborhood. The real estate dealer either hopes to purchase properties cheaply from Whites and resell the properties to Blacks at a substantial profit or simply to turn over properties to earn commissions.

Redlining refers to the practice by lending institutions of withholding mortgage financing from potential buyers in neighborhoods that are undergoing economic transition to a lower-income group. If mortgage funds are not available, the price of housing will tend to fall, speeding the process of change. Insurance companies have also been accused of redlining by refusing to insure (or charging higher premiums for) houses in certain areas or refusing to provide automobile insurance for residents in those areas.

There are laws against some forms of blockbusting and redlining. However, both may occur in subtle ways. A broker may intimate that a racial change is occurring without being explicit (e.g., "The character of the area isn't what it once was"), or a lending institution may place barriers to a potential borrower in a redlined area that are difficult to detect. Although both blockbusting and redlining are frequently proposed theories that stimulate neighborhood transition, the extent that they actually affect neighborhood transition is unknown.

Another factor that can speed the rate of neighborhood change is the level of maintenance. Galster (1987) investigated the decision of homeowners to repair and maintain their houses. He found that both sociological and economic factors affected the upkeep decision. Social factors include the solidarity of the neighborhood and the expectation that it might deteriorate. A neighborhood going through the filtering process may have a social environment that discourages reinvestment. Economic factors include the potential for capital gains. The expected capital gains from a maintenance investment is affected by the anticipated appreciation and the expected length of tenure. If individuals plan to move in the near future or if they anticipate declines in property values, there will be less investment.

Porell (1985) showed that when landlords reside in the building they rent they tend to maintain the property better than absentee landlords do. By implication, the findings also suggest that when landlords live in the neighborhood, they will better maintain rental units. If landlords move from the neighborhood in the course of the filtering process, the quality of the housing stock may fall, quickening the filtering process.

The filtering-down theory also has important policy implications for development officials. Most important, the theory suggests that housing of the poor may be improved if new construction is encouraged for the upper and middle classes. However, this process will help low-income families only if the new housing units the poor occupy as the result of filtering are less expensive than previously and do not deteriorate during the filtering process.

Olsen's (1969) model of the filtering process indicated that in the long run the price of a unit of housing services would be determined by the cost of production. Therefore, in the long run, the housing stock would evolve through disinvestment to the level that residents could afford to construct and maintain. Unless they were willing and able to pay the cost of additional housing services, their housing standard could not be improved. Hence filtering could not improve the housing standards of low-income groups in the long run. However, in the case of housing, the "long run" is generations, so filtering may indeed result in better housing for trailing groups.

Weicher and Thibodeau (1988) provided empirical evidence that filtering improved housing conditions of low-income groups and that it was quantitatively an important mechanism. They found that about one less substandard housing unit was occupied during the 1970s for each new housing unit built during the 1960s. Although the ratio of reduced substandard occupancy to new construction will change depending on market conditions, their findings suggest that filtering is an important way to increase the supply of housing services to low income groups. Whether it is more effective to improve the housing conditions of the poor directly rather than relying on the filtering process is an issue that remains subject to debate.

The Trade-Off Model

The trade-off model explains the predominance of high-quality housing on the city perimeter in terms of the trade-off between access to central locations and household demand for space (Muth, 1969). The model is based on the assumption that as incomes rise the rate at which households are willing to substitute access for cheaper land changes.

Space Versus Access

The model starts with the proposition that the land near the CBD is the most desired location because it provides greatest access to work and other amenities. Desirability decreases with distance from the CBD. Picture a household at location M in Figure 11.2. The location at M represents the optimal trade-off for the household between access to the central city, on the one hand, and lower land costs, on the other. Each household has two factors to consider in choosing its location. One consideration is the amount of space that it prefers. The larger the amount of space the household desires, the farther from the city center the household will tend to locate, all other things being equal. Second, costs of travel into the city must be considered. Travel costs include the out-of-pocket costs and opportunity costs of foregone activities while traveling. Empirical studies have shown that time costs of commuting are valued at about 25% of the traveler's hourly wage. These opposite pulls determine the slope of the individual access/price trade-off curve.

As the income of the family located at M increases, the household will want more land. The desire for more land will tend to tilt the locational choice toward the periphery where land is cheaper. However, the increased income will also increase the opportunity costs of commuting. The increased oppor-

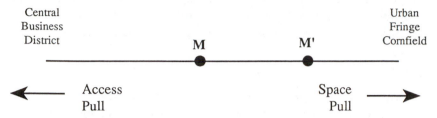

Figure 11.2. Space versus access as income rises. Initially, the household is in equilibrium at point M. As income increases, the household will relocate because the desire for more space plus the cheaper land near the fringe is stronger than the increased pull of the desire for better access. A relocation to M' would reflect the stronger space pull caused by the income increases.

tunity cost of travel will tend to orient the optimal location toward the city's center where access is best. Which pull will dominate cannot be determined theoretically.

Evidence in the United States indicates that the outward movement effect is much greater than the travel cost effect. Therefore, neighborhoods of higher-income families are more likely to locate in the metropolitan area's outer ring. Many South American and European countries have not experienced the tendency of families to move farther from the city center as incomes increase. The contrast suggests (not surprisingly) that the trade-off is affected by attitudes regarding the value of nonwork time, images of the city-preferred living accommodations, and other socio-psychological factors.

Trade-Offs in the Multiple Nuclear City

There are increasingly multiple points within a metropolitan area that represent points of substantial access. The CBD is no longer the controlling access point in most major metropolitan areas. During the past 20 years, jobs have shifted from the central city to suburban locations, so the assumption of minimum transportation costs at the CBD are unrealistic for most families. The CBD remains the site of the plurality of jobs, but many large business agglomerations exist throughout most metropolitan areas.

In light of the new realities of urban form, the trade-off theory should be modified to describe households as examining trade-offs between a variety of jobs and residential locations. Within limited areas, land costs may actually decline, moving toward the central city. However, the generalization that preferences for increased space are more easily attainable at the urban fringe remains valid, particularly if newly constructed housing is desired.

The Cultural Agglomeration Model

The filtering and trade-off models explain the emergence of neighborhoods with similar incomes. Cultural factors are also important in neighborhood formation. People often believe they will find congenial friends or mates (or mates for their children) if they live near people like themselves. Thus neighborhoods of individuals with similar social characteristics will form based on social desires and agglomeration economics.

The services that some ethnic groups desire may be provided economically only if economies of scale can be achieved. Therefore, groups may form neighborhoods around stores that reflect their buying patterns. Aged individuals may congregate in neighborhoods that provide certain services, whereas families in the child-rearing stage may be overrepresented in a neighborhood with recreational facilities and good schools. Ethnic groups may form neighborhoods around a church. The changing demographic composition of a neighborhood portends a change in the services available in the area. Besides the forces that draw like groups together, there are discriminatory processes at work that tend to isolate poor and minority families.

Socially homogeneous neighborhoods have been criticized. Sarkissian (1976) argued that greater socioeconomic diversity in neighborhoods would

- help promote a stable social mix of community leaders
- provide alternative role models for individuals in the lower class
- encourage artistic diversity
- encourage cultural cross-fertilization
- increase opportunities for the poor
- reduce social tension
- avoid residential instability
- help prepare residents for life in a diverse world

The desirability of neighborhood diversity has been recognized and encouraged in some local development programs. However, the forces tending to segregate households along income and racial lines continue to be strong.

The Tiebout Model

Tiebout (1956) developed an informative model that describes the relationship between local government programs, taxes, and housing prices. His model represents an ingenious and useful application of the fundamental concepts of supply and demand. The Tiebout model is normally considered part of the public finance literature because it emphasizes the role of government services as a main attractor and taxes as a major detractor in creating neighborhood amenities. The model is discussed here because it also has implications for neighborhood change. In fact, in a metropolitan context, a small suburb is similar to the neighborhood as a reference point. There are four necessary postulates of the model.

First, a house purchased in a particular area embodies a bundle of services that vary depending on government activity. For instance, the housing services in a particular neighborhood may or may not include garbage collection, adequate police service, and quality public schools. These government-related services are in addition to the private housing services of the shelter and land. The model can be extended to include nongovernmental amenities that neighborhood residents receive, such as prestige, sociable neighbors, and quiet.

Second, individuals form preferences for an area based on the public services and other features of the external environment together with the private services of the house.

Third, different levels of service provisions will often result in different tax burdens among municipalities. Other things equal—that is, assuming equal service levels—the higher the tax burden the smaller will be the housing demand in a jurisdiction. Negative features of the neighborhood, such as unsafe conditions, higher insurance premiums, and pollution, can be treated similar to increased taxes.

Fourth, individuals differ in their preference and willingness to pay for private housing services and also for the goods associated with housing in a particular neighborhood. In other words, some individuals will be willing and able to pay different amounts for packages of neighborhood amenities and disamenities.

To understand the implications of the Tiebout model, assume that the legislative body in a small suburb voted to construct a major sports facility to include tennis courts, swimming pools, and a gymnasium with an indoor track, weight rooms, and sauna. The facility would be available free to community residents only. Property taxes would increase by an average of $100 per household per year to finance the project. The tax boost includes maintenance and repayment of bonds issued to support construction. How will the change in the amenity-disamenity mix affect housing prices and the characteristics of individuals living in the neighborhood?

First, some residents will be deterred from living in the area because the higher taxes are more of a burden to them than the value they place on the sports facility. In other words, they would no longer be willing to pay as much as they previously would have paid for a house in the same area. Demand among this group will decrease. Conversely, other individuals will be attracted to the municipality because they value the services of the sports complex more than they object to the extra costs. Thus some individuals will move out of the suburb to avoid the high taxes while others will move into the area because they want access to the complex.

The process of housing adjustment is best illustrated by the supply and demand model. Assume there are two groups of individuals, one termed the"sports nuts" and the other the "misers." The sports nuts are willing to pay for the extra facilities; the misers are not. The responses can be analyzed by reference to Figure 11.3. Prior to the sports complex construction, the demand by the two groups may have been similar. Thus the pre-sports-complex demand curve D in Figures 11.3a and 11.3b is the same for both the sports nuts and the misers. After the increase in services and taxes, however, the demand for housing in the area increases among sports nuts and decreases among misers. The isolated effect of the sports nuts is to increase prices from $500 to $600 per month. The isolated effect of the misers is to decrease housing prices from $500 to $400. The combined effect depends on which group has the largest shift in demand. Figure 11.3c is drawn on the assumption that the sport nut effect outweighs the miser effect. Hence housing prices rise to $580. Of course, the combined outcome could have resulted in lower property values; it depends on tastes and preferences.

The adjustment process is also accompanied by spatial rearrangement of households. The misers will sell their property to both avoid higher taxes and capture the higher prices that the sports nuts are willing to pay. When they sell their properties, misers will move to an area providing a better service/tax mix for their preferences. Sports nuts, however, will move into the suburb. In Tiebout's (1956) words, spatial arrangement amounts to "lumping together of all similar tastes for the purpose of making joint purchases" (p. 417).

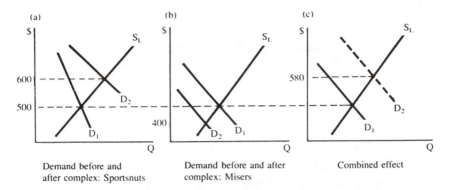

Figure 11.3. The Tiebout model. The public improvements made the community more desirable for some residents, but the higher taxes to finance the improvements made the community less desirable for others. The combined effect cannot be determined theoretically, although in this example the net effect was to increase property values.

Individuals "voted with their feet" for the combination of amenities and disamenities they preferred.

The Tiebout hypothesis has been tested on several occasions. Oates (1969b), for instance, found that, ceteris paribus, "property values would be higher in a community the more attractive its package of public goods" (p. 940). Oates was the first to show that property tax increases tend to be capitalized into the current value of property. School expenditures exert a particularly significant positive impact in the municipalities examined by Oates. Clotfelter (1975) documented spatial rearrangement as a result of school desegregation using the Tiebout model as the basic theoretical framework. Jud and Bennet (1986) showed that school quality has been a significant factor in shaping interurban locations even holding racial composition constant. Differences in property insurance have also been shown to affect housing prices (MacDonald, Murdoch, and White, 1987).

An important implication of the Tiebout model is that individuals select areas that provide their preferred mix of services and taxes. Better services and lower taxes will increase housing demand within the area. Individuals will express their preferences by attempting to move into the district—a process termed "voting with their feet." If property values increase more than property values in nearby jurisdictions, one may infer that a possible reason may be that local officials are providing a desired mix of taxes and services. Some observers have suggested that relative changes in housing prices by a measure of the performance of public officials. However, nongovernmental actions, such as establishment of an attractive shopping center nearby or a neighborhood escort service for the elderly, will also change the amenity-disamenity mix.

The Aggregate Economic Fallout Model

Hill and Bier (1989) developed a model of neighborhood change that links changes in the economic base to neighborhood formation. Changes in the national economy may affect particular local sectors, and these impacts are, in turn, translated into changes in neighborhood characteristics. Their model suggests that neighborhoods have identifiable links to occupations and industries in the local economy. For instance, one neighborhood may have a disproportionate number of residents who are blue-collar workers in an automobile plant. Another neighborhood may be composed primarily of high-income professionals in the service sector, such as lawyers and bankers. A layoff in the automobile plant is likely to result in deterioration and lower property values in the neighborhood linked to the auto sector. Neighborhoods with occupational-industrial mixes that are not linked to the auto sector would be affected only indirectly. Hill and Bier used data from Cleveland to show that both the positive and negative effects of industrial and occupational changes in the local economy spilled into neighborhoods where workers lived, affecting poverty levels and housing costs.

Recap of Neighborhood Change Models

The five models of neighborhood formation and change complement one another. The filtering model best explains the adaptive adjustments that occur during neighborhood change. The trade-off model explains why wealthy families lead the suburbanization movement and create a process that allows filtering to occur. The concept of mobile externalities also shows how pressures from within the urban center can create pressures for wealthy families to move outward. The concept of social agglomeration helps explain social, economic, and ethnic characteristics of neighborhoods. The Tiebout model shows how neighborhood characteristics affect housing prices and how individuals "vote with their feet" for neighborhood characteristics and public services associated with a property. Neighborhood characteristics are also affected by macroeconomic forces. Although in some instances one model may have more explanatory power than another, in most cases each model provides an important perspective on neighborhood development.

Housing Segregation

Residential segregation is an obvious characteristic of most American cities. Economic prospects of Blacks and other minorities are hurt by housing discrimination in several important ways. First, their housing choices are limited. Blacks and other groups tend to be confined to areas that may not suit their housing preferences and may not offer attractive appreciation potential. Second, because of housing patterns, Blacks and other minorities may have less access to jobs on the metropolitan periphery where jobs are growing most rapidly. Geographic segregation raises search costs for suburban jobs. Most jobs are obtained through informal referrals from other employees or signs posted in stores, so it is difficult for individuals in distressed neighborhoods to know of job openings. Furthermore, it has been speculated that housing segregation contributes to the difficulty a member of a minority group has in attaining suburban clerking jobs because there will be fewer minority customers. Consequently, suburban retail stores may be more likely to discriminate. Third, confinement of minorities in inner-city neighborhoods may also contribute to higher travel costs if a suburban job is obtained. Besides the negative impact on minorities, housing segregation may contribute to an atmosphere that hinders economic development prospects for the metropolitan region (Rusk, 1993). Thus reducing housing segregation will have a positive economic consequence.

The existence of segregated housing markets does not prove housing discrimination. Housing segregation could result from factors other than discrimination. First, the relatively low incomes of Black families and other minority groups could account for a significant amount of segregation as low-income households locate in areas of low-quality housing.[2] However, income differences would not account for the segregation of low-income Blacks from low-income Whites. The degree of racial discrimination is much greater than would be anticipated based on income. Second, the social agglomeration model implies that segregated neighborhoods could result from a voluntary process. However, several empirical studies have shown that Blacks are more segregated than other ethnic minorities, a finding that suggests that racial differences are recognized in the operation of housing markets.

There are several mechanisms of segregation. First, Blacks may hesitate moving into White neighborhoods because they fear they will not be welcome. Second, landlords and home sellers often deliberately discriminate. Although discrimination on the basis of race is illegal, subtle forms of discouragement can have the effect of maintaining all-White neighborhoods. Third, real estate salespersons steer minority buyers into areas already dominated by the particular minority group and fail to inform Black buyers of homes for sale in White areas. Salespersons have defended this practice by saying they try to show buyers houses in neighborhoods where the buyers would want to live, yet the effect is to maintain housing segregation.

Several studies by the U.S. Department of Housing and Urban Development examined practices of racial discrimination. Black couples and White couples responded separately to housing advertisements (Yinger, 1986). The analysis indicated that Black couples experienced some form of discrimination when responding to 27% of the advertised vacancies. The extent of discrimination was higher in the case of rental housing than in owner-occupied housing. The primary mechanism appears to be that housing agents promote their economic interests by abiding by the racial prejudice of current or potential customers. Another study in Dallas (U.S. Department of Housing and Urban Development, 1979) found that Hispanics were likely to experience the same level of discrimination as Blacks did.

Financial institutions also engage in discrimination against Black neighborhoods through their lending practices (Shlay, 1989). Several empirical studies have shown that lenders are less likely to extend loans in Black neighborhoods, even after holding constant for housing values and community income. The difficulty that homeowners experience in getting loans means that the housing stock occupied by Blacks will tend to be renter rather than owner occupied. This may decrease neighborhood stability. Worse yet, lack of mortgage loans will decrease property values because few individuals can afford to purchase a home without a mortgage. As property values soften, few potential buyers will be interested in buying in the area, continuing a cycle of decline.

⊠ Housing Policy Debates

Local officials have considerable latitude in designing urban housing programs. Several policy issues need to be addressed in the development of local housing programs. The issues are described here as polar positions to

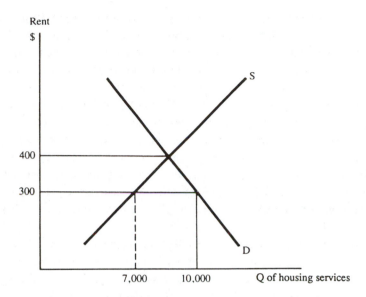

Figure 11.4. Rent control. The controlled rent of $300 per month will result in a shortage of 300 units of housing services.

make the distinctions as sharp as possible. However, policymakers often must select the appropriate middle ground.

Rent Control Versus Market Forces

The role of rent control in local housing policy is a perennial issue. Several cities have enacted rent controls. Tenant groups in cities where rents have increased rapidly have pressured their local legislators to enact controls. Rent controls take many forms. In some cities, rents are allowed to increase at a given amount per period. Often, the controls are lifted when one tenant moves and a new base is established. Even within a city, some units may be rent controlled and others not, depending on the time, the location, and the conditions of construction.

In spite of the variety of rent controls, the issue is generally analyzed by the simple supply and demand curve shown in Figure 11.4. The market rent per unit of housing services is $400 per month. However, the rent is controlled at $300 per month. Consequently, more housing services are demanded at the controlled price than building owners are willing and able to supply.

The arguments for rent control are generally based on equity. Proponents of rent control argue that tenants may be exploited if building owners are allowed to raise rents according to what the market will bear. The reasons for increases are frequently attributed to neighborhood or communitywide factors as opposed to actions of individual property owners. Therefore, tenants, as part of the community, might be as entitled to some of the benefits of increased community desirability as much as property owners are. Furthermore, the buildings subject to control are already in existence and were built based on rent expectations in a previous period. Consequently, rent-control proponents view rent increases (above increases needed for tax and operating cost factors) as windfalls. Luger (1986) has shown that there are instances in which rent controls serve the interests of a majority of the voters, so rent controls may make political sense.

Opponents of rent control believe that rent controls are inefficient. They point out that if rents are prevented from increasing, property owners will reduce the housing stock. The housing supply will shrink until the supply is consistent with the lower-than-market rents. Mechanisms for decreasing the quantity of housing services include reducing maintenance levels, abandonment, providing fewer amenities, and lower rates of new housing construction.

Furthermore, the problem of rationing will remain. If rents are below the equilibrium, building managers will have to select incoming tenants. Criteria for choosing which tenants will occupy below-market-rent properties could include race and a willingness to pay kick-backs to the managers (an under-the-table means of raising rents).

New measures to skirt the intent of rent controls may also be attempted. Landlords may convert rental units to condominiums or tear down a rent-controlled building and construct a new one that is either not subject to controls or subject to a less restrictive set of controls. Instances of property owners deliberately cutting heat or vandalizing their own buildings to encourage tenants to leave have been reported. Moorehouse (1987) has shown that landlords have lowered the benefits that tenants receive from rent control by reducing housing maintenance and other techniques. However, some benefits continue to accrue to tenants even after 25 years of rent control.

Proponents of rent control have argued that many abuses can be avoided by a well-designed and administered rent-control law. However, most economists oppose rent controls because of the inherent inefficiency and because the administrative costs needed to prevent abuses are substantial.

Income Support Versus Housing Assistance

One of the classic arguments in welfare economics is that individuals would be better off receiving cash grants rather than an equal-valued amount of in-kind transfers. Consider a family receiving $200 per month as a rent supplement. The traditional argument is that if the family were given $200 in cash rather than a housing grant they would be better off. At the very least, the family would continue to spend the money on housing, so they would be no worse off. If they choose to spend the funds to purchase an alternative mix of goods—say, $100 on housing and $100 on food—then they must be better off because each individual is the best judge of his or her own welfare (and as a corollary, parents are the best judges of their children's welfare). Therefore, if the purpose of housing programs is to improve the lot of the families they are designed to serve, income rather than housing subsidies of various types should be given.

There are two rebuttals. First, individuals may not know what is best for themselves. Second, individuals may know what is best for them, but they may not know what is best for society. Substandard housing is not only an undesirable (and possibly the most visible) manifestation of poverty, it may also create other social problems such as arson, street crime, homicide, and so forth. Thus aid designed to alleviate housing conditions is intended to help ameliorate problems in the larger society while helping the direct recipients. The argument about cash grants versus strings-attached transfers is a variant of the more general question of how much discretion recipients of aid should be allowed. The trend in housing policy has been toward greater discretion in choice of housing, but the cash transfer argument has not been accepted as policy.

A housing experiment conducted by the U.S. Department of Housing and Urban Development indicated that the income elasticity of demand for housing among low-income families is quite low. A 10% increase in income may induce individuals to spend only 3% to 4% more for housing. Thus, if given a cash grant, the recipient will likely use only a small percentage of the grant to upgrade his or her housing. Even if housing vouchers are provided, households will substitute the voucher and use the money they would otherwise have spent on housing for other purposes.

In practice, it is very difficult to prevent families from substituting some housing assistance for other goods. For instance, suppose a family was spending $300 per month on housing prior to receiving assistance. Suppose the government provides a $100-per-month housing subsidy. If the family moves to a $325 per month unit, then $75 of the housing assistance will be used for nonhousing assistance. The substitution could occur even if the government assistance were provided in the form of a $100 voucher that could be used only for housing.

Supply Versus Demand Side Assistance

A related debate concerns whether housing assistance should be provided by increasing the housing stock or by providing low-income families with the means to rent better housing through vouchers or other types of assistance.

One advantage of a supply-side strategy is that the construction or rehabilitation of low-income housing units will create additional jobs, albeit temporary ones. Some economic development officials have successfully combined housing rehabilitation with training in the building trades for low-skilled unemployed persons. Increases in housing supply will also reduce rents. The lower rents will not only help individuals directly receiving assistance but may lower other rents as well. Lower rents will leave families with more discretionary income that will be spent largely on goods and services purchased locally.

Demand-side assistance can deliver assistance efficiently and at a lower cost than new construction. Also, the assistance can be targeted according to need and increased or decreased as needs change. Under voucher programs, low-income consumers have greater choice than when they must choose between public housing or publicly subsidized rehabilitation units.

Ghetto Dispersal Versus Ghetto Improvement

The problem of housing segregation has led many policymakers to argue that policies should strive to disperse the large concentrations of Blacks in the inner city. If assisted housing were more integrated, Blacks would have better opportunities to secure jobs in suburban areas and lower travel costs if they obtained suburban jobs. Furthermore, if more Blacks were represented in currently nearly all-White areas, employers would be less likely to discriminate against Blacks in hiring practices. Provisions of subsidized housing in the suburbs and enforcement of fair-housing laws have been the primary tools to encourage housing desegregation.

An alternative policy approach has been termed the "gilded ghetto." Some observers believe that dispersing Blacks and other minorities to the suburbs would not open up significant job opportunities because discrimination in hiring practices will persist. Furthermore, dispersal of Black populations throughout the metropolitan area would likely weaken Black political strength. Assuming voters are more likely to vote for someone of the same race, Blacks would have a difficult time being elected if a metropolitan area were spatially integrated. However, Black political control of urban ghettos is virtually assured. Thus Blacks are more likely to be assured of some representation in city, state, and national legislatures.

Dwelling Unit Versus Neighborhood Development

Closely related to the previous issue is the question of whether the focus of policies should be to improve the house or to improve the larger environment in which low-income families live. The condition of housing units among the poor has improved dramatically since the 1940s, yet there has been little improvement in the public perception of the "problem" of slums. The home itself may be but a small part of the environment. Social programs to eliminate crime, provide recreation, and clean up neighborhoods may be equally important.

⊠ Neighborhood Commercial Development

Much of the neighborhood focus has been on maintaining a viable housing stock that will attract residents. Commercial development is also part of neighborhood development. In fact, there is a vicious circle between business development, housing, and neighborhood change. As the population declines, businesses lose customers and are more likely to fail. As neighborhood businesses close, the area will likely become less attractive for residents. Furthermore, the closure of neighborhood businesses results in local job loss. Additional problems may emerge, such as building abandonment, negative community images, and crime. In light of the web of related problems, many local development planners have focused efforts on neighborhood business development. One of the early movements for neighborhood development has been termed "ghetto economic development." In part, the interest in neighborhood economic development was encouraged by a belief that some neighborhoods are cut off from the mainstream metropolitan economy.

A traditional economic approach to neighborhood development is to view the area as a small city. Low-income communities in particular are considered as having few products or services, including skilled labor to export. However, such neighborhoods have high imports because families must purchase most of their products outside the neighborhood because there are few local businesses. Thus income tends to leave the area quickly (i.e., the neighborhood multiplier is small).

Neighborhood and community groups are often concerned about traditional economic development programs because they believe that local economic development officials place too much emphasis on helping big businesses or focus excessively on downtown developments at the expense of small, neighborhood businesses. Economic development officials may consider programs to help low income neighborhood businesses or to improve the neighborhood infrastructure as "welfare" programs rather than economic development programs. Thus neighborhood programs may receive less attention and funds. Consequently, parts of a city may prosper while low income neighborhoods decline. To address this concern, many neighborhood organizations have attempted to serve as a political power base to help the small, neighborhood businesses deal with city hall.

Wiewel and his associates (1993) identified several forms of neighborhood economic development:

- *Business retention* programs use neighborhood organizations to promote the stabilization of existing businesses and industrial districts. Community organizers may play a leadership role in assessing business needs. Neighborhood groups may also help neighborhood businesses secure low-interest loans, tax breaks, or technical assistance. Often, small businesses may not even know that such city programs are available, and neighborhood-based business development efforts can help provide such information.

- *Commercial revitalization* has an entire commercial district as a target. Often, it is more effective to stabilize a neighborhood business strip by focusing on the entire area rather than on individual businesses. Neighborhood groups may sponsor events designed to attract consumers to the district. They may encourage the formation of special districts for possible tax breaks or infrastructure assistance. Tax incremental financing has been used in commercial revitalization strategies. Tax incremental financing is based on the idea that improvements in property values in a target neighborhood should be respent in that district. Thus, if a business group secures resources to improve the physical appearance of the commercial district, the increased revenues that the city receives from imported property values will be respent in ways that continue to benefit the neighborhood.

- Some effort to encourage the *formation of new businesses* can help strengthen a neighborhood's economic base. Increases in local businesses mean that the income of residents will more likely be spent in the neighborhood, creating jobs through a multiplier effect. Businesses that take advantage of neighborhood features such as historic areas may attract spending from elsewhere. Entrepreneurship development is one way to encourage the development of new neighborhood businesses. The entrepreneurship strategy has the perspective that human resources in a neighborhood are underused. This strategy not only requires the training of neighborhood residents in entrepreneurial skills, but socioeconomic support needed to encourage innovation and risk may also be useful. Neighborhood entrepreneurs may know the resources and needs of the neighborhood better than nonresident investors and accordingly they will be in a better position to spot new business potential.

- Both encouragement of new business and support for existing businesses usually require capital. Financial institutions have been reluctant to extend loans to poor, inner-city neighborhoods in part because of the perceived higher risk. Also, many large financial institutions are not used to dealing with small, neighborhood businesses that may have unconventional accounting and business practices (Blair and Endres, 1994). Therefore, neighborhood development includes *encouraging local capital accumulation and investment.* Many community groups work with banks and other lenders to ensure that neighborhood businesses receive an adequate share of loans. The Community Reinvestment Act requires some financial institutions to document the share of loans made to various neighborhoods. It has been a tool for neighborhood groups to monitor capital flows into the neighborhood. Another strategy to increase the availability of capital has been the formation of community-based banks. Such institutions attempt to channel their assets into local businesses.

- Many inner-city neighborhoods are home to structurally unemployed workers. Neighborhoods can serve as the base for *job training and education* programs that will provide workers with the skills they need to secure jobs that later may be the source of additional neighborhood spending. Often, such programs can be provided in neighborhood schools, and the job skills that are taught may match neighborhood needs. Sometimes, large neighborhood businesses can be encouraged to hire newly trained neighborhood workers.

- Neighborhood groups may operate through direct political action to secure and increase *government programs,* such as construction that will make the neighborhood more attractive and thus support businesses. For instance, a commercial beautification program that might include new lighting, curbing, and store-front improvements may attract customers to local businesses. Such programs might not be forthcoming in neighborhoods with little political power.

There are numerous community groups that have made significant contributions to a city's economic development efforts. Some local development officials have been successful in learning the culture and customs of groups in such neighborhoods and have, therefore, been able to contribute to economic development successes. Similarly, community leaders have learned the "language of business." However, other local development officials have resisted working with small community or neighborhood groups because they see such activity as "welfare" and not economic development (Fitzgerald, 1993).

⊠   The Informal Economy: An Alternative Strategy

Many inner-city neighborhoods have hidden economic development resources in the form of informal economic activity (Blair & Endres, 1994). Informal economic activity may be defined as both extralegal and illegal-criminal transactions that are not properly reported to appropriate governmental agencies, such as the Internal Revenue Service. Most illegal activities clearly harm economic development efforts. However, activities that are otherwise legal but unreported are an important hidden development asset of primary concern here.

The potential development impact of the underground economy may be indicated by considering its size. The consensus of expert opinion is that the informal economy constitutes between 16% and 20% of national income. Feige (1989) suggested that the informal sector began to significantly outpace the mainstream economy in the mid-1970s, and future growth is likely to continue to outpace the formal economy.

Inner-City Neighborhoods

The informal economy is suspected to be particularly strong in inner-city neighborhoods where effective economic development policies may be needed most. One reason for its strength is that the opportunity cost of participating in informal activities is lower for individuals without mainstream employment opportunities. Second, informal activities allow individuals to circumvent means tests for certain government programs. Some families may find that combining government support and informal earnings is a feasible response to declining real value of government transfer programs. Third, a dense net of social and institutional relationships characteristic of some urban neighborhoods has been shown to be useful in supporting the formal economy. Word of mouth is important in informal activity. Fourth, the "cover" function is also provided in an inner-city environment because many commercial operations are small proprietorships in which tax avoidance is relatively easy and work rules or other regulations can be skirted. Fifth, inner-city neighborhoods have a higher portion of minorities, female-headed households, and immigrants. Case studies suggest that such groups are likely to participate in informal activities. Finally, lower incomes among inner-city residents may make it worthwhile for them to exert the extra effort necessary to find informal suppliers who may provide goods and services at a lower cost.

Development Policy

By focusing only on potential loss of tax revenue, many policymakers may fail to recognize potential policy implications that may help incorporate the productive informal economy into mainstream economic development planning.

First, urban policymakers may find it useful to systematically monitor productive informal activities. Such an approach may be critical to understanding changes in inner-city neighborhoods. Toward this end, observation techniques of anthropology will be as important as traditional survey research because informal sector participants are naturally reluctant to answer questionnaires honestly.

Second, the role of the informal sector in providing support for unemployed workers or individuals receiving public assistance is an important function of the unobserved sector. Many individuals combine welfare and other transfer payments with earnings from informal work. To the extent that informal activity enables welfare recipients and the working poor to maintain higher consumption levels, the extra spending will contribute to the support of neighborhood retail businesses. Furthermore, earnings from informal activities supplement transfer payments and may moderate pressure to increase welfare programs.

Informal work opportunities also provide a safety net for some workers who have income and wealth above the level to qualify for many public assistance programs but who are experiencing transitory unemployment. Income from informal activities may be a critical part of a financial package (including draw-down of savings, unemployment compensation, the earnings of additional family members, and so forth) that helps maintain at least a near-comparable living standard for some time after a layoff.

Third, for many new job entrants, the informal sector can be a "sandbox" in which they learn skills and make contacts that can lead to mainstream jobs.

Individuals with low productivity may develop both social and technical job skills that often help them obtain mainstream jobs. Minimum-wage laws, employer payroll taxes, and some work rules add to the cost of labor. Under these conditions, employers may find it unprofitable to hire low-productivity workers in the mainstream economy. Workers can be hired at lower cost in the informal sector. In the best cases, employees will use these experiences to increase their productivity and obtain better, mainstream jobs. Administrators of job-training programs may wish to build on informal experiences by encouraging individuals to participate in training programs while continuing their informal work. Unfortunately, some casual labor conditions may actually discourage job-skill enhancement by not rewarding improvements and not punishing sloppy work habits.

A strong case can be made for benign neglect in the enforcement of welfare work rules. It is reasonable to suppose that individuals who received public assistance while working off-the-books would have a better chance of becoming self-supporting than someone who received only public assistance. Informal work can often provide opportunities to develop contacts, skills, and work habits that enhance employment prospects in the formal sector, thus reducing public assistance dependency.

Fourth, because of their small size, informal activities tend to be very entrepreneurially oriented—and therefore good targets for entrepreneurial development programs. For some informal businesses, movement into the mainstream economy can stimulate growth by providing greater access to capital, encouraging advertising, and presenting opportunities for linkages and other mainstream firms. A challenge for policymakers is to help move informal businesses into the mainstream economy without destroying them. Movement into the formal economy might be expedited by a process that gradually imposes the requirements of mainstream businesses.

The job-creation process in the urban United States can be illustrated in the case of a small, informal business. A woman who provides off-the-books day-care services in her home may find it advantageous to report only a fraction of her income. As her business and care skills improve, she may recognize advantages of starting a formal, licenced facility with a few employees. Consequently, some or all of her services may shift from the informal to the formal sector. Development officials could play several roles in encouraging this process, including helping the business owner visualize the growth potential, advising the proprietor regarding various aspects of starting a business, minimizing complicated regulations, and assisting with start-up capital. Jane Jacobs (1969) described the economic development process as "adding new work to old." As development planners work with informal enterprises to add new, formal sector work, a useful twist on this well-known strategy may develop.

⊠ Summary

Housing improvements are often a direct objective of economic development. At the same time, attractive neighborhoods contribute to a community's quality of life and hence can be an important tool. The housing market can be analyzed using traditional supply and demand concepts. However, care must be taken to understand what the supply and price represent. It is useful to describe the quantity axis as "units of housing services" rather than a physical quantity. Price may be expressed as sale price of a stock of housing or as rent for a periodic flow of housing services. By discounting the present value of rents, one can convert between rents and sale prices.

The hedonic pricing model splits the housing service bundle into detailed components and uses statistical techniques, such as regression, to value each of the components. Characteristics that affect price include features of the property itself and those of the surrounding area. The market comparison approach is a "quick and dirty" application of the hedonic pricing method.

Real estate markets are imperfect, characterized by few buyers and sellers and imperfect information. Consequently, bargaining is an important part of real estate transactions, and specialists are needed to assist buyers and sellers. There is also a range of uncertainty regarding price.

Four complementary models of neighborhood formation were described. According to the filtering model, as their incomes rise, upper-income groups tend to purchase new housing on the urban periphery. The vacated houses become available to lower-income groups. The trade-off model emphasizes the space versus access trade-off. As incomes increase, the pull of cheaper space near the urban fringe increases more than the pull toward the central business district due to the desire for better access. Social forces are also important factors in neighborhood formation because individuals with similar tastes and backgrounds often live in the same areas. The Tiebout model describes the process in which individuals "vote with their feet" to live in the neighborhood that provides the best combination of housing unit, neighborhood amenities, public services, and housing prices. Improvements in neighborhood amenities, public services, and taxes become capitalized into property values. The aggregate economic fall-out model links neighborhood change to larger economic changes.

Residential segregation is significant in most American metropolitan areas. Housing patterns appear to be detrimental to economic prospects for African Americans and other minorities and may contribute to an atmosphere that hinders economic development.

Many policy analysts have been dissatisfied with existing low-income housing assistance programs. Issues include rent control versus market forces, income support versus housing assistance, supply versus demand assistance, ghetto dispersal versus gilding, and dwelling unit versus neighborhood development.

Strengthening commercial establishments has been a centerpiece of neighborhood development. Forms of neighborhood commercial development include business retention, commercial revitalization, new business formation, local capital accumulation, neighborhood-based job training, and direct government programs, such as construction. The informal or underground economy is active in many neighborhoods and offers a basis for building a neighborhood economy.

⊠ Notes

1. This section may be skipped without loss of continuity.
2. The lower incomes of Blacks could, in turn, be attributed to discrimination.

APPENDIX

⊠ Hedonic Pricing and
the Quality of Life

The importance of the quality of economic life has been discussed at various points thus far. It is an industrial location factor and is also a residential location factor. Early studies measured the quality of life with surveys. Individuals were asked to rank and weigh the value of various amenities and disamenities. Based on the survey findings, metropolitan areas and individual neighborhoods could be compared. The quality-of-life index for a region could be expressed as

$$QLI_j = \sum_{i=1}^{n} A_{ij} V_i ,$$ (11A-1)

where

QLI_j = quality of life index for region j
A_{ij} = quantity or level of amenity factor i in region j
V_i = value placed upon amenity i

The value of an amenity factor (V_i) could be positive or negative. For instance, sunshine is an amenity and thus would be valued positively, whereas particulate matter in the air would be a disamenity and would carry a negative value. Accordingly, areas with high levels of highly valued amenities and low values for disamenities would have a high QLI.

269

Although survey data may reflect opinion, relative values of various amenities are more difficult to assess. The majority of individuals surveyed may say that congestion is a disamenity. What are they willing to give up to relieve congestion? Although surveys may reflect opinion, economists normally prefer to use values reflected by market activity. Although surveys are useful, many individuals have difficulty estimating the actual monetary value of amenities such as sunshine, and economists normally prefer to use values reflected in the market. Market values represent actual behavior regarding the selective worth of amenities.

To better quantify amenities' values, economists have used hedonic pricing techniques. Rosen (1974) suggested that a location is a bundle of wages, rents, and amenities. Individuals will trade off among elements in the bundle. For instance, someone may accept lower wages and pay higher rents in order to live in an amenity-rich area. Roback (1982) showed that interregional differences in amenity differences are reflected in land rent differences and/or wage differences. If individuals are in spatial equilibrium—that is, if they have no incentives to move and if the local housing and job markets are in equilibrium—then the premiums or discounts accepted by individuals in their wages and rents will reflect the value they place on amenities associated with that area. Amenities should decrease wages and/or increase housing costs, whereas disamenities should be associated with the higher wages and/or lower housing costs, other things equal.

Blomquist, Berger, and Hoehn (1988) developed two hedonic models to explain differences in rents and wages. Their sample consisted of over 34,000 housing units in 253 counties. The housing equation expresses housing expenditures as a function of characteristics of the housing unit (age of structure, number of units at an address, number of baths, and so forth) and 16 county amenities (shown in column 1 of Table 11.A1):

$$HE = f(CIH_1 \ldots CIH_n, A_1 \ldots A_{16}), \qquad (11A\text{-}2)$$

where

HE   = monthly housing expenditures
CIH_i = characteristics of the individual housing units
A_j = level of 16 county-level amenities.

Similarly, the wage equation reflects both individual workers' characteristics (age, education, race, etc.) and the same 16 county-level amenities used in the housing equation:

$$W = f(IWC_1 \ldots IWC_n, A_1 \ldots A_{16}), \qquad (11A\text{-}3)$$

TABLE 11A.1 Linearized Parameter Estimates, Full Implicit Prices, and Quality-of-Life Index Components

Amenity Variable (wage sample mean and unit of measurement)	Monthly Housing Expenditure Equation[a]	Hourly Wage Equation[b]	Full Implicit Price[c] (in dollars)
Precipitation (32.0 inches per year)	−1.047	−.0144	23.50
Humidity (68.3%)	−2.127	.0065	−43.42
Heating degree days (4,326 per year)	−.0136	−.0001	−.08
Cooling degree days (1,162 per year)	−.0760	−.0001	−.36
Wind speed (8.89 miles per hour)	11.88	.0961	−97.51
Sunshine (61.1% of possible)	2.135	−.0091	48.52
Coast (.330, = 1 if county on coast)	32.51	−.0310	467.72
Violent crime (647 per 100,000 population per year)	.0434	.0006	−1.03
Teacher-pupil ratio (.0799 teachers per pupil)	635.3	−5.451	21,250.00
Visibility (15.8 miles)	−.8302	−.0026	−3.41
Total suspended particulates (73.2 micrograms per cubic meter)	−.5344	−.0024	−.36
NPDES effluent discharges (1.51 county)	−7.458	−.0051	−76.68
Landfill waste (477 hundred million metric tons per county)	.0095	.0001	−.11
Superfund sites (.883 per county)	13.42	.1069	−106.07
Treatment, storage, and disposal sites (46.4 per county)	.2184	.0013	−.58
Central city (.290, = 1 if residence in central city)	40.75	−.4537	645.02
R^2	.6624	.3138	

SOURCE: Glenn C. Blomquist, Mark C. Berger, and John P. Hoehn, "New Estimates of the Quality of Life in Urban Areas," *American Economic Review,* March 1988, pp. 89-107.
NOTES: a. The dependent variable is actual or imputed monthly housing expenditures. Control variables included in the housing-hedonic regression but not reported are units at address, age of structure, stories, rooms, bedrooms, bathrooms, condominium status, central air, sewer, lot size exceeds 1 acre, renter status, and renter interaction terms for each of these variables.

b. The dependent variable is annual earnings divided by the product of annual weeks worked and usual hours per week. Control variables included in the wage-hedonic regression but not reported are experience (age-schooling-6), experience squared, gender interaction with experience and experience squared, race, gender, gender interaction with race, marital status, gender interaction with marital status, gender interaction with children under 18, schooling, disabled, school enrollment status, dummies for five of six broad occupation groups, and percentage industry covered by unions.

c. The full implicit price is the sum of the annual housing expenditure and wage differentials. To obtain an annual household full implicit price, the housing coefficients are multiplied by 12 (months per year) and the wage coefficients are multiplied by (1.54) (37.85) (42.79), the product of the sample means of workers per household, hours per week, and weeks per year.

where

W = hourly wage rate

IWC = individual worker characteristics

A_i = level of the 16 amenities

The amenity parameter estimates for both the housing and wage equations are shown in Table 11.A1. The parameter estimates for characteristics of the individual housing units (CIH_i) and individual worker characteristics (IWC_i) were calculated but are excluded from the table.

Humidity is an example of a disamenity. Column 1 of Table 11A.1 indicates that housing prices fell ($2.127 per month) and wages increased ($.0065 per hour) in an area for each percentage increase in humidity. However, the teacher-pupil ratios caused rents to increase and wages to fall, indicating that individuals were willing to accept higher rents and lower wages to live in areas with a higher teacher-to-pupil ratio, presumably indicating a better quality of education.

For some amenities, the values given by the housing equation and the wage equation are inconsistent. For instance, the effluent dischargers variable decreases monthly housing expenditures by $7.458 per discharger, suggesting that it is a disamenity. It also decreases the wage rate by $.0051 per hour, suggesting that the presence of effluent dischargers is an amenity. To determine whether effluent dischargers is an amenity or a disamenity, it is necessary to determine whether the wage effect or the housing effect is larger. The addition of the housing and wage variables will also allow a value to be set on each amenity.

Column 3 of Table 11A.1 shows the sum of the annualized housing expenditure and wage differentials. To annualize the housing coefficient, the monthly differential is multiplied by 12. To annualize the wage coefficient, the hourly differential is multiplied by the average number of hours worked per year. The annual amenity value is determined by changing the sign of the housing differential (to show a positive value for the amenity) and adding the annualized values for housing and rent to provide the estimate of amenity value shown in column 3 of Table 11A.1. For instance, in the case of effluent dischargers, it is not surprising that the housing effect (which indicated a disamenity) outweighs the wage differential. The results indicate a marginal amenity value of $76.68 for water effluent discharges. The value of the central-city amenity factor is interesting. Although central-city housing expenditures are lower than else-where in the metropolitan areas as are wages of central-city residents, these appear to be the result of other factors in the hedonic models. When the value of living in the central city is isolated, that is, when other amenities exist (other things held equal), central-city residence has a positive amenity value of $113.

Column 3 shows the implicit price for each quality-of-life indicator. The implicit price represents V_1 (monetary value of an amenity) in Equation 11A-1. Because the level of each amenity factor is known for each county in the study, a quality-of-life index can be constructed through the application of Equation 11A-1. The estimated value of each of the 16 amenity factors was multiplied by that amenity's level in each metropolitan area and the results summed.

TABLE 11A.2 Quality-of-Life Index Values[a] for Large Metropolitan Areas[b] (in dollars)

Denver-Boulder, CO	1,197.36
San Diego, CA	980.83
Phoenix, AZ	870.69
Anaheim-Santa Ana-Garden Grove, CA	803.49
Nassau-Suffolk, NY	687.80
Los Angeles-Long Beach, CA	667.64
Tampa-St. Petersburg, FL	191.57
San Francisco-Oakland, CA	139.55
Riverside-San Bernardino-Ontario, CA	135.46
Philadelphia, PA; New Jersey	9.21
Washington, D.C.; Maryland; Virginia	5.08
Newark, NJ	−11.48
Atlanta, GA	−25.74
Seattle-Everett, WA	−124.18
Cleveland, OH	−190.62
Pittsburgh, PA	−330.90
New York, NY; New Jersey	−369.20
Minneapolis-St. Paul, MN; Wisconsin	−372.20
Dallas-Fort Worth, TX	−399.70
Baltimore, MD	−422.70
Chicago, IL	−822.80
Houston, TX	−948.40
Detroit, MI	−968.00
St. Louis, MO; Illinois	−990.10

SOURCE: M. Berger and G. C. Blomquest, "Income, Opportunities and the Quality of Life of Urban Residents," in *Urban Change and Poverty,* edited by M. G. H. McGeary and L. E. Lynn. (Washington, DC: National Academy Press, 1988.)

NOTES: a. The Quality-of-Life Index (QOLI) is measured in 1979 dollars. The difference in index values represent the annual premiums that households are willing to pay for differences in amenities in different metropolitan areas. The values reported are taken from a study by Berger et al. (1987) that ranks 185 metropolitan areas by quality of life.

b. Listed are 29 standard metropolitan statistical areas (SMSAs) with a 1980 population exceeding 1.5 million. The 1980 definition of an SMSA is used. Boston (Massachusetts) and Miami (Florida) are omitted because sufficient data were not available to estimate the parameters for the QOLI. The mean QOLI for the 24 SMSAs is −11.95.

Table 11A.2 shows the quality-of-life index for several major metropolitan areas (Berger and Blomquist, 1988, p. 96). Whether the results are consistent with popular expressions of where the areas with a high quality of life are will be left to others to decide. The main point is that Blomquist and his associates illustrated a technique allowing quality-of-life comparisons between counties. To compare quality of life among neighborhoods within a county, a similar technique could be used but the variables indicating life quality would have to reflect factors for which neighborhood-level data are available, and the wage variable might not be useful because a metropolitan area is usually a single geographic labor market.

12

Metropolitan Government and Finance

When we think about the role of government in economic development, there is a tendency to focus on activities that directly affect business decisions such as subsidies, special infrastructure, tax abatements, and so forth. However, a more important role may be performing a variety of traditional tasks well, creating an overall atmosphere that encourages economic development. A well-functioning government can contribute to the elusive but important "business climate."

The primary purpose of this chapter is to examine major public finance issues as they relate to local economic development.

⊠ Governmental Functions in a Spatial Context

Local governments that either over- or underprovide government services can detract from economic development prospects. Musgrave (1959), in a classic analysis of federal government functions, concluded that government has three basic functions: maintaining a stable economy, providing an adequate distribution of income, and ensuring the appropriate production of goods. A single local government cannot significantly affect national economic growth. They lack tools of monetary and nonfiscal policy, yet economic development directly represents local stabilization activities. This section will describe distribution and allocation activities that influence economic development, although the roles are less recognized.

Distribution

Distribution activities refer to government activity designed to ensure the appropriate distribution of income. It is generally believed that income distribution activities should be a function of the federal government. If a state or local government attempted excessive redistribution programs, an influx of the poor and an exodus of the wealthy could be anticipated. In practice, state and local governments have a variety of small redistribution programs. Many local services are provided primarily because they help the poor. The most widely discussed welfare program is Aid to Families with Dependent Children (AFDC), which is principally a state program although it receives federal monies. Many analysts have contended that state differences in AFDC payments influence the potential recipients' choices of residence. Counties and other local governments have general relief programs, food pantry programs, and so forth, so there are variations in benefit levels even within a metropolitan area.

Distribution activities are conceptually distinct from the government decisions regarding what types of goods to produce (allocation). Nevertheless, state and local governments are continually mixing distribution and allocation functions. For instance, there are many services that are financed by tax dollars, yet they are received more or less equally by everyone in the district. The cost of the service falls disproportionately on the wealthy, who tend to pay more taxes.[1] Therefore, many goods and services provided by local governments tend to redistribute income even when the purpose of the local program is not redistributive.

Allocation

Allocation activities deal with the goods-providing functions of government. State and local governments probably have a major role in the allocation of resources. Three types of goods provided are pure public goods, goods with externalities, and merit goods.

Pure Public Goods

Pure public goods can be consumed by one person without diminishing the consumption of that same good by anyone else (i.e., the marginal cost of an extra consumer is zero) and where exclusion of potential consumers is not feasible. If goods have either of the characteristics of a pure public good, the private market will not provide the good in optimal quantities. If the marginal cost of an additional person consuming the good were zero, then why should anyone be excluded even if they could not pay? But if no one paid, how would production be financed without tax subsidies?

National defense is a classic example of a pure public good. Everyone consumes the same amount of national defense, and nonpayers cannot be excluded. If national defense were financed privately, rational individuals (in the economic sense of utility maximizing) would refuse to pay because their contribution would not affect the level of services received. This is a typical free-rider problem.

There are also goods that have characteristics of "publicness" only within the confines of a smaller geographic area, such as police or fire protection. Within a jurisdiction, everyone may receive similar benefits regardless of whether or not they pay. For instance, streets that are safe for taxpayers are also safe for nontaxpayers. It is also often impractical to exclude nonpayers from many types of amenities, such as a riverfront walkway. Accordingly, governments must provide public goods if they are to be provided at all (and force individuals to pay through the coercive means of taxation). The shared nature of some public goods implies that more than one business can benefit from some expenditures. Consequently, infrastructure improvements that enhance business prospects for a variety of firms or even projects that help firms in a particular cluster may have a greater "bang for the buck" than narrowly focused subsidies that assist only one company.

The Tiebout Model Again

The Tiebout model has important implications for the allocation activities of local governments. Tiebout (1956) showed that under certain conditions individuals would move to communities that provided their preferred mix of government services and taxes. Individuals would "vote with their feet." The conditions necessary for citizens to vote with their feet are more closely approximated in the context of residential choice within a metropolitan area than in the context of interstate or international locational choice because relocation costs are lower.

Eberts and Gornberg (1989) used the Tiebout model as the framework for their hypothesis that if local governments were forced to compete with one another they would operate more efficiently. Inefficient governments would be constrained by citizens voting with their feet. They found that the greater the number of general-purpose governments within a metropolitan areas, the smaller the share of personal income given to government. In other words, competition among general-purpose governments constrains local public spending.

Externalities

Goods with externalities (spillovers) are another instance where local governments should alter the allocation choices of the private sector to ensure that the proper quantity of goods is produced. Externalities may be either positive or negative. Positive externalities provide benefits to third parties, whereas negative externalities impose costs on third parties. The market will tend to underproduce goods that have positive externalities and overproduce commodities with negative externalities. Furthermore, externalities may be produced by either production or consumption processes.

Local governments face two kinds of externalities. First, they must deal with externalities that occur strictly within their jurisdictions. For instance, a crowded shopping area may impose negative externalities on nearby residents. Second, local and regional governments must address externalities that spill over to or from neighboring jurisdictions. For instance, jurisdiction A could allow a large shopping mall to be constructed on A's side of the boundary separating A and B. Jurisdiction A's actions could create externalities in the form of congestion, noise, and air pollution for residents of jurisdiction B. Problems of interjurisdictional spillovers often require methods for coordinating local actions such as grants or regulations imposed by higher governmental units. The use of grants to encourage activities with positive externalities and withholding grants to discourage regional externality activities are discussed later in this chapter. One important interjurisdictional externality follows from local job creation efforts. If community A subsidized the expansion of a new plant, many of the employees may live in neighboring jurisdiction B. The residents in B may receive positive spillover effects due to city A's economic development program.

Merit Goods

The provision of merit goods by public intervention in the market economy is controversial. There are goods or services considered so meritorious that the market will not provide them in the optimal quantities. Higher education and health care are examples of a merit good. The private benefits from higher education may be sufficient to ensure that education will be provided in optimal quantities, but because society values education so much, the allocation branch may encourage additional production. Merit goods may play an important role in creating a community image and building a reputation for a high quality of life.

⊠ Size and Scope of Local Governments

This section explores two perspectives on government size. The traditional approach to optimal size has been to examine the economically efficient (lowest cost) size of production to determine the appropriate size of government. More recently, however, decision-making costs have been viewed as the most important consideration in determining government size.

Economies and Diseconomies of Scale

Some economists have argued that the appropriate size for a local government should be the population size that will allow the government to provide services at the lowest average cost.

There are three serious problems regarding the minimum-cost approach. First, Oates (1969a) and others have shown that costs are influenced by the type of people being served. If, for example, a given input of community police services is associated with a higher degree of safety on the streets, then the members of that community are less prone to engage in crime. Likewise, the more able and highly motivated the pupils in a certain school are, the greater may be the potential for independent study. Hence the optimum class size or the need for special educational services may depend on the type of students.

A second criticism of the minimum-cost approach to optimal city size is that it fails to recognize that governments perform many functions, from managing airports to providing social services. The relationship between average cost and population may be different for each function. Consequently, the lowest-cost population size depends on the number and type of services provided by local governments.

A third drawback with the minimum-cost approach is that it fails to recognize that communities may purchase selected government services from other cities. The size of the purchasing unit does not have to be the same size as the producing unit. For instance, a small city may enter into an agreement with another jurisdiction to pay a part of the cost of the fire department in return for fire protection. Because local governments do not have to produce all the services they provide, low average production costs need not be a factor in determining optimum government size. A large city may generate substantial economies of scale in fire protection. A small city may receive the benefits of the scale economies by purchasing fire protection from a large city at a cost that reflects the scale economies. The ability of communities to develop shared services offers potential for significant efficiencies.

Decision-Making Costs

Another approach to local government size is to examine the decision-making ability of citizens as size changes. Do decisions reflect citizen preferences and are the costs of reaching a decision low? There are three aspects of decision-making costs: preference mismatches, decision-making effort, and intergovernmental spillovers.

Preference Mismatch

If the set of goods and services provided by the government does not match the preferences of residents, then a preference mismatch exists. Preference mismatches are a necessary cost of public action. The larger the political jurisdiction, the greater the number of citizens who will be dissatisfied with the mix of public services and taxes. The mismatch between preferences and government performance is a political externality. Reducing political externalities reduces decision-making costs.

What government size best satisfies the preferences of voters? The most efficient size for satisfying individual preferences would be a government serving only one person. In this case, an individual's preferences can be accommodated exactly. However, because of the nature of governmental functions, outputs must be shared; so, one person/one government is not feasible.

Assume that if the actual level of service exceeds or falls short of an individual's preference by a given percentage, he or she becomes dissatisfied. The greater the gap between the service level and the preferred level, the greater the dissatisfaction. The preference of the median voter is the most likely outcome of a two-party democratic process. The extent of dissatisfaction

is a decision-making cost. If citizens have relatively homogeneous preferences for the level and type of service provision as indicated by the small
spread of opinion, the extent of dissatisfaction will be small. Such communities are well positioned to work in a cooperative manner for community goals,
including economic development. Areas where preferences are diverse and
far apart are likely to experience high levels of dissatisfaction.

Citizen Effort and Governmental Scope

Decision-making costs are also influenced by the effort or resources
required to make wise decisions. Consequently, the decision-making effort
depends on the number of issues that voters are expected to decide. On the
one hand, proliferation of many jurisdictions usually makes decision making
harder because voters must know more potential officeholders. On the other
hand, if there were only one general-purpose government, specific issues
might not get the attention they deserve. Citizens would vote for representatives who would reflect their preferences only on some issues. High-
profile issues, such as abortion or crime, might dominate voter attention,
whereas issues like the need to separate garbage might receive no attention.

Thus, in attempting to minimize decision-making costs, the scope of
government should balance the ability of voters to express their opinions on
specific issues with the information costs that would exist if a separate
representative or unit of government existed for narrow sets of public issues.

Intergovernmental Spillovers Reconsidered

Earlier, the many externalities associated with economic development
were discussed. These externalities occur when one government unit imposes
on (or provides services to) residents of another jurisdiction. The potential for
intergovernmental spillovers can influence the appropriate size and scope of
local government. Everything else equal, intergovernmental spillovers should
be minimized. Obviously, the larger the political jurisdiction, the fewer the
intergovernmental spillovers. However, larger government units may increase
the preference-mismatch problem.

The suburban/central-city exploitation thesis is based on the idea of intergovernmental spillovers. The thesis is that suburban residents benefit from the
services provided by the central city, but they do not pay their fair share of the
cost. For example, suburban residents use central-city roads but do not pay

central-city property taxes. Because so many suburban residents work in the central city, they use many central-city services during the day. Suburban residents also use cultural and recreational facilities often found in the central city. Accordingly, the charge has been made that suburban residents exploit residents of the central city. The empirical evidence for central-city exploitation is mixed (Green, Neenan, and Scott, 1976; Neenan, 1972; Ramsey, 1972).

Central-city/suburban spillovers are particularly cogent in the job creation process because many of the high-paying jobs held by suburban residents are located in the CBD. The efforts to maintain a viable downtown help suburban residents. These economic interdependencies have caused many metropolitan areas to create institutions that encourage interjurisdictional cooperation in the area of economic development. The presence of interjurisdictional spillovers in economic development supports the idea that cities and suburbs should cooperate more in economic development efforts.

⊠ Intergovernmental Grants

The crazy quilt of intergovernmental relationships provides a background for understanding the role of intergovernmental grants. This section presents the rationale for intergovernmental grants, followed by a discussion of the types of intergovernmental grants and their effect on the behavior of other units of government.

Intergovernmental Grants, Coordination and Cooperation

Two reasons are generally given for intergovernmental grants. First, there is a need to encourage positive spillovers. Second, some intergovernmental grants are necessary to rectify fiscal disparities among jurisdictions. Grants to rectify fiscal disparities have both equity and efficiency objectives, as unequal fiscal treatment may result in inefficient relocation of households. Because grants are used to coordinate activities of smaller units of government, grants almost always flow from larger units of government to smaller units.

Efficiency and Spillovers

Externalities among local governments are common. For instance, excellent parks in one jurisdiction may be used by residents of another jurisdiction.

In this case, nonpayers will receive a positive externality. Economic theory suggests that when positive externalities exist, the good in question tends to be underprovided. When negative spillovers are present, the good tends to be overproduced.

Positive externalities flow from a variety of activities, including public parks, police services, roads, and so forth. The external benefits that flow from economic development constitute one of the reasons for the rapid growth in economic development grants from federal, state, and county governments to local jurisdictions. A single jurisdiction might encourage economic development to the point where program costs equal benefits to the jurisdictions, but the state (or some other higher level of government) might wish that the jurisdiction went beyond that point to achieve additional benefits for neighboring jurisdictions. To encourage additional economic development spending, the state might put additional monies in the form of grants for economic development purposes.

Jurisdictions can also be encouraged to reduce negative externalities through the use of intergovernmental grants. For instance, grants for sewage improvements reduce the water pollution that affects downstream communities. Expressed differently, water purification carries positive externalities and a grant to increase purification efforts will increase the level of this output.

Equity

A second reason for having intergovernmental transfers is to ensure that unequal burdens are not placed on individuals living in jurisdictions with different taxing abilities. Often, poor districts with small tax bases must impose higher tax rates on their residents, yet the district collects less total revenue than more affluent communities do. This imbalance is a particular issue in the funding of education.

Suppose individuals A and B earn equal incomes, but A lives in a rich city and B lives in a poor city. Further assume that their tastes and preferences are the same and that taxes are proportionate to income. Given the assumptions, it would be advantageous to be a resident of the wealthy community because the local tax burden would be smaller. To receive the same services, B would pay more taxes than A. This situation violates the tax principal that "equals should be treated equally." Thus transfers to ensure that A and B receive equal fiscal residuum may be appropriate.

Furthermore, given the potentially disadvantageous tax treatment of B, an incentive would exist for B to relocate to the richer community. There are two potential efficiency problems that arise from the fiscal incentive to live in a wealthy jurisdiction. First, the rich political jurisdictions will get richer and the low-income residents in the poorer district will be more isolated. Excessive income segregation could also result in increased racial and social problems. Second, the provision of public services is often characterized by congestion costs. Migration could increase costs in the richer jurisdiction, and increased congestion could reduce the quality of services.

Types and Consequences of Intergovernmental Grants

Frequently, economists distinguish between matching grants in which the size of the grant depends on the level of local spending and lump-sum (fixed amount) grants. Another typology is between categorical grants that must be used for a particular purpose and block grants that can be used for a wide range of purposes.

Matching and Lump-Sum Grants

The amount of intergovernmental transfers depends on the level of the recipient government's spending in the case of the matching grant. The lump-sum grant is a fixed amount. To compare matching and lump-sum grants, assume that the transfers are not financed through taxes on residents in the recipient area. Thus only the effect of the grant would be examined, excluding how the grant was financed.

Matching grants have two effects that tend to encourage the grantee to increase spending on the service being supported by the grantor. First, the matching grant will lower the relative price of the activity being encouraged. This is called the substitution effect. Second, an income effect exists because the grant will increase the revenue and hence the spending ability of the jurisdiction receiving the grant. The recipient jurisdiction will tend to spend more on all activities, including the target activity. In the case of lump-sum grants, local spending ability will increase (income effect), but there will be no substitution effect. Although the grant may be directed toward a particular activity (e.g., a $10 million grant to support education), relative prices will not change. Hence a local government could simply reduce its own outlays on the target activity and use the grant to maintain existing activity levels. For instance, economic development programs may have been funded at $10 million annually from the general revenue fund after the community received a lump-sum $25 million grant for economic development. The general fund outlays may be cut by $25 million, so the total economic development spending remains $100 million.

Matching grants are more likely than lump-sum grants to encourage spending on the activity the grantor has targeted. Because the matching grant has the effect of lowering the relative price of the target activity, city officials are likely to provide more of the lower-priced activity. Bell and Bowman (1987) compared the consequences of matching and lump-sum grants given by the state of Minnesota to its cities. They found that matching grants are the most stimulative and even cause local taxes to increase so that the localities may take advantage of the match. Lump-sum grants increased the level of local services but did not influence the level of taxes.

The theoretical analysis of spending effects indicates that matching grants may be the preferred type of transfer if the grantor government wants to stimulate an activity. An activity that creates positive spillovers for residents of other jurisdictions such as economic development might be a candidate for a matching grant. However, if the purpose of the transfer is to equalize fiscal abilities without interfering with local decision making, the lump-sum grant may be preferable.

Categorical and Unrestricted Grants

Categorical grants are transfers that the granting agency earmarks for a rather narrow range of spending purposes. For instance, a state road-improvement grant would have strictly limited purposes. Categorical grants may be either lump sum or matching. In contrast, unrestricted grants may be spent on a variety of purposes, so they will not tend to stimulate one type of spending program over another. Consequently, the recipient jurisdiction has more discretion in determining how to spend the unrestricted funds. However, the term "unrestricted" should not be taken literally because no grant is totally unrestricted.

Advocates of unrestricted grants believe that the smaller units of government are closer to the problem and best know how to spend the funds to satisfy local needs. Furthermore, a dollar of unrestricted funds is worth more to the recipient jurisdiction than a dollar that must be spent in a particular way. Thus explanation was that the same level of benefits could be achieved with smaller but less restricted grants. The return of authority to state and local governments has been termed "devolution," a policy that favors unrestricted grants.

Opponents of unrestricted grants have argued that they merely reshuffle money rather than accomplish any clearly defined goal. Furthermore, the administrative costs of sending money to Washington, D.C. or a state capital and then back to local governments is high. However, unrestricted grants may improve fiscal equity if they return more funds to the poorer jurisdictions than they take.

⊠ Guidelines for Evaluating Taxes

A fair or efficient tax system at the state and local level can be an important economic development tool. Businesses consistently rank taxes as an important location and expansion factor. This section first discusses general criteria for evaluating taxes: efficiency, equity, and revenue elasticity.

Tax Efficiency

An efficient tax is one that does not alter outcomes of private economic activity unintentionally. An income tax, for instance, can be considered inefficient because a high income tax may encourage some individuals to work less. A head tax, on the other hand, will not distort the work/leisure choice because the taxpayer cannot escape the tax by working less. However, some taxes may deliberately distort prices to correct for other imperfections in the economy. Hence a tax on a polluting product may be efficient even if it alters existing incentives.

There is a saying that "an old tax is a good tax." Once the market has adjusted to a tax, it may be more disruptive to remove an existing tax and replace it with a theoretically more efficient one. The old tax-good tax principle implies that stability is an important efficiency characteristic.

Tax Equity

The main criteria for judging the fairness of a tax are the ability-to-pay and the benefits-received principles. The ability-to-pay principle asserts that taxes should be levied based on a person's ability to pay. Because income is a major indicator of ability to pay, the principle is usually interpreted as implying that high-income families should pay more taxes.

The benefits-received principle links tax payments to benefits received from governments. The benefits-received principle is most useful in situations where benefits of the government program accrue directly to the recipient and where the value the recipient places on the good is easily determined. A motor fuel tax is based on the benefits principle because it is assumed that the use of motor fuel represents use of roads. Direct-user charges for public services, such as garbage collection, are an increasingly popular form of user fees.

Tax Shifting

Tax shifting must be considered when examining either efficiency or equity. The determination of tax equity is difficult because the party that actually pays the tax to the government may be able to pass the tax forward to consumers or backward to producers. If a tax can be passed to someone other than the initial payer, the tax is said to have been shifted. The party that actually has a reduction in income because of the tax bears the "tax incidence."

Figure 12.1 illustrates the shifting process. Suppose S_1 and D represent the original supply and demand curves prior to the imposition of a tax. Then a tax is imposed on taxi trips equal to $1 per trip. Assume that cab drivers are responsible for collecting the tax. The initial effect of the tax will be to reduce the supply of taxi trips at each price the consumer pays. This is shown by the backward shift of the supply curve to S_2. The new equilibrium price will be $2.75. In this case, 75 cents of the tax has been shifted forward to the consumer who now pays 75 cents more than before the tax, and 25 cents is shifted backward to the driver. Often, the fare might be expressed "$1.75, plus $1 tax." When expressed this way, it appears the consumer is bearing the full incidence, but, in reality, the price of the taxed service drops, forcing the producer to bear part of the burden.

The relative elasticities of supply and demand determine the extent of shifting. If firms face consumers with inelastic product demand (i.e., prices can be increased without consumers significantly decreasing their purchases), producers will be able to shift a high portion of the tax forward to consumers, but if consumer demand is elastic, producers will have difficulty passing taxes forward. Similarly, if the product being taxed has an inelastic supply, as would be the case if the resources used in production had few alternative uses, the tax would tend to be shifted backwards to producers. Producers with greater options would tend to avoid the tax and it would be shifted to consumers. Shifting prospects have important implications for metropolitan taxing policies.

Suppose a small jurisdiction imposes a sales tax on a particular type of store. Consumers could easily avoid paying it by shopping at competitive

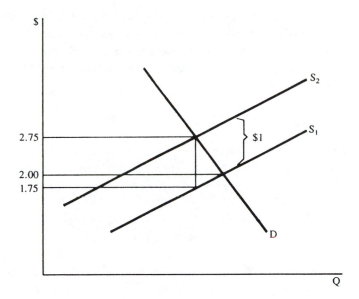

Figure 12.1. Tax shifting. Out of a $1 tax, 75 cents will be shifted forward. In this example, 25 cents will be shifted backward. The extent of shifting depends on the elasticities of supply and demand.

stores outside the taxing jurisdiction. Because consumers have elastic demands for products sold within one specific jurisdiction in a metropolitan area, it is difficult for owners to shift the tax to consumers. Thus the incidence will fall on the store owner. If the store was not making excess profits before the tax, it could easily be driven out of business. Similarly, local taxes on businesses that sell their products in competitive national or international markets may be harmful to the firm and the community. However, a statewide sales tax is more likely to be shifted forward to consumers. Because consumers have fewer nontaxed options, their demand will be less elastic.

Supply elasticity is also an important determinant of tax shifting. Factors of production with elastic supplies can move to untaxed areas, whereas immobile factors of production cannot avoid the tax. Building on the previous example of a sales tax, if shop owners were mobile and able to relocate to an untaxed district, they could escape the tax.

The property tax is considered to be borne primarily by property owners in the very short run because the supply of property is inelastic. Thus the tax will not affect supply or demand, and therefore rents will not increase. However, beyond the very short run, the housing supply could decrease as investors cut back on upkeep and new construction slowed. Thus the longer the time period, the greater the likelihood that increases in property taxes will be passed forward to renters.

Revenue Elasticity

Another important characteristic of taxes is their revenue elasticity, their elasticity with respect to growth in the economy. One measure of tax-revenue elasticity is

$$RE = \frac{\text{Percentage change in tax revenues}}{\text{Percentage change in national income}}. \qquad (12\text{-}2)$$

Most communities want a tax base that increases at least proportionally to national income. However, they also desire a revenue source that is stable during economic downturns because local expenditures are difficult to reduce during downturns. Often, these two goals conflict.

⧖   Reasons for Fiscal Problems

Overcoming fiscal problems is one of the motives for economic development. Local fiscal problems are also a deterrent to economic development. This section examines fiscal problems among local governments. First, the meaning and measure of fiscal stress is discussed. Next, several major ideas about causes of fiscal stress are presented. The reasons for fiscal stress are generally complementary rather than mutually exclusive explanations.

Measuring Fiscal Stress

There are two approaches to measuring fiscal stress. The "funds flow" approach identifies city government fiscal or budgetary characteristics. This approach implies that the causes of fiscal stress can be traced to budget management. If a budget is poorly managed, any city, no matter how wealthy, could experience fiscal stress. Measures of fiscal stress include current account surplus or deficit as a percentage of revenue and average debt service costs as a percentage of total revenues. These and related fiscal measures have been combined into rather complicated indexes.

The "socioeconomic" approach employs demographic characteristics in association with governmental fiscal measures. This approach implies that an area's fiscal health can be determined by comparing resources and needs. Needs are determined by socioeconomic characteristics, such as community income, infrastructure age, population change, and per capital income. The level of spending needed to bring the local government to a certain norm, such as a U.S. average, is compared to the ability to support that norm, such as community wealth or income. Thus areas with a high ratio of needs to resources will have high fiscal stress regardless of the area's budgetary deficit or surplus.

Productivity and Baumol's Disease

Baumol (1967) viewed the inherent nature of local government services as a contributing reason for fiscal problems. He argued that many local governmental activities are service intensive and therefore less likely to benefit from cost-saving technologies. For instance, law enforcement technologies are unlikely to replace police officers. In his model, goods and services are divided into technologically progressive activities and activities not susceptible to substantial productivity increases. Whereas the first type of activities was called progressive, the second type, which Baumol believed constituted most public activities, was considered nonprogressive. Baumol contended that the most important reason for an increase in productivity is that capital and knowledge can be substituted for labor for some activities. For other activities, labor is practically the end product, so it is difficult to increase labor productivity. The division of goods and services into only two sectors is procrustean, but it is a useful classification for his purposes.

Baumol assumed that wage differentials (adjusted for skills and working conditions) between the two sectors would remain about equal. If the differential temporarily increased, workers would move into the higher-wage sector until the initial wage differences were reestablished. Baumol also assumed that the wages of workers in the progressive sector would rise based on increases in productivity.

As productivity in the progressive sector increases, wages will increase. Because workers in the nonprogressive sector can substitute for workers in the progressive sector (at least in the long run), nonprogressive wages will also increase. In the progressive sector, the wage increases will not cause price to increase because the wage increases will be offset by increases in productivity. However, in the nonprogressive sector, the wage increases will not be matched by productivity increases, so prices will rise.

Baumol believed that public sector services tended to be nonprogressive because it is difficult to apply technology to many areas of social services. There is a fixed or nearly fixed ratio of service providers to recipients. For instance, a public school teacher may find it difficult to increase class size beyond 25 students. The ratio of pupils to teacher may be increased slightly by using computers and other educational technology, but the scope of such productivity enhancements is limited. Yet if teachers' pay is to remain in line with compensation in other occupations, the per-pupil cost of education will rise. If local governments provide a disproportionate share of nonprogressive services, there will be a tendency for taxes to increase or for local governments to face fiscal crisis. The increased productivity in the progressive sector will provide society with the extra wealth to continue to be able to purchase nonprogressive services, but Baumol's point is that government cost increases should be expected. Understanding the reasons for the tendency of urban governmental costs to increase may diminish some voter opposition to tax increases. Nevertheless, governments should look for opportunities to use technologies to minimize costs in those areas where such adaptations are possible.

Federal Mandates and Regulations

Mandates are responsibilities imposed on one level of government by another. Normally, the federal government, the judiciary, or state governments impose duties on local governments. Mandates may be required directly or as a condition for receiving aid. In either case, local governments are usually effectively forced into actions that may increase their costs. It has been estimated that local governments face over 1,200 federal mandates (Lovell and Tobin, 1981).

Cumulative Economic Decline and Fiscal Issues

Fiscal problems can lead to cumulative decline. For instance, a city facing a small fiscal problem may have to raise taxes or lower spending in ways that reduce the attractiveness of the community. As attractiveness diminishes, individuals may relocate to another city. The potential to relocate due to local fiscal policies is greater in metropolitan areas than in isolated cities because in metropolitan areas it is much easier to change residences without changing jobs. Thus the tax base will shrink, leading to more revenue loss and/or service cutbacks.

Service cutbacks may cause property values to fall, aggravating fiscal problems in several ways. First, individuals purchase houses with some hope of building equity through appreciation. If property values fall, this expectation of appreciation could be diminished, causing further decline in real estate prices. Second, the decline in property values may cause tax rates to increase. If revenue requirements are unchanged and there are no compensating increases in other revenues, then the tax rate would have to increase in proportion to the decline in the tax base. Economic development may be discouraged. Third, the drop in property values may cause the composition of the community to change. Particularly if lower-income groups that required expensive public services moved into the city, the demographic change would add to the fiscal stress.

Population declines can also contribute to cumulative fiscal distress even if demographic changes do not occur. Many of the costs of urban infrastructure are fixed, regardless of population size. The maintenance costs of sewers and roads, for instance, will vary little with population size. Yet most local revenue sources depend on population size. Tax revenues may decline more rapidly than the expenditures required to provide desired services. Thus the fiscal problems will increase, leading to further population loss.

Cumulative decline is not inevitable, and many cities have stabilized their fiscal position after a major fiscal crisis. The choices made by political leaders and other public groups may halt successive rounds of service cuts or tax increases. The health of the private sector economy can help avoid cumulative decline if there are business expansions that compensate for the initial fiscal shortfall. Nevertheless, there is a danger that once a local fiscal unit raises taxes or cuts services it may find itself on a slippery slope of decline.

⊠ Fiscal Strategies and Tools

Many areas face substantial fiscal pressures. Often, annually-balanced budget requirements further reduce local options. The federal deficit and fiscal strain in many states have made further increases in intergovernmental revenues an unlikely source of additional funds. Consequently, local governments are looking for alternative solutions. This section describes some of the innovative fiscal strategies and decision-making tools being used by local governments.

Privatization and Shedding Responsibilities

Many individuals consider private sector activities more efficient than public operations. The private sector has been shown to provide some services at a lower cost than governments charge. If the private sector is in fact more efficient than government, citizens may be better served if private businesses provided services traditionally provided by governments. Even if efficiency were not a concern, financially pressed governments might want to shed some activities and let them be provided by businesses if an effective demand for the service exists.

Local governments have also attempted to act more like private producers by relying on user fees that are similar to private sector prices. Governments can act more like private organizations if agencies charge appropriate prices.

Privatization can also be achieved when local governments contract with private firms to provide a service the government previously provided. For instance, a school district may contract with a private institution to provide special testing services. Private organizations have been hired to provide such services as school lunches, transportation, and safety programs. Franchises have been used to privatize public services. A local government may grant the right to provide certain services to private producers. The private provider may charge the public for the services; however, the price and conditions are regulated by the terms of the franchise agreement. Several states use a franchise system to collect fees for automobile license plates.

Voucher systems allow the government to pay for a stipulated service level, but the choice of provider is left to the individual. The voucher will support a minimum level of service, so if recipients wish to spend in excess of the voucher amount, they may do so with their income. The individual is responsible for arranging for the services, and the service will normally be produced by a private source. Food stamps are the most well known type of voucher, and recently, the federal government has provided housing assistance through a voucher. Many observers have proposed using vouchers in education. Although vouchers are not widely used by local governments, their popularity is increasing.

Traditionally, local governments have relied on volunteers to provide many services, and the interest in using volunteers is increasing. The use of volunteers in schools, social service agencies, and other organizations has been viewed as a way to expand services at modest costs. Recently, the concept of volunteerism has been expanded as governments have negotiated formal arrangements with businesses called *public-private partnerships.*

Intergovernmental Rearrangements

Several types of intergovernmental rearrangements have been suggested to relieve pressures on local governments. These include reassignment of functions, regional tax-base sharing, and annexation.

Reassignment of Responsibilities

The reassignment of responsibilities is a solution that usually involves shifting the financial burden upward where the ability to pay is perceived to be greater. There are two limiting problems, however. First, as fiscal responsibility shifts upward, there is a tendency for control to shift upward, too. Yet many programs are best controlled and administered at the local level where opportunities and needs can be seen more clearly. Thus the ability to shift programs upward is hindered by the propensity to lose local control. Second, higher units of government may not necessarily have greater fiscal ability than the combined local jurisdictions. After all, a state's taxable base is ultimately equal to the individual areas that make up the state.

Tax Sharing

Under tax sharing, increases in metropolitan taxes are shared among local jurisdictions. For instance, suppose industry and the property tax base are growing in a northern suburb while the central-city tax base declines. Under a tax-sharing system, the growing district might turn over a certain percentage of the increase in taxes to the central city as well as to other local jurisdictions.

Tax sharing has been supported for two reasons related to economic development. First, employment growth often depends on a variety of regional factors, including a vibrant downtown area. Expenditures of the central city often make the entire region more attractive to industry, so the central city should benefit from growth that occurs elsewhere in the region. Second, tax sharing may reduce the zero-sum game, that is, reduce intrametropolitan competition among jurisdictions attempting to enlarge their tax base. Such destructive competition has resulted in such generous tax abatements that even jurisdictions with increasing employment and industrial tax bases fail to increase their revenues.

Annexation

Many communities have attempted to solve fiscal problems through annexation. If a city annexes industrial or commercial areas, it may expand its tax base by more than the cost of providing services to the annexed area. Likewise, annexation of undeveloped land can provide sites for the growth of future taxable property.

Rusk (1993) has suggested that annexation is one of the principal determinants of central city success. Unfortunately, there are several drawbacks to using an annexation strategy. First, only a limited number of central cities can benefit from annexation because they are surrounded by previously incorporated suburban jurisdictions and it is usually difficult to annex an incorporated area. Furthermore, although annexation may help increase per capita income in a city, it may do little for the inner-city populations still trapped in a vicious cycle of economic decline. For the region as a whole, annexation may be an example of place prosperity that ignores the welfare of people in those places. For the metropolitan region as a whole, one community's annexation gain is often another's loss. Third, many suburban areas resist annexation by major cities because of the poor image and other problems that central cities have.

User Charges and Fees

User charges have grown rapidly during the 1980s. They are consistent with the benefits-received principle as they require the users of a service to pay all or part of its cost. Sometimes, "sliding scale" fees are used that link the user charge to income. Thus an ability-to-pay standard also can be applied to user fees. The recent popularity of user fees can be attributed to four factors. First, they help ration public services and thus alleviate pressures to produce more. When a good or service is free, it tends to be used until consumers receive no more utility from an extra unit. Second, user fees can help reduce congestion. By increasing the user fee, usage can be reduced. Well-designed user fees can also be used to spread usage away from peak-use times. Third, user charges provide decision makers with information regarding citizen valuation of goods and services. If a small user fee causes usage to fall drastically, policymakers may conclude that most users place a low value on it. Finally, user charges are a revenue source. Because many communities face tight budgets and political pressures to increase spending, additional revenue sources are usually welcome.

However, there are important limitations to user fees. Principally, user charges are generally only appropriate for goods that could be provided privately. Thus public swimming pools and other recreation facilities are susceptible to user charges. However, goods with characteristics of nonexcludability are not suitable for collection of user fees, nor are services and transfers designed to correct for problems of income distribution. Often, local governments face stiff opposition when they impose user fees because of a type of fiscal illusion held by the public. Some citizens believe they will have to pay for something they previously received for "free." The political problem of establishing user fees is aggravated by the fact that users of some services where user fees could be applied constitute a well-defined group that can lobby effectively to avoid charges on its use of services.

⊠ Fiscal Impact and Benefit-Cost Studies

Fiscal impact and benefit-cost studies are useful tools for economic development planners. Fiscal impact studies can be used to assess the effect of development projects on the government treasury. Benefit-cost studies analyze not only fiscal impacts but other costs and benefits that may accrue to citizens (Blair, 1992).

Fiscal Impact Studies

Fiscal impact analyses are useful for forecasting the effects of economic development and other projects on an area's fiscal health. Local economic development officials should consider fiscal impacts in planning and supporting new ventures. They vary greatly in scope and detail. However, there are certain steps that are common to most fiscal impact studies. A formula developed by Muller and Dawson (1972) provides a basic framework:

$$\text{NFI} = W - (X + Y) \qquad (12\text{-}3)$$

where

W = present value of development-linked revenue

X = present value of development-linked operating expenditures
Y = present value of development-linked capital expenditures
NFI = net fiscal impact

Although the net fiscal impact formula is very clear conceptually, in practice it is usually difficult to estimate the various components.

Estimating Revenues

Local revenues can be divided into property tax revenues, sales tax revenues, income tax revenues, intergovernmental transfers, and user charges/fees. Separate calculations may be made for each type of revenue. The importance of specific types of revenue sources will vary from district to district.

Residential developments are likely to generate most revenue through the property tax. The approximate value of new residential properties will be known when a fiscal impact study is undertaken because developers normally know the price range of houses in their development. Therefore, increased property tax revenues are relatively easy to estimate by multiplying the effective tax rate by the increase in the tax base. Revenues from sales taxes and income taxes may be more difficult to determine because they depend on residents' shopping and work patterns. However, based on these patterns and the income levels that could be assumed based on the value of the residences, reasonable estimates may be derived. Intergovernmental transfers depend primarily on population size and the number of school-aged children, although other factors may enter some grant formulas. Family size can be estimated from the type of residential development proposed, so roughly accurate estimates of intergovernmental revenues may be obtained.

Property tax revenues from commercial developments are also fairly easy to estimate based on the value of the proposed development stated in the zoning request or building permit. Local payroll tax revenues may also increase to the extent that employment increases. Sales taxes will increase to the extent that sales increase. An analyst must be careful to adjust revenue estimates if increased sales or employment come at the expense of other local businesses.

Estimating Operating Expenditures

A major difficulty in measuring operating expenses is that costs may remain fixed when usage increases by a small amount, so that marginal costs are near zero. Such might be the case for small increases in road use. Other governmental services may face sharply increasing marginal costs as demand increases, as might be the case if new roads were required to accommodate development-related traffic increases. In the absence of data on marginal cost, analysts often assume that the marginal cost of public services will equal average cost.

Operating expenses for residential developments may be analyzed by considering whether demand for government services is concentrated among low-income households, increases with income, changes with the size of the units constructed, and varies in other relevant variables. Such considerations may be compared to the type of project being proposed. Operating expenses of commercial enterprises may be estimated based on average costs of similar businesses in the area.

Estimating Capital Expenditures

Capital expenditures caused by new development include the following:

1. Facilities that are linked directly with the proposed project, such as sewer lines or fire stations.
2. Facilities that would have been constructed regardless of the new development but in which new residents will share.
3. Facilities that will have to be constructed because of the new development but which will be shared by other residents.

Theoretically, only the marginal costs of a new development are relevant. However, marginal costs are seldom the basis for evaluating a development's capital costs because they are difficult to determine and may differ from citizens' concepts of the fair-share burden. In practice, the new project is normally charged for the entire cost in the first instance. In the second case, the new development may not be charged for any of the costs or an average cost may be assigned. In the third case, the development may be charged for a disproportionate share of the incremental costs.

Benefit-Cost Analysis

Benefit-cost analysis is a decision-making tool that can be used to improve governmental decision making by going beyond narrow fiscal impacts and examining a broader range of costs and benefits. It attempts to measure the social costs and social benefits of public projects. If the benefits outweigh the costs, then the presumption is that the community would be enhanced by the project. If, however, the costs exceed the benefits, then the aggregate value of the resources required to build a project is greater than the benefits placed upon the output. The former case is intended to be the public sector equivalent of a profitable business venture, and the latter case is the counterpart to an unprofitable business.

The formula central to benefit-cost analysis is

$$B/C = \sum_{i=1}^{n} B_i \Big/ \sum_{i=1}^{n} C_i , \qquad (12\text{-}4)$$

where

B/C = benefit cost ratio

$\sum_{i=1}^{n} B_i$ = the sum of the discounted value of social benefits (0 = present year)

$\sum_{i=1}^{n} C_i$ = the sum of the discounted value of the social costs

The concept of benefit-cost analysis is simple: measure and compare the benefits and costs. Yet there are conceptual difficulties and implementation problems. Social costs and benefits will differ from private costs and benefits if there are spillover effects or externalities. The private costs of producing a commodity are borne by the producer. A social cost might also include the effects of pollution on residents near the factory. Total social costs include both private costs and spillover effects.

The inclusion of all benefits and costs in the decision is the key element in understanding the difference between benefit-cost analysis and the private decision-making process. However, the comprehensive perspective creates an implementation problem: The consequences—both good and bad—that stem from a project are too numerous and often too small to measure.

Steps in Benefit-Cost Analysis

The discussion of potential difficulties of benefit-cost analysis suggests that benefit-cost studies should be structured and implemented to avoid potential abuses. The eight steps required in developing a benefit-cost study are briefly summarized:

1. *Describe the nature of the project.* This step is necessary because the purposes of benefit-cost studies are not always the same, and the purposes may affect methodology. Benefit-cost analysis can be either a decision-making tool or an evaluative tool. For example, one study may answer the question "Should the school be built?" and another "Should the school have been built?" There may also be relevant constraints that will affect the outcome or nature of the study. For example, a budgetary constraint may prevent analysis of a bigger project that might appear better.

2. *Delineate the set of choices.* Benefit-cost analysis is not feasible for comparing all governmental projects. In describing the choice set, the analyst should specify alternative projects being considered. In the simplest case, where only one project is being considered, the issue may be whether the benefit-cost ratio is greater than a certain level. The choice will become more difficult if projects are mutually exclusive or otherwise interdependent.

3. *Describe the benefits and costs of the project.* This step and the next are possibly the most difficult in the analysis. The benefits and costs should include not only direct but also indirect impacts. The analyst might even choose to discuss "speculative effects," so that those factors that might or might not result would at least be mentioned. One of the significant lessons learned from evaluations of federal urban programs is that unintended and unanticipated effects often turn out to be more significant than planned impacts. An important dimension of the description of the costs and benefits is the time period in which they occur. The further in the future the costs and benefits take effect, the less weight they will be given.

4. *Estimate the monetary value of the costs and benefits.* Techniques and examples for estimating social benefits are the following:

- The benefits of a road can include time savings valued at the traveler's hourly wage in addition to direct transport-cost savings.
- The value of mass-transit facilities includes the benefits to automobile drivers, who will save time because mass-transit facilities reduce driving time.
- Public housing benefits have included the estimated value of crime prevention.
- The value of public parks and other recreational facilities has included the price paid for admittance to similar private facilities plus the value of travel time saved because of the nearness of the facility.
- Surveys have been used to determine what individuals might be willing to pay.
- The increased property values of land near public improvements have been a measure of benefits of parks.
- Flood-control projects have included the value of the increase in agricultural output.

Of course, there are still significant estimation problems with attempts to quantify elusive outcomes. All attempts to estimate value are subject to criticism. Some analysts prefer simply to list or set aside some qualitative benefits.

5. *Select a discount rate.* The selection of the discount rate for government projects is a controversial aspect of benefit-cost analysis. Because most government development projects involve large current expenditures and provide a flow of benefits over many years, a low discount rate increases the net present benefits and hence also increases the number of projects that can be justified. Among the possible discount rates that can be used are these:

- Private rate of return, because it represents the opportunity cost of capital used in the project
- A rate slightly lower than the private rate of return, to adjust for the risk of public projects
- The rate at which the government borrows
- A rate that reflects appropriate concern for future generations

There is as yet no final resolution of the discount rate issue. Although the conceptual problems inherent in this step may be great, a rate is usually selected based on rates in effect at the time of the study.

6. *Discount the costs and benefits.* The first five steps are preliminary to the actual calculation. Once the appropriate benefits, costs, and discount rates are established, this step is mechanical.

7. *Perform sensitivity analysis.* While not always necessary, repeating the fifth and sixth steps with different assumptions provide an indication of how sensitive the results are to changes in the discount rate or in values placed on some intangible benefits. If the results are sensitive to small changes in, say, the value of time savings resulting from construction of a road, then doubt will be cast on the project.

8. *Describe conclusions and caveats.* Many benefit-cost studies leave the impression that if the benefit-cost ratio is greater than 1 it is obvious that the conclusion should be to construct the project. However, if a result is sensitive to the discount rate or to one of the variables that the analyst could only roughly estimate, then the conclusion would be in doubt. There could be a discussion of how the inclusion of qualitative variables may have affected the analysis. Furthermore, because of budget constraints the cutoff point for government projects may be a benefit-cost ratio greater than 2 rather than

greater than 1. Also, funding a project with the highest benefit-cost ratio may not maximize the difference between the total benefits and total costs. Consequently, the reasoning behind any cutoff point should be discussed.

Conceptual and Implementation Issues

The theoretical justification for benefit-cost analysis is that when a project's benefits outweigh project costs, net social wealth will increase. With the increase in social wealth, the government could redistribute income so as to make at least one person better off without making anyone worse off (called a Pareto move). Society may decide not to redistribute income because it prefers the existing distribution; but as long as everyone can be potentially better off, the project should be undertaken. Thus benefit-cost analysis is based on efficiency rather than equity criteria.

One method for dealing with the distributional issue is to assign different weights to various income groups. Thus $1 of benefits or costs to a low-income family could be weighted by a factor of 1.2 or 1.7. Whatever the weight (even if all are weighted equally), the analyst is making a value judgment, not a scientific judgment. Some writers have suggested a "balance sheet" approach whereby the benefits and costs that accrue to individuals in different income categories are separated.

Several criticisms of benefit-cost analysis have been discussed in the literature. One criticism is that all the costs and benefits cannot be counted. Because almost every action sets off numerous second-, third- and greater-order consequences, tracking down and valuing all the ramifications is impossible. Still, benefit-cost studies should attempt to count the costs of the major consequences. An analyst may have to assume that unforeseen or remote costs and benefits balance out.

A second criticism has been that local governments cannot afford to undertake all projects for which the benefit-cost ratios are greater than 1. Consequently, another standard must be developed to select among projects. Most analysts recognize this point. As a result, benefit-cost studies are more appropriate as a guide to an agency selecting among similar projects than as a guide to a legislature trying to allocate funds among very different projects, such as health and road maintenance. A small agency may also lack the resources to undertake all projects with positive benefit-cost ratios, but it could have a decision-making rule requiring benefit-cost ratios of over, say, 1.5, before a project could be undertaken.

The presence of intangible costs and benefits presents another problem. It is nearly impossible to place a monetary value on some activities. Frequently, critics suggest that because we cannot place a value on a human life, benefit-cost studies are not appropriate to projects where such issues are involved. However, some benefits and costs that cannot be valued may be set aside and the benefits or costs expressed as "$10,000,000 plus or minus fewer health problems for 100 people." The decision makers must then determine how to handle the trade-off.

Finally, critics contend that benefit-cost studies remove decisions from the political decision makers and place them in the hands of technocrats. When benefit-cost techniques are employed, citizens lose the ability to engage in debates and affect outcomes. It is true that benefit-cost studies can be used to "snow" people and make a political decision appear to be only a technical decision. However, this abuse can be avoided in well-implemented studies.

⊠ Summary

Most public programs influence economic development prospects either directly or indirectly, intentionally or unintentionally. Economic development officials are often involved in many phases of local government.

The federal government has a dominant influence in stabilization activities through monetary and fiscal policy. Local governments lack the capacity to controll overall levels of economic activity, but local economic development efforts are a form of stabilization policy. Distribution functions are also difficult to implement at the local level because migration may negate efforts to transfer income from one group to another. However, modest redistribution efforts occur at the local level. Most state and local government activities are designed to influence the allocation of resources. Allocation activities include the provision of public goods and adjusting market outcomes for externalities and merit goods.

Many observers examine economies of scale to determine the appropriate size of local governments, but some economists argue that local governments can purchase services from elsewhere, so there is no need to have a government large enough to achieve economies of scale. More recently, economists have claimed that decision-making costs should be the key factor in determining government size. Three important aspects of decision-making costs are preference mismatches, decision-making effort, and intergovernmental spillovers.

Intergovernmental grants are used to improve the efficiency in the allocation of goods that spill over from one jurisdiction to another. They are also used to encourage fiscal equity among individuals living in different jurisdictions. A variety of types of intergovernmental grants can be used to influence how local governments react to a grant from another unit of government.

Taxes have been evaluated according to their efficiency, equity, and revenue elasticity. The property tax is an important source of local government revenue. Unfortunately, the property tax does not score well on any of the three criteria. Shifting of taxes through price changes can drive a wedge between the party responsible for collecting the tax and the individuals who actually pay the tax.

Urban fiscal problems include fiscal stress, lack of productivity increases in the provision of public services, federal mandates and regulations, underfunded obligations, perverse incentives, and cumulative decline. Strategies and tools for improving local government decisions include privatization, annexation, tax sharing, and user fees. Fiscal impact and cost-benefit studies are useful tools for fiscal management. Urban development specialists should understand the strengths and limitations of these tools.

⊠ Note

1. Taxes are regressive, proportional, or progressive according to whether they take a lower, proportional, or higher percentage of income as income rises. The wealthy generally pay more taxes in absolute dollars under each type of rate structure.

13

Planning, Futures Studies, and Development Policy

Economics, futures studies, and urban planning are important aspects of the economic development process. Urban planners need reasonable estimates regarding the likely course of future events so as to anticipate needs and develop policy responses. Economics is usually at the heart of planning processes because planners are interested in economic outcomes, economic methods are used in the planning process, and economic factors constrain what can be done. The influential planner, George Sternlieb (1986) described the orientation of planners to economic concerns when he said, "In a word we have all suddenly become economists" (p. 154). Most applied urban economists work closely with planners. Planners in turn are influenced by the thinking of future thinkers. In practice, it is often difficult to determine whether someone engaged in planning or policy development has an academic background as an economist, planner, futurist, or is from some other field.

Futurists and planners have learned a great deal from economists, but economists can also learn from futurists and urban planners. This chapter reviews some of the ways futurists and urban planners view urban and regional economic development. It should stimulate thought, speculation, and wide ranging thinking about urban futures and how to influence the course of future events.

⊠ Futurist Perspectives

The process of thinking about the future is frustrating because nobody knows what the future holds. Yet decision makers want to know the future. Most decisions require at least implicit assumptions about the future so some type of futures analysis is almost unescapable. Often, such decisions have an implicit assumption—the future will be pretty much like today. That assumption is often roughly accurate—but not always. Often, we look back on events and realize that they could or should have been anticipated.

Futurists, like economists, are careful not to imply that they can "predict" the future. Rather, they use phrases like "trend analysis," "scenarios," "forecasts," and "projections" when describing what the future might be like.

Futurist thinking is diverse, and some generalizations can be useful to illustrate the futurist perspective. This section examines four such areas.

Concern With Values and Attitudes

Economics has been called the science of values. Choice is the observable reflection of values, yet economists generally take individual values as given. Economists are generally concerned with how individuals behave, *given* a set of values. Futurists are concerned with changing values. They ask what value changes are likely to occur and how those changes may affect the way we will live.

Two general theories of value change have been popular. Constancy theories suggest that, in the course of time, value conflict will be recognized. These value conflicts will create political and personal agitation. Eventually, one of the values will prevail or a third value that rationalizes the conflicting values will emerge. The choices made by individuals as well as social institutions will change to reflect the value shift. The classic example of a conflict of values is the existence of slavery in a country that professed that "all men are created equal." The conflict between these two values created a "house divided," and new institutions emerged. A weakness of the value conflict theory is that conflicting values are not uncommon, but there is no satisfactory explanation of when the conflicts will result in reconciliation.

Another view is that values are functional and values will change if they no longer serve the individual or society. For instance, the right of private property is functional because (among other things) it contributes toward economic efficiency. However, the values of private property have had to give way when they conflict with other social goals. Taxation requires individuals to give up their private property, yet some taxation is necessary to social maintenance. A weakness of the functional theory is that there may be a "metavalue" that determines what is functional and what is not. Value changes may be reflected in changing public opinions and behavior changes.

Several possible value changes that may affect urban development are the following:

The Income-Leisure Trade-Off

If individuals become more interested in leisure activities, the importance of the city as a place for consumption will increase relative to its importance as a site of production. Efforts to protect the quality of life reflect a planning strategy associated with a stronger preference for leisure.

Importance of Friends and Family

The high level of mobility in U.S. society in part reflects a preference for monetary success even when it requires moving from family and friends. A value change whereby individuals placed a greater importance on stable social relationships could decrease interregional mobility. In response, the neighborhood might become a more important urban building block. Public policy could tilt toward a jobs-to people approach relative to the people-to-jobs approach. However, technological changes in transportation and communications could make it easier to maintain relationships over distance. So the tendency toward increased population mobility could continue in spite of such a value shift.

Attitudes Toward Race and Gender

Sargent (1980) argued that the central city has been identified with masculine pursuits and imagery such as aggressive, energetic, powerful, and dangerous. This imagery has contributed toward the desire to separate home life from the central city. As the lives of men and women become more similar, the environment they use may become less differentiated by economic and domestic functions.

Race relations are one of the most distinguishing characteristics of American cities. They contribute toward political tension and other urban problems. Increased respect for individuals regardless of race (or ethnicity) would affect urban life. It would increase the access that individuals have to parts of the urban environment currently considered out of bounds because of subtle or not so subtle social barriers. However, a variety of negative consequences could be anticipated if racial attitudes deteriorate and urban areas became more segregated. Urban planners generally believe that improved race relations would greatly improve the life quality of urban areas.

Communal Versus Individual Consumption

Americans tend to value privacy and individual consumption more than shared consumption. Concerns about sharing common areas was an attitude that had to be addressed before condominiums were widely accepted. Urban living offers numerous sharing possibilities. It might be economical for neighbors to share a lawn mower or even take turns mowing combined lawns. Local governments might provide more semipublic goods if joint consumptions were valued more highly (i.e., more public or club facilities and fewer private swimming pools). The possibilities for joint consumption are many, but Americans today prefer private consumption. A significantly different urban environment could be imagined if shared consumption were more highly valued.

Technological Change

Technological change includes new ways of organizing activity. Technology does not have to be embodied in a machine. For instance, the reorganization of a plant so that employees became more efficient could reflect a change in technology even if no new machines were used. Futurists are concerned with the impacts that technological changes can have. In fact, technological forecasting is a strong subarea of futures studies. Futurists are concerned not only with what new technologies may be developed but how they will affect society.

Coates (1982) described five important ways that new technologies may affect urban development:

1. Technologies can affect the hierarchical relationship among regions. For instance, declines in transportation costs have expanded the hinterland of major metropolitan areas.

2. Technological change will affect the internal structure of cities. For instance, the automobile contributed to urban decentralization. More recently, advances in technology have made possible the creation of urban megastructures, such as domed stadiums, that have affected the organization of urban regions.

3. Technological innovations will develop in response to urban problems. Although technological developments will undoubtedly present solutions for many serious problems, most futurists believe it unwise to simply assume that a "technology fix" will negate the need to anticipate alternative solutions. Behavioral changes may be more efficient solutions to problems than technological innovations.

4. Technology has effects through what is displaced. New technology usually replaces something else. For instance, technological changes that replace certain jobs continue to provide challenges to economic development planners.

5. Technology will interact with other trends to create changes that are difficult to anticipate. In the past, the technology of food production and the trend toward two-income households have interacted to stimulate the fast- and frozen-food industries.

Systems Orientation

Like economists, futurists have a systems orientation. They realize that because of the interrelatedness of subsystems a change will have repercussions on variables. "You cannot change just one thing," a systems thinker quipped. Futurists usually assume a more open system and often take a global perspective. Economists usually limit their analysis to a few variables, such as prices or quantities of a good. Although no one can examine all of the changes that spring from an event, futurists try to track a wider variety of the repercussions because they are less limited by boundaries of academic disciplines.

Related to the systems perspective is the realization that most change can create additional, unanticipated problems. Would public policy have been as supportive of the automobile had decision makers anticipated costs including 50,000 deaths annually, hundreds of thousands of injuries, billions of dollars of property damage, urban sprawl, oil dependency, and unwanted pregnancies? Of course, the benefits of the automobile may still outweigh the costs, but even desirable changes have some undesirable impacts.

Harman (1974) listed some important "problems of success" that affect local economic development:

- Prolonging the life span results in overpopulation and problems of old age.
- Automation of work results in dislocated workers.

- Advances in communication and transportation result in pollution, information overload, and vulnerability of a complex society to break down.
- Efficient production systems result in dehumanization of some work.
- Affluence results in increased energy use and pollution.
- Satisfaction of basic needs results in revolutions of rising expectations.
- Economic growth results in inequality between rich and poor countries.

The fact that improvements bring more challenges is reflected in science fiction writer Isaac Asimov's observation that that there are no happy endings in history, only crises that have passed. The same concept is embedded in the thinking of most economists who recognize the elusiveness of happiness—the problem of virtually unlimited human wants and limited resources.

Nevertheless, the idea of progress has been embedded in the worldview of most Westerners since the 1700s. History tends to be viewed as a movement from a less desirable state toward a more desirable one. This perspective is almost unanimously shared by futurists, planners, and economists.

Importance of Timing

Economists recognize the importance of time in forecasting. Anyone can correctly forecast an economic expansion or recession, for eventually such an event will occur. Yet such forecasts do little good unless the forecast explains when the event will occur. Futurist writers often are not precise about the timing of events when they describe qualitative or speculative trends. (Futurists are more speculative than economists.)

The future has been categorized as follows:

1. Immediate future: starting now and extending generally up to 1 year in the future
2. Near term future: 1 to 5 years from now
3. Middle-range future: 5 to 20 years from now
4. Long-range future: 20 to 50 years from now
5. The far future: more than 50 years from now

Economic forecasts tend to be in the "now" or immediate future. Planners for government and business tend to operate in the near term and middle-range future. Futurists tend to think in the middle-range and long-range future.

Futurists are very sensitive to how rapidly change occurs, and many futurists believe that the rate of change is accelerating. Furthermore, if a society makes a particular project a high priority, it can often be accomplished quickly. For instance, it required only four years to develop the nuclear bomb once the decision had been made to give that goal a high priority. Eight years after President Kennedy announced the goal of reaching the moon we were there. Of course, the scientific knowledge base for accomplishing these goals took centuries to develop. Yet at the time the goals were announced, most people considered them unattainable in the near future.

⊠   Planning Perspectives on Development Policy

Planning is an established profession. Planners need the ability to understand what the future could be (called an image of the future), the ability to understand how the future could be different, and the ability to describe the means to achieve desirable futures.

The term "planner" frequently connotes an urban land use planner. However, land use planning is only one type of planning activity. Near term, middle-, and long-range planning has become an important function in both public and private sectors. Private firms, such as real estate development companies, engage in planning. Almost all major corporations engage in some types of strategic planning. Most large cities and counties have planning departments to help accomplish a variety of goals, including economic development. A social service agency or a transportation authority might use a planner to develop goals and strategies for specific activities. The discussion below is primarily concerned with urban planning in the public sector; however, the principles are applicable to private planning as well.

The Planning Process

Most planners agree that the planning process is important because it serves as a vehicle for participants to think about the future. The process is generally considered more important than the document, or "plan," that results from the process. Often, "plans" are put on the shelf, yet the thinking that went into the plans has significant influence. Figure 13.1 illustrates a generic planning process. The principal steps are goal articulation (increase employment) and projections (employment growth will be too slow if nothing changes), intervention choice (a low-interest loan program), and implementation (create an economic development bank). Goal articulation requires a vision of what the city should look like

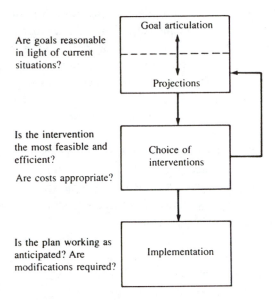

Figure 13.1. The planning process. Feedback may also be part of the planning process, resulting in goals being revised or new interventions selected.

at some time in the future. Future goals should be based on a realistic understanding of what is possible rather than on a wish list. Interventions are required to alter likely outcomes. Finally, the implementation process should feed back into the plan so it can be updated to reflect changing circumstances.

Goals and Projections

Many cities have master plans that set out future goals. Historically, urban master plans have been strong in describing physical development goals, such as where the new shopping centers, sewage treatment facility, and other developments will be. They have been weak in describing social goals, such as decreasing unemployment.

Goals must be developed from a base of where the community is and where it will be if current trends continue and resources are available to affect change. Goals should be realistic. Consequently, planners need to understand and analyze the community before or simultaneously with the development of goals.

The selection of the most appropriate goals is more difficult in public than in private planning. Private companies often have a clear goal: profits or stockholder wealth. Public agencies have a variety of goals that reflect competing interests within the community. For instance, the goal of open space could conflict with the goal of industrial employment growth.

Besides determining where the community is now, it is important to determine where the community will be if current events run their course. How well can analysts predict the future? Some things can be predicted very well, such as demographic composition. Other elements of the urban future are easy to predict, but local official control the outcome. For instance, the land use pattern might be predictable if locally a particular land use pattern was a high political priority. However, most aspects of the urban future are neither easy to predict nor controllable.

Comparing goals with projected outcomes in the absence of deliberate interventions is necessary to determine whether intervention is necessary. Frequently, goals must be changed if they are unrealistic in view of the existing situation and the nonintervention projections.

Selection of Interventions

What changes could be made to alter the course of events in order to achieve desired goals? There are many ways to achieve particular ends. Planners usually consider a variety of interventions to achieve particular goals.

A first step in selecting interventions is to determine whether proposed interventions are feasible. Can the intervention be implemented given the community values, political patterns, budget constraints, and national trends. A proposal that cannot be implemented is seldom useful. It is also necessary to determine whether the intervention will actually bring about the desired goal. Like a less than adequate dosage of medication, some policies may be insufficient to accomplish the tasks. Many proposed interventions may be rejected at this stage.

Because an end can be achieved through a variety of interventions, the planning process should select one of the various feasible interventions. The criterion for evaluation can include the intervention that is the most likely to produce the desired outcome, the least costly, has the lowest risk of negative outcomes, is likely to contribute to other desirable outcomes, and so forth. Selecting among feasible interventions can be complicated because some interventions may affect more than one planning goal. Therefore, an intervention that is less efficient in achieving one particular goal may be preferred because it helps achieve other goals.

Implementation

Many, many plans have failed because planners have not been concerned with implementation. The plan may sit on the shelf, or unanticipated snags may result in a scrapping of the plan. Many planners believe that a plan should be updated regularly. These rolling plans require a link to the implementation process so the plan can be modified to reflect unanticipated events or implementation problems. A 10-year plan might require revisions every 2 years. The fact that a plan must be modified to reflect changes in the environment does not mean the initial plan was inadequate.

A suboptimal plan may be better that a technically "best" one if the suboptimal plan has the support of the individuals involved in implementation. During implementation, cooperation of many persons is required. An excellent plan introduced in an uncooperative environment will probably be sabotaged. Furthermore, unanticipated events normally require changes in a plan, and these same changes provide opportunities for the individuals charged with implementing the plan to undermine it. The more broadly based the planning process, the more likely that individuals responsible for implementing the plan will support it. Of course, some plans must be introduced in situations where the implementors are hostile, as might be the case when one political action reverses a previous plan of action. In this case, implementation can be very difficult.

Common Themes in Economic Development Plans

Economic development planning has significantly increased in importance in the past 15 years. Today, large- and medium-size cities have either economic development plans or a strategic plan of which economic development is a major part. Numerous consulting firms specialize in economic development planning, and many states provide financial assistance for such planning. There is a wide variety of economic development plans, reflecting differing regional resources and opportunities and differing philosophies of the planners.

Blakely (1989) suggested that the nature of plans reflects the economic circumstances and community interests (including, presumably, potential

| | | In Response to | |
		Opportunities	Threats
	Reactive	Recruitment	Impact
Historic or Futures		Planning	Planning
Orientation	Proactive	Strategic	Contingency
		Planning	Planning

Figure 13.2. Types of local planning. Planning may take a historic or futures orientation and may be in response to opportunities or threats.

conflicts of interest) that initiated the planning process. He identified four types of plans, depending on whether the plan was designed to take advantage of opportunities or respond to threats and whether the plan was reactive or proactive. Accordingly a 2×2 matrix, shown in Figure 13.2, can be used to describe the types of local economic plans.

Recruitment planning in Blakely's model represents efforts to take advantage of emerging opportunities by attracting firms in new or fast-growing industries. For instance, if it were evident that many industries had locational requirements that could be satisfied best if space in industrial parks were available, many communities would begin planning for the development of such facilities. Impact planning represents attempts to respond to a negative event, such as a plant closing, and a public feeling that "something must be done." Both recruitment and impact planning represent reactions to past events.

Strategic and contingency planning are intended to anticipate events and develop appropriate responses. Contingency planning involves developing appropriate responses to anticipated events. A danger of contingency planning is that plans dealing with an adverse economic situation could lead to the expectation of decline, leading to a self-fulfilling prophecy. For instance, if economic discussion were dominated by how the region would respond to the loss of a mill, potential suppliers to the mill might be deterred from locating there because they believed the planners knew the mill was going to close. Strategic planning is comprehensive and long range. It examines merging external opportunities and includes plans to take advantage of such opportunities.

The goals of economic plans often take several forms. Some plans emphasize process goals. In other words, the goals are to change the economic environment so as to make the locality attractive to businesses. Other plans contain specific goals, such as "create 5,000 new manufacturing jobs." One drawback of plans that have very specific goals is that it may be difficult to determine whether specific jobs are attributable to local efforts or are fortuitous.

Allardice and Giese (1987) examined the economic development plans of states in the Seventh Federal Reserve District. They found several common themes in the reports. Of particular importance was decreased emphasis on industrial recruitment ("smokestack chasing") and more emphasis on helping firms and industries already in the area. This change in approach is often justified by the fact that most new jobs are created by expansion of existing facilities rather than by new start-ups or relocation. Second, although strengthening technology continues to be important, there is a realization that the high-tech sector will account for only a small percentage of future jobs. The key point stressed in recent studies is the application of advanced production processes and product innovation to traditional activities. Thus Michigan's emphasis on robotics technology follows from the increased importance of robotics in automobile production as do many state technology transfer programs. Third, the reports analyzed by Allardice and Giese indicated a trend toward cooperative coalitions between governments, universities, labor groups, and businesses. Universities are frequently assigned roles in stimulating the transfer of technology. Finally, international trade is being incorporated into regional planning strategies. Not only are planners suggesting strategies for encouraging exports abroad, but attracting investments from abroad is an important feature of development plans.

Most of the recommendations identified in the state plans are also reflected in local plans (Fosler, 1988). Local plans often target specific industries with special potential and provide suggestions to market the community for improving the city's image.

Plans are often put away and forgotten. But, increasingly, they call for the creation of an ongoing organization to monitor implementation, with specific tasks assigned to appropriate organizations. For instance, a university-based group might monitor and update the plan through annual reports while a preexisting group, such as the Chamber of Commerce, might be charged with the task of enhancing the metropolitan area's image. Special ongoing committees of key public and private individuals might also be assigned tasks called for in the plan.

Planning and Policy Paradigms

In developing images of the future and community goals, most analysts have a perspective about the kind of future that is likely and desirable. These images help shape the planning process. For instance, if a planner has a basically optimistic worldview he may envision the future of pleasant cities. However, distopian pictures of the future have been described by a number of influential futurists.

A paradigm is a reflection of the spirit of thought. Different models may be incorporated within a paradigm. Gappert (1982) described four paradigms that affect the way we view urban futures:

1. The technocratic perspective is concerned mainly with rationality and efficiency. Development planners with this perspective suggest that the city should develop efficient social arrangements.
2. The utopian perspective suggests that improvement can be achieved by the proper application of knowledge, resources, and good intentions. It attempts to define very clear patterns that will characterize the future city.
3. The pragmatic humanistic paradigm is concerned with the quality of human behavior. It recognizes that behavior can increase the efficiency of urban activities and emphasizes the importance of urban leadership and political coalitions in developing a satisfactory future.
4. Strategic reconstructionism emphasizes the development of large-scale projects that may create or exploit new opportunities.

Of course, elements of each perspective may be incorporated in a single plan.

Another way to look at economic development planning is to consider various models or development paths for a community. Some analysts might consider "decline economies." Such a view might project a decline in an area's economic base. Other planners have suggested the development of "knowledge based" cities (Knight, 1987) whereby urban regions will prosper by gaining international preeminence in a specialized knowledge cluster. Menlo Park, California, and the Golden Triangle in North Carolina are examples of knowledge-based economies. "Leisure cities" represent another future development path. Examples are Sun City, Arizona, and Orlando, Florida. Many cities are employing a "neighborhood" vision to strengthen their local economies. By strengthening local neighborhoods, development planners hope to strengthen the internal economy. Older northeastern cities have tended to adopt strong neighborhood approaches to local economic development. Many other visions of urban futures can be sketched, and elements of various visions have been incorporated into plans for the same urban region. A believable development path will help focus economic development planning models.

⊠ Planning and Futures Studies Tools

The tools that economists bring to the study of urban futures are powerful. They include modeling, forecasting, other econometric techniques, and, perhaps most important, the ability to deduce outcomes from a set of assumptions. There are some tools, however, that are unfamiliar to many economists. This section describes three tools that can be used in the planning and futures analysis: delphi forecasting, scenario development, and gaming.

Delphi Forecasting

Delphi forecasting is useful in developing answers about future events for which technical knowledge is required and where judgment is an important ingredient. The delphi technique is a way of combining the opinions of experts while allowing some feedback and discussion.

To illustrate the use of the delphi forecast, suppose you wish to know if and when a new regional airport will be necessary. First, a questionnaire might be sent to a group of experts asking when or if a new airport will be needed. An explanation of their reasoning and their degree of confidence in their response might also be requested. After the responses have been tabulated, the results would be sent to the panel of experts and the question asked again. In the second round, the experts would be able to reevaluate their original forecast in light of the opinions and information given by other experts. For instance, one expert might have said a new regional airport would be required by 1995 because of traffic control problems. Another expert might have replied that new technologies in traffic control would relieve the congestion problem without the need for an additional facility. Faced with the new information, the individual who thought the airport would be needed in 1995 might revise the estimate to, say, 2005. The second-round projections would be informed by the results of the first round. Generally, the expert opinions will converge after successive rounds, as indicated by Figure 13.3.

The delphi technique is quite versatile. The rounds can be conducted by mail, phone, face-to-face, computer network, or other means. The moderator can instruct the panel to accept certain assumptions as given so various alternatives can be explored. For instance, an assumption about regional population growth could be built into the question regarding the need for a new regional airport. Cross-impact analysis can be combined with futures

Percentage in agreement

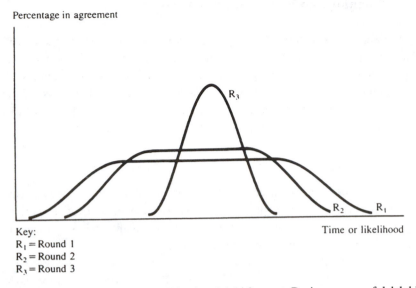

Key:
R_1 = Round 1
R_2 = Round 2
R_3 = Round 3

Figure 13.3.   Convergence of opinion in a delphi forecast. During a successful delphi, the opinions of experts will tend to converge.

analysis so that the impacts forecast in one set of delphi conferences can be used as assumptions in other delphi studies or to insure that events projected in various studies are consistent.

Two significant dangers of delphi forecasting should be noted. First, situations where the results represent an averaging of ignorance should be avoided. The usefulness of an expert panel will be negated if the questions are about things with which the respondents are unfamiliar. However, the experts need not have similar backgrounds. In fact, it may be useful to include experts in a variety of fields in some forecasts. Second, a dominant personality can sometime force individuals to conform to an opinion simply to avoid being contrary. The moderator should be particularly careful not to dominate the expert panel.

Games

Games are characterized by the assignment of a role to various participants. Individuals behave as they believe they would given their role. The game should be structured so that the participants face constraints similar to the situation being simulated. An urban game might include such roles as mayor, land developers, factory owners, and workers. A game master would create a situation and set parameters. As the game proceeds, the players might make demands on each other, form coalitions, or negotiate particular outcomes. The games are useful in helping players grasp the complex interactions that might be involved in real-life situations. The rules of the game might be changed to determine how the outcome would differ under different situations.

Games have been a major tool in military planning. War games often involve actual soldiers, but war games can also be played in a more abstract setting. Military games played by think tanks such as the RAND Corporation help demonstrate the problems with a strategy of "massive retaliation" and helped demonstrate the need for flexible responses in addition to all-out war.

Scenarios

A scenario is a plausible story. It is a description of a series of events that the writer could imagine happening. Although scenario writing appears simple, the technique can be quite useful. If the details of how an event could possibly occur cannot be plausibly described, it is an improbable event. For instance, if no one can imagine the series of events that would lead to the development of an enclosed football stadium, then that event is unlikely to occur. Similarly, if the only events that can lead to the development of an enclosed stadium are improbable than the end result is also improbable. Conversely, if the occurrence of an event can be described as the logical outcome of a series of likely intermediate events higher probability should be given to the scenario. Often, when a historian looks back on an event the steps that led to it appear logical and predictable. With hindsight it may appear that a scenario of the future could have been written easily.

Scenario development seems simple because we are so familiar with the technique. Many novels are scenarios. Samuelson's correspondence theorem suggests that it is not sufficient to *say* that a condition can be achieved, we must also *show* how it can be achieved. A scenario is a way of describing how a future state can be achieved. Developing a plausible scenario that leads to a nonobvious conclusion about the future is a difficult but valuable exercise.

Social Scanning

Social scanning is a rather simple technique. It consists of monitoring newspapers and other current events and attempting to spot trends. Futures analysis may formalize the process by selecting a group of monitors from different fields. Thus one team member might be asked to focus on value changes while another might focus on technological or governmental trends. The scanning group may meet occasionally to discuss the trends they have identified (or hypotheses) and determine potential interactions. Trends that tend to reinforce one another are more likely to be realized. For instance, an environmental consciousness and the problem of pollution reinforce each other, suggesting that "environmental concerns" will be a long-term trend.

⌘ **Summary**

Almost by definition, economic development is a forward-looking subject. Economic development planners must think strategically and plant seeds that may bear fruit only after many years. The purpose of this chapter was to develop a future perspective on local economic development.

Futurists have diverse points of view; yet there are common threads in their analyses. Futurists avoid suggesting that they can predict the future. They describe likely events if certain trends prevail or if certain changes occur. Sometimes, they speak of "alternative futures." Concerns about value changes, technological developments, the interrelatedness of social and ecological systems, and the importance of timing are important in futures analysis. All of these factors can be critical in economic development planning.

Planners need to be able to understand future possibilities and the ability to describe the means of achieving desirable futures. Planners in both the public and the private sector frequently rely on economic paradigms. Most planners believe that the planning process is as important as a final document or plan. The planning process can be a vehicle for thinking about the future. A three-step planning process would include the development of goals and projections, selection interventions, and implementation. In developing future images and goals, most analysts have perspectives about the kind of future they believe is likely and/or desirable.

Several useful tools are available for planning and futures analysis. First, delphi forecasting can be used to help understand the future by drawing on expert opinion. Games can be used to simulate the possible course of events. A well-structured game includes realistic constraints on the behavior. Third, scenarios are descriptions of events that could evolve from the current flow of events. The more realistic the scenario, the more likely the future event will occur. Finally, social scanning attempts to identify trends that will affect the locality through an organized monitoring of newspapers and other current services.

⬚ References

Allardice, David R., and Alenka S. Giese. 1987. "Economic Development Efforts in the Seventh District." *Economic Perspectives,* September-October, 32-37.

Allen, David N., and David J. Hayward. 1990. "The Role of New Venture Formation/ Entrepreneurship in Regional Development." *Economic Development Quarterly* 4 (1): 55-63.

Ashton, D. J., and B. K. Sternal, 1978. *Business Services and New England's Export Base.* Boston: Federal Reserve Bank of Boston.

Bartik, Timothy J. 1984. "Business Locational Decisions in the U.S.: Estimates of the Effects of Unionization, Taxes and Other Characteristics of the States." *Journal of Business and Economic Statistics* 3: 14-22.

Bartik, Timothy J. 1988. "Measuring the Benefits of Amenity Improvement in Hedonic Price Models." *Land Economics* 64 (2): 172-83.

Bartik, Timothy J. 1991. *Who Benefits From State and Local Economic Development Policies?* Kalamazoo, MI: Upjohn Institute.

Bartik, Timothy J. 1992. "The Effects of State and Local Taxes on Economic Development: A Review of Recent Research." *Economic Development Quarterly* 6 (1): 102-10.

Baumol, William J. 1963. "Interaction of Public and Private Decisions." In *Public Expenditure Decisions in the Urban Community,* edited by H. S. Schaller, pp. 1-18. Baltimore: The Johns Hopkins Press.

Baumol, William J. 1967. "The Macroeconomics of Unbalanced Growth: The Anatomy of Urban Crisis." *American Economic Review* 513: 415-26.

Baumol, William J. 1986. "Productivity Growth, Convergence, and Welfare." *American Economic Review* 76 (5): 1072-85.

Beauregard, Robert. 1993. "Constituting Economic Development: A Theoretical Perspective," in *Theories of Local Economic Development: Perspectives from Across the Disciplines,* edited by R. Bingham and R. Mier, pp. 267-83. Newbury Park, CA: Sage.

Bell, Michael E., and John H. Bowman. 1987. "The Effects of Various Intergovernmental Aid and Local Own-Source Revenues: The Case of Property Taxes in Minnesota Cities." *Public Finance Quarterly* 15 (3): 282-97.

Berger, Mark C., and Glenn C. Blomquist. 1988. "Income, Opportunities and the Quality of Life for Urban Residents." In *Urban Change and Poverty,* edited by M. G. H. McGeary and L. E. Lynn. Washington, DC: Committee on National Urban Policy, National Research Council.

Berry, Bert L. and W. L. Garrison. 1958. "Functional Bases of the Central-Place Hierarchy," *Economic Geography* 34: 304-22.

Beyers, W. B., and M. J. Alvine. 1985. "Export Services in Post Industrial Society." *Papers of the Regional Science Association* 57: 33-45.

Blair, John P. 1992. "Benefits from a Baseball Franchise: An Alternative Methodology." *Economic Development Quarterly* 6 (1): 91-95.

Blair, John P. and Carole R. Endres. 1994. "Hidden Economic Development Assets." *Economic Development Quarterly* 8(3): 286-91.

Blair, John P., Rudy H. Fichtenbaum, and James A. Swaney. 1984. "The Market for Jobs." *Urban Affairs Quarterly* 20 (1): 64-77.

Blair, John P., and Robert Premus. 1987a. "Choosing a Location for an Industrial Facility: What Influences the Corporate Decision Maker?" *Perspective* 14: 72-85.

Blair, John P., and Robert Premus. 1987b. "Major Factors in Industrial Location: A Review." *Economic Development Quarterly* 1(1): 72-85.

Blakely, Edward J. 1989. *Planning Legal Economic Development: Theory and Practice.* Newbury Park, CA: Sage.

Blinder, Alan S. 1987. *Hard Heads, Soft Hearts: Tough Minded Economics for a Just Society.* New York: Addison-Wesley.

Blomquist, Glenn C., Mark C. Berger, and John P. Hoehn. 1988. "New Estimates of the Quality of Life in Urban Areas." *American Economic Review,* March, 89-107.

Bloomberg, Warner, and Rodrigo Martinez Sandoval. 1982. "Hispanic-American Urban Order: A Border Perspective." In *Cities in the 21st Century,* edited by G. Gappert and R. Knight, pp. 112-32. Beverly Hills, CA: Sage.

Borjas, George J. 1987. "Immigrants, Minorities and Labor Market Competition." *Industrial Labor Relations Review* 40 (3): 382-92.

Borts, George. H., and Jerome Stein. 1964. *Economic Growth in a Free Market.* New York: Columbia University Press.

Bowen, Harry P., Edward E. Leamer, and Leo Sveikauskas. 1987. "Multicountry Multifactor Tests of the Factor Abundance Theory." *American Economic Review,* December, pp. 791-809.

Bradford, David F., and Henry H. Kelejian. 1973. "An Econometric Model of the Flight to the Suburb." *Journal of Political Economy,* May, pp. 566-89.

Burgess, Ernest W. 1952. "The Growth of the City." In *The City,* edited by R. Parks, E. Burgess, and C. McKenzie. Chicago: University of Chicago Press.

Carlino, Gerald A. 1980. "Contrasts in Agglomeration: New York and Pittsburgh Reconsidered." *Urban Studies* 17 (3): 39-54.

Carlton, D. 1983. "The Location and Employment Choices of New Firms: An Econometric Model with Discrete and Continuous Endogenous Variables." *Review of Economics and Statistics* 65:440-49.

Charney, A. H. 1983. "Intraurban Manufacturing Locational Decisions and Local Tax Differentials." *Journal of Urban Economics* 14:184-205.

Chinitz, R. 1961. "Contrasts in Agglomeration: New York and Pittsburgh." *American Economic Review* 51 (2): 1-12.

Clark, Gordon L. 1983. *Interregional Migration, National Policy and Social Justice.* Totowa, NJ: Rowman and Allanheld.

Clotfelter, Charles T. 1975. "Spatial Rearrangement and the Tiebout Hypothesis: The Case of School Desegregation." *Southern Economic Journal* 24 (2): 263-71.

Coates, Joseph F. 1982. "New Technologies and Their Urban Impact." In *Cities in the 21st Century,* edited by G. Gappert and R. Knight, chap. 10. Beverly Hills, CA: Sage.

Conway, McKinley. 1986. *A Technology Review and Forecast for Development Strategists.* Atlanta, GA: Conway.

Council on Environmental Quality. 1972. *The Third Annual Report.* Washington, DC: Government Printing Office.

Crane, Steven E. 1993. "Developing a Leading Indicator Series." *Economic Development Quarterly* 7(3): 267-81.

Doeringer, Peter B., and David G. Terkla. 1992. "Japanese Direct Investment and Development Policy." *Economic Development Quarterly* 6 (3): 225-71.

Eberts, Randall W., and Timothy J. Gornberg. 1989. "Can Competition Among Local Governments Constrain Government Spending?" *Economic Review* 24 (1): 2-9.

Erickson, Rodney A. 1987. "Business Climate Studies: A Critical Evaluation." *Economic Development Quarterly* 1 (1): 62-72.

Fagan, Mark, and Charles F. Longino, Jr. 1993. "Migrating Retirees: A Source for Economic Development." *Economic Development Quarterly* 7 (1): 98-106.

Fitzgerald, Joan. 1993. "Labor Force, Education, and Work." In *Theories of Local Economic Development,* edited by R. Bingham and R. Mier, pp. 125-146. Newbury Park, CA: Sage.

Feige, Edgar L. 1989. "The Meaning and Measurement of the Underground Economy." In *The Underground Economy,* edited by E. L. Feige, pp. 51-53. New York: Cambridge University Press.

Forrester, Jay. 1969. *Urban Dynamics.* Cambridge: MIT Press.

Fortune, Inc. 1977. *Facility Location Decisions.* New York: Fortune, Inc.

Fosler, R. Scott. 1988. "Economic Development: A Regional Challenge for the Heartland." *Economic Review* 73: 10-19.

Friedman, Milton. 1962. *Capitalism and Freedom.* Chicago: University of Chicago Press.

Galster, George C. 1987. *Homeowners and Neighborhood Reinvestment.* Durham, NC: Duke University Press.

Gappert, Gary. 1982. "Future Urban America: Post Affluent or Advanced Industrial Society?" In *Cities in the 21st Century,* edited by G. Gappert and R. Knight, pp. 1-9. Beverly Hills, CA: Sage.

Giese, Alenka, and William A. Testa. 1988. "Can Industrial R&D Survive the Decline of Production Activity?" *Economic Development Quarterly* 2 (4): 326-38.

Gillis, William. 1987. "Can Service-Producing Industries Provide for Regional Economic Growth?" *Economic Development Quarterly* 1 (3): 249-55.

Grant, Alexander & Co. 1985. *General Manufacturing Climates of the Forty-Eight Contiguous States of America.* Chicago: Alexander Grant.

Green, Howard L. 1959. "Hinterland Boundaries of New York City and Boston in Southern New England." In *Readings in Urban Geography,* edited by H. M. Mayer and C. F. Kohn, pp. 15-32. Chicago: University of Chicago Press.

Green, Kenneth V., William B. Neenan, and Claudia D. Scott. 1976. "Fiscal Incidence in the Washington Metropolitan Area." *Land Economics* 52: 13-31.

Guntermann, Karl L., and Stefan Norrbin. 1987. "Explaining the Variability of Apartment Rents." *American Real Estate and Urban Economics Association Journal* 15 (4): 321-39.

Hanson, Russell L., and Michael B. Berkman. 1991. "Gauging the Rainmakers: Towards a Meteorology of State Legislative Climates." *Economic Development Quarterly* 5 (3): 213-28.

Harman, Robert. 1974. "The Coming Transformation in Our View of Knowledge." *The Futurist* 8 (3): 15-24.

Harris, J. R., and M. P. Todaro. 1970. "Migration, Unemployment and Development: A Two Sector Analysis." *American Economic Review* 60: 126-42.

Haug, Peter, and Philip Ness. 1993. "Industrial Locations Decisions of Biotechnology Organizations." *Economic Development Quarterly* 7 (4): 390-402.

Heckman, John S. 1982. "Survey of Locational Decisions in the South." *Economic Review,* June, pp. 6-19.

Heckscher, E. F. 1919. "The Effect of Foreign Trade on the Distribution of Income." *Economisk Tidshift* 21: 497-512.

Hill, Edward W., and Thomas Bier. 1989. "Economic Restructuring: Earnings, Occupations and Housing Values in Cleveland." *Economic Development Quarterly* 3 (2): 123-34.

Hirschman, A. O. 1972. *Strategies of Economic Development: Processes and Problems.* New York: John Wiley.

Hoover, Edgar M. 1948. *The Location of Economic Activity.* New York: McGraw-Hill.

Huff, David L. 1963. "A Probabilistic Analysis of Shopping Center Trade Areas." *Land Economics* 39: 81-90.

Isard, Walter. 1975. *Introduction to Regional Science.* Englewood Cliffs, NJ: Prentice Hall.

Jacobs, Jane. 1969. *The Economy of Cities.* New York: Random House.

Jones, Bryan D., and Lynn W. Bachelor. 1984. "Local Policy Discretion and the Corporate Surplus." In *Urban Economic Development,* edited by R. D. Bingham and J. P. Blair, pp. 245-67. Beverly Hills, CA: Sage.

Jud, G. Donald, and D. Gadar Bennet. 1986. "Public Schools and the Pattern of Intraurban Residential Mobility." *Land Economics* 62 (4): 362-70.

Kasarda, John O. 1988. "Jobs, Migration, and Emerging Urban Mismatches." In *Urban Change and Poverty,* edited by M. McGeary and L. Lynn, pp. 176-194. Washington, DC: National Academy Press.

Keil, Stanley R., and Richard S. Mack. 1986. "Identifying Export Potential in the Export Sector." *Growth and Change* 55:1-10.

Kieschnick, Michael. 1981. *Taxes and Growth: Business Incentives and Economic Development.* Washington, DC: Council of State Planning Agencies.

Klaasen, L. H., and A. Pawlowski. 1982. "Long-Term Forecasting, Meditations of Two Pitfall Collectors." *Man, Environment, Space, and Time* 2 (1): 17-28.

Knight, Richard V. 1987. "Governing the Post-Industrial Metropolis—Building the Global City." Paper presented at Milan, Italy.

Kozlowski, Paul J. 1987. "Regional Indexes of Leading Indicators: An Evaluation of Forecasting Performance." *Growth and Change,* Summer, pp. 62-73.

Levy, John M. 1985. *Urban and Metropolitan Economics.* New York: McGraw-Hill.

Lichtenberg, R. M. 1960. *One-Tenth of a Nation.* Cambridge, MA: Harvard University Press.

Little, James T. 1980. "Contemporary Housing Markets and Neighborhood Change." In *Residential Mobility and Public Policy,* edited by W. V. Clark and E. More, pp. 126-49. Beverly Hills, CA: Sage.

Losch, August. 1954. *The Economics of Location.* New Haven, CT: Yale University Press.

Lovell, Catherine, and Charles Tobin. 1981. "The Mandate Issue." *Public Administration Review* 41: 318-31.

Luger, Michael. 1986. "The Rent Control Paradox: Explanations and Prescriptions." *Review of Regional Studies* 16 (3): 25-41.

MacDonald, Don N., James Murdoch, and Harry L. White. 1987. "Uncertain Hazards, Insurance and Consumer Choice." *Land Economics* 63 (4): 361-71.

Mansfield, Edwin. 1991. *Microeconomics: Shorter Seventh Edition.* New York: Norton.

Mills, David E. 1989. "Is Zoning a Negative Sum Game?" *Land Economics* 65 (1): 1-12.

Mills, Edwin S., and Bruce W. Hamilton. 1984. *Urban Economics.* 3d ed. Glenview, IL: Scott, Foresman.

Moorehouse, John C. 1987. "Long-Term Rent Control and Tenant Subsidies." *Quarterly Review of Economics and Business* 27 (3): 6-24.

Morgan, W. 1964. "The Effects of State and Local Tax and Financial Incentives on Industrial Location." Ph.D. diss., University of Colorado.

Morrill, R. L. 1987. "The Structure of Shopping in a Metropolis." *Urban Geography* 8: 97-128.

Morse, George. 1990. "Moving from R @ E's to Jobs." In *The Expansion and Retention of Existing Businesses*. Ames: Iowa State University Press.

Muller, Thomas, and Grace Dawson. 1972. *The Fiscal Impact of Residential and Commercial Development*. Washington, DC: Urban Institute.

Musgrave, Richard A. 1959. *The Theory of Public Finance*. New York: McGraw-Hill.

Muth, Richard F. 1969. *Cities and Housing*. Chicago: University of Chicago Press.

Myrdal, Gunnar. 1957. *Economic Theory and Underdeveloped Regions*. London: Duckworth.

Neenan, W. B. 1972. *Political Economy of Urban Areas*. Chicago: Markham.

Norgaard, Richard. 1984. Coevolutionary Development Potential." *Land Economics* 60: 159-76.

Oates, Wallace E. 1969a. "On Local Finance and the Tiebout Model." *American Economic Review* 59: 957-71.

Oates, Wallace E. 1969b. "The Effects of Property Taxes and Local Public Spending on Property Values: An Empirical Study of Tax Capitalization and the Tiebout Hypothesis." *Journal of Political Economy* 77:957-70.

Oates, Wallace E., E. P. Howrey, and William J. Baumol. 1971. "An Analysis of Public Policy in Dynamic Urban Models." *Journal of Political Economy* 79: 142-53.

Ohlin, B. 1933. *Interregional and International Trade*. Cambridge, MA: Harvard University Press.

Olsen, Edgar. 1969. "A Competitive Theory of the Housing Market." *American Economic Review* 59:612-21.

Papke, Leslie E. 1987. "Subnational Taxation and Capital Mobility: Estimates of Price Elasticities." *Motivational Tax Journal* 40 (2): 141-203.

Persky, Joseph, David Ranney, and Wim Wiewel. 1993. "Import Substitution and Local Development." *Economic Development Quarterly* 7 (1): 18-29.

Porell, Frank W. 1985. "One Man's Ceiling Is Another Man's Floor: Landlord Manager Residency and Housing Conditions." *Land Economics* 61 (2): 106-18.

Pred, A. R. 1966. *The Spatial Dynamics of U.S. Urban-Industrial Growth*. Cambridge: MIT Press.

Pred, Allen. 1977. *City-Systems in Advanced Economics*. New York: John Wiley.

Premus, Robert. 1982. "Locational High-Technology Firms and Regional Economic Development." U.S. Congress, Joint Economic Committee Report. Washington, DC: Joint Economic Committee.

Ramsey, D. D. 1972. "Suburban-Central City Exploitation Thesis: Comment." *National Tax Journal* 25: 599-604.

Reilly, William J. 1931. *The Law of Retail Gravitation*. New York: Pillsbury.

Rhoads, Steven E. 1985. *The Economists' View of the World: Government Markets and Public Policy*. New York: Cambridge University Press.

Ricardo, David. 1911. *Principles of Political Economy and Taxation*. London: J. M. Dent & Son.

Richardson, Harry. 1978. *Urban Economics*. Hinsdale, IL: Dryden.

Roback, Jennifer. 1982. "Wages, Rents and the Quality of Life." *Journal of Political Economy* 90 (6): 1257-78.

Romans, T., and G. Sabrahamanyan. 1979. "State and Local Taxes, Transfers, and Regional Economic Growth." *Southern Economic Journal* 46:435-44.

Rosen, S. 1974. "Hedonic Markets and Implicit Prices: Product Differentiation in Pure Competition." *Journal of Political Economy* 82:34-55.

Rubin, Barry M., and Rodney A. Erickson. 1980. "Specification and Performance Improvements in Regional Econometric Forecasting Models: A Model for the Milwaukee Metropolitan Area." *Journal of Regional Science* 20 (1): 11-35.

Rubin, Herbert J. 1988. "Shoot Anything That Flies: Claim Anything That Falls." *Economic Development Quarterly* 2 (3): 236-51.

Rusk, Dean. 1993. *Cities Without Suburbs.* Washington, DC: Woodrow Wilson Center.

Sargent, Susan. 1980. "Masculine Cities and Feminine Suburbs" *Signs* 5: 93-108.

Sarkissian, Wendy. 1976. "The Idea of Social Mix in Planning: A Historical Review." *Urban Studies* 13 (3): 27-38.

Schmenner, Roger. 1982. *Making Business Location Decisions.* Englewood Cliffs, NJ: Prentice Hall.

Schmenner, Roger W. 1981. "Locational Decisions of Large Firms: Implications for Public Policy." *Commentary,* January, pp. 3-7.

Shlay, Anne B. 1989. "Financing Community: Methods for Assessing Residential Credit Disparities, Market Barriers and Institutional Reinvestment Performance in the Metropolis." *Journal of Urban Affairs* 11 (3): 201-23.

Siegan, Bernard. 1970. "Non-Zoning in Houston." *Journal of Law and Economics* 13: 71-113.

Skinner, G. W. 1964. "Marketing and Social Structure in Rural China—I." *Journal of Asian Studies* 24: 3-33.

Skoro, Charles L. 1988. "Ranking of State Business Climates." *Economic Development Quarterly* 2 (2): 138-52.

Stabler, J. C., and P. R. Williams. 1973. "The Changing Structure of the Central-Place Hierarchy." *Land Economics* 49: 454-58.

Steponaitis, V. P. 1981. "Settlement Hierarchies and Political Complexity in Nonmarket Societies: The Formative Period of the Valley of Mexico." *American Anthropologists* 83: 320-365.

Sternberg, Ernest. 1991. "The Sectoral Cluster in Economic Development Policy: Lessons from Rochester and Buffalo, New York." *Economic Development Quarterly* 5 (4): 342-56.

Sternlieb, George. 1986. "Grasping the Future." In *New Roles for Old Cities,* edited by E. Rose, chap. 14. Brookfield, VT: Gower.

Storey, David J., and Steven G. Johnson. 1987. "Regional Variations in Entrepreneurship in the U.K." *Scottish Journal of Political Economy* 34 (2): 161-73.

Swaney, James A. 1981. "Externality and Community." *Journal of Economic Issues* 15: 610-27.

Thisse, Jacques-François. 1987. "Location Theory, Regional Science and Economics." *Journal of Regional Science* 27 (4): 519-28.

Thompson, Wilbur. 1984. "The City as a Distorted Price System." In *Urban Economic Issues: Readings and Analysis,* edited by S. Nehay and G. Nunn, pp. 13-21. Glenview, IL: Scott, Foresman.

Thompson, Wilbur R. 1968. *A Preface to Urban Economics.* Baltimore: Johns Hopkins University Press.

Thompson, Wilbur R. and Philip R. Thompson. 1987. "Alternative Paths to the Revival of Industrial Cities." In *The Future of Winter Cities,* edited by G. Gappert, pp. 233-250. Newbury Park, CA: Sage.

Tiebout, Charles. 1956. "A Pure Theory of Local Public Expenditure." *Journal of Political Economy* 64: 416-24.

Tiebout, Charles. 1962. *The Community Economic Base Study.* New York: Committee for Economic Development.

Tolchin, Susan, and Martin Tolchin. 1987. *Buying Into America.* New York: Time Books.

U.S. Department of Housing and Urban Development. 1979. *Measuring Racial Discrimination in American Housing Markets.* Washington, DC: Department of Housing and Urban Development.

U.S. Department of Housing and Urban Development. 1988. *The President's National Urban Policy Report, 1988.* New York: U.S. Department of Housing and Urban Development.

Van de Berg, Leo. 1986. *Urban Systems in Dynamic Society.* London: Gower.

Voith, Richard. 1992. "City and Suburban Growth: Substitutes or Complements?" *Business Review,* pp. 341-57.

Warner, Paul D. 1989. "Alternative Strategies for Economic Development: Evidence from Southern Metropolitan Areas." *Urban Affairs Quarterly* 24 (3): 389-411.

Wasylenko, Michael. 1984. "The Effects of Business Climate on Employment Growth in the States Between 1973 and 1980." Report for the Minnesota Tax Study Commission.

Weicher, John L., and Thomas G. Thibodeau. 1988. "Filtering and Housing Markets: An Empirical Analysis." *Journal of Urban Economics* 23: 21-40.

Weiss, Leonard W. 1972. "The Geographic Size of Markets in Manufacturing." *Review of Economics and Statistics* 54: 255-57.

Weiss, Steven J., and Edwin C. Gooding. 1970. "Estimation of Differential Employment Multipliers in a Small Regional Economy." In *Regional Economics: A Reader,* edited by H. Richardson, pp. 55-67. London: Macmillan.

West, Douglass, Balder Von Hohenvalken, and Kenneth Kroner. 1985. "Tests of Interurban Central-Place Theories." *Economic Journal* 95: 101-17.

White, Sammis B. 1987. "Reservation Wages: Your Community May Be Competitive." *Economic Development Quarterly* 1 (1): 18-29.

Wiewel, Wim, Michael Teitz, and Robert Giloth. 1993. "The Economic Development of Neighborhoods and Localities." In *Theories of Local Development: Perspectives From Across the Disciplines,* edited by Richard D. Bingham and Robert Mier, pp. 80-99. Newbury Park, CA: Sage.

Yinger, John. 1986. "Measuring Racial Discrimination with Fair Housing Audits: Caught in the Act." *American Economic Review,* December, pp. 881-93.

⬗ Index

Access:
    central city, 248
    proximity versus, 211
Administrative regions, 19-20
African Americans:
    segregation and, 255-256, 260
    unemployment and, 27
Agglomeration economies, 74-75, 95-103,
        227-228
Aggregate economic fallout model, 254
Agriculture:
    mechanization of, 79
    metropolitan statistical areas and, 17
Airports, location decisions and, 63
Allardice, D. R., 315
Allen, D. N., 140
Allocative government functions, 275-278
Altruistic behavior, 4
Alvine, M. J., 128
Amenities, value placed on, 269-272
Annexation, 294
Appalachian region, 19
Ashton, D. J., 128
Assets, rate of return on, 172, 210, 232
Assumptions, economic analysis and, 2-3

Bachelor, L. W., 36, 177-178
Bartik, T. J., 51, 52, 172, 240
Baumol, W. J., 30, 183, 289-290
Beaten-path effect, migration and, 196, 197
Beauregard, R., 15

Beautification programs, 179
Bedroom suburbs, 17, 83
Behavior:
    altruistic, 4
    analyzing individual, 3-4
    productivity and, 26
    rational, 4
Benefit(s), 1
    economic development and, 168-170
    future, 14
    intangible, 302
    job growth, 176
    marginal private, 9
    marginal social, 9-10
    spillovers, 27
Benefit-cost comparisons:
    efficiency and, 5-6
    government programs and, 297-302
Bennet, D. G., 253
Berger, M. C., 270, 271, 273
Berkman, M. B., 53
Berry, B. L., 78
Beyers, W. B., 128
Bier, T., 254
Biotechnology firms, 98
Blair, J. P., 174, 207, 263, 264, 295
Blakely, E. J., 313
Blockbusting, 246
Blomquist, G. C., 270, 271, 273
Bloomberg, W., 205
Booth, D. E., 140
Borjas, G. J., 206

Borts, G. H., 200
Bowen, H. P., 191
Bradford, D. F., 183
Branch plants, 181
Break-even quantity, 72
Buildings, physical life of, 228-229
Bureaucratic organizations, urbanization and, 15
Bureaucrats, incentives and, 36-37
Burgess, E. W., 244
Business(es):
    clusters of, 16, 69, 227-228
    linkages between pairs of, 96-97
    retention programs, 262
Business centers, 16
Business climate, location decisions and, 53, 59
Business cost-reduction approaches, 180-181
Business cycle analysis, 155
Business formation, 263
    time lags and, 173
Business location. See Location decisions
Business ties, 42

California, Asian investments in, 207
Capital:
    availability of, 140-141
    flows, 198-199
    local accumulation, 263
    opportunity costs of, 13
    supply of, 171-172
Capital expenditures, local governments and, 297
Carlton, D., 54
Categorical grants, 284
Census data, 19, 154
Central business districts, 224-228, 280-281
Central cities:
    access to, 248
    annexation and, 294
    image of, 230
    investments in, 199
    metropolitan statistical areas and, 17
    outmigration and, 182
    suburbs benefiting from services of, 280-281
    See also Inner cities
Central city housing, low-quality, 226

Central-place theory, 66, 74-84
Ceteris paribus (other things equal) assumption, 2
Chicago, filtering-down theory and, 244
Chinitz, R., 137
Circular flow model, regional growth and, 120-126
Cities, 15
    attractiveness of, 290-291
    economic functions of, 79
    growth stages, 116-120
    hierarchical system of, 66, 74-80, 119
    innovations moving among, 201
    interdependence and, 80
    master plans, 311-312
    metropolitan statistical areas and, 17
    migration and, 194
    networks of, 66, 82-83
    optimal size, 278-279
    percent of residents in, 19
    quality of life and, 307
    race relations and, 306-307
    trading patterns among, 74
    urban development and, 307-308
    See also Central cities; Inner cities; Metropolitan areas; Urban areas
Citizens:
    consumer choices, 37
    uninformed, 35
Clark, G. L., 203-204
Class conflicts, 7
Clawback clauses, 178
Climate:
    housing prices and, 272
    urban growth and, 141
Clotfelter, C. T., 253
Coates, J. F., 307-308
Coefficient of specialization, 112-113
Collective actions, 3
Commercial development:
    neighborhoods and, 261-264
    revitalization and, 262
    strips and, 226-227
Commodity flows, 189-208
Commodity market, 121
Community, business location decisions and, 42
Commuting, 17, 83, 248-249
Comparative advantage, 189-191
Compensation differentials, 193

Competition:
  among localities, 169
  barriers to entry and, 173
  for markets, 69-74
  in government, 34
  location decisions and, 70
  market size and, 66
  real estate transactions and, 242-244
Competitive advantage, 146
Computers:
  at-home work and, 230
  quality of energy for, 54
  site-selection and, 59
Congestion, 28, 29, 119, 174, 246, 294
Conservative economists, 6-7
Consolidated metropolitan statistical area, 18
Construction costs, 218
Consume, marginal propensity to, 130
Consumers:
  immigration and, 205
  location of, 69, 82, 88
  location preferences, 70
  uncertain behavior of, 88
Consumption:
  individual versus communal, 307
  law of demand and, 2-3
  marginal private benefits and, 9
  prices and, 7
  purchases outside area and, 129
  utility maximizing, 4
Contingency planning, 314
Corporate income taxes, 52
Corporate site selection process, 56-60
Cost(s), 1
  altering, 13-14
  future, 14
  government programs, 297-302
  intangible, 302
  marginal, 13
  marginal social, 10
  of economic growth, 173-174
  profit formula and, 12-13
  relative, 190
  subsidies, 179
  zoning and, 233
Cost of living, migration and, 193
Cost spillovers, 27
Counties, metropolitan statistical areas and, 17
Crane, S. E., 155

Crime, 23, 182, 246
Cultural agglomeration model, 250
Cultural facilities, 15, 51
Cumulative causation, 182-183

Data, measurement errors and, 154
Dawson, G., 295
Decision making:
  benefit-cost analysis and, 297-302
  business location and, 41-65
  individuals and, 3-4
  land use, 218-222
  local government size and, 279-281
  market and, 7
  opportunity costs and, 13
  profits and, 12-14
  public choice perspective, 34-37
  rational, 4
Deductive models, 2-3
Delphi forecasting, 317-318
Demand:
  economic development and, 9
  efficiency and, 9-10
  export-base theory and, 127-139
  export sector and, 170
  for land, 248-249
  housing and, 238-240, 244-246, 251, 259
  land use and, 216-217
  law of, 2-3
  local growth and, 170-171
  location and, 67-69
  marginal social benefits and, 9-10
  market areas and, 66, 67-74
  prices and, 7-10
  rents and, 257-258
  spatial setting, 66, 67-69
  threshold, 72-73
Demand curve, 2-3, 8
  externalities and, 29
  stability of, 67
Demand density, 73, 79
Developer goals, 215-216
Development officials, 222-223
Development rights, transferable, 235
Devolution, 284
Diminishing marginal utility, 29
Direct and indirect coefficients, table of, 161-162

Direct coefficients, table of, 160-161
Discretionary subsidies, 180
Discrimination:
  arbitrary, 27
  housing and, 255-256, 260
Display variety agglomeration, 100
Distance, changing perceptions of, 92
Distribution, government functions, 275
Doeringer, P. B., 207
Doughnut city, 226
Dwelling unit development, 261

Eberts, R. W., 276
Econometric models, 149-155
Economic analysis:
  assumptions and, 2-3
  econometric models, 149-155
  externalities and, 27-33
  ideological perspectives, 6-7
  importance-strength survey, 157-159
  individual behavior and, 3-4
  input-output, 159-166
  metropolitan statistical areas and, 17
  models and, 2-3
  policy debates and, 4-7
  public sector and, 33-39
  shift and share analysis, 145-149
  simulation models, 149-150
Economic development:
  common themes in, 313-315
  defined, 14-15
  demand and, 9
  directed, 234
  economic growth and, 14
  equity and, 15
  external benefits and, 168-170, 282
  fiscal impact studies and, 295-297
  futurist perspectives, 305-310
  human capital strategies, 180-181
  import substitution and, 136
  income and, 14-15
  input-output analysis and, 164
  land use and, 209-237
  local competition for, 174-181
  localization economies and, 98
  low wages and, 22-27
  market areas and, 66-94
  market logic and, 1-21

politicians and, 35
public finance issues, 274-278
public sector and, 33
quality of life and, 15, 51
regional growth and, 116-144
services and, 128
social concerns and, 22-40
special interest groups and, 35
subsidies and, 174-180
supply-side theories of, 139-142
targeting activities and, 184-185
unemployment and, 22-27
Economic development agencies, growth of,
  36
Economic growth, 6
  beneficiaries of, 168-174
  costs of, 173-174
  cumulative, 182-183
  disequilibrium, 182
  econometric models and, 149-155
  economic development and, 14
  export-base theory of, 127-139
  external benefits from, 168-170
  importance-strength survey, 157-159
  innovations and, 199-203
  input-output analysis and, 162-166
  monetary flows and, 120-139
  movement between stages, 119-120
  opponents of, 173-174
  regional, 116-144
  shift and share analysis, 145-149
  taxes and, 52
Economic indicators, local leading, 155-156
Economic man, 34
Economic structure, 95-115
Economic theory, econometric models and,
  150
Economics:
  housing, 238-244
  of migration, 193-197
  planning process and, 304
Economies:
  agglomeration, 74-75, 95-103, 227-228
  cohesive forces in, 95-115
  efficient, 5
  informal, 264-267
  localization, 97-100
  open, 121
  urbanization, 100-102

Economies of scale:
  infrastructure and, 100-101
  production and, 67, 73, 79
Economists:
  conservative versus liberal, 6-7
  radical, 7
  worldview of, 1-7
Educated citizenry, benefits of, 11
Education:
  attracting business and, 14
  economic development and, 15
  positive externalities and, 29
  quality of life and, 51
  skilled labor and, 202, 263
Efficiency:
  demand and, 9-10
  government activities and, 33-39, 292
  policy issues, 5-6
  supply and, 9-10
  taxes and, 285
Eminent domain, 232
Employment:
  coefficient of specialization and, 112-113
  export, 108-112, 127-128, 135, 151
  export-base approach and, 131-133
  labor migration and, 193
  market for, 174-176
  minimum wage effects, 24
  share of national, 145-146
  temporary, 178
  See also Job creation; Labor
Employment concentrations, 103, 107
Employment growth, time path of, 201-202
Employment impact studies, 134-135
Employment level, demand for labor and, 25
Employment location quotient, 106-107
Endres, C. R., 263, 264
Energy costs, location decisions and, 54, 59, 229-230
Entitlement programs, 180
Entrepreneurship, 140, 185, 263
Environmental concerns, location decisions and, 62
Environmental impact statements, 217-218
Equity:
  economic development and, 15
  policy and, 6
Equity capital, 141
Erickson, R. A., 59

Escheat, 232
Ethical issues, externalities and, 33
Ethnic neighborhoods, 19
Export(s):
  comparative advantage and, 190-191
  demand for, 170
  economic growth and, 116-117, 127-139
  monetary flows and, 123
  permanent increases in, 125-126
  primacy of, 135
  productivity increases and, 137
  regional growth and, 116-117
  service firms and, 137, 138
Export-base theory of growth, 127-139, 151-152
Export employment, 108-112, 127-128, 135, 151
Export income, 131
External benefits, economic development and, 282
External-economy industries, 103-104
Externalities, 27-33
  government and, 7, 11-12, 277
  intergovernmental, 280-282
  land use and, 212, 217
  negative, 11
  positive, 11

Factor mobility, 192
Fagan, M., 197
Fairness, public policies and, 6
Family:
  importance of, 306
  two-income, 42
Farm Belt, immigrant labor and, 205
Federal mandates, 290
Federal subsidies, 178-179
Feedbacks, 137-138, 185
Fichtenbaum, R. H., 174
Filtering-down theory, 244-248
Financial services, property value and, 224
Fiscal impact studies, 295-297
Fiscal improvement, 169-170
Fiscal problems, local government and, 288-291
Fiscal strategies, 291-295
Fixed costs, economies of scale and, 73
Floor area ratio, 235-236

Forecasting:
    Delphi, 317-318
    econometric models and, 150
    importance of timing and, 309
Foreign investment:
    in industrial sector, 206-207
    political climate and, 54
Foreign workers, 205
Formal income model, 128-131
Forrester, J., 186
Fosler, R. S., 315
Free-rider problem, 276
Freight absorption, 82
Friedman, Milton, 7
Friends, importance of, 306
Fringe benefits, for employees, 49, 51
Functional regions, 16
Future, predictions of, 153-154
Futures studies tools, 317-320
Futurists, economic development and,
    305-310

Galster, G. C., 247
Games, futures studies and, 318-319
Gappert, G., 316
Garrison, W. L., 78
Gender, attitudes toward, 306-307
Geographic immobility, 26
Ghetto dispersal, 260-261
Ghetto improvement, 260-261
Giese, A., 203, 315
Gifts received, 123
Gillis, W., 128
Gooding, E. C., 151
Goods:
    merit, 277-278
    poorly defined nature of, 178
    See also Public goods
Gornberg, T. J., 276
Government:
    accountability and, 37
    efficiency and, 33-39, 292
    externalities and, 7, 11-12, 32
    functions, 274-278
    housing demand and, 251
    income distribution and, 275
    income transfers and, 123
    invisible hand in, 37

    metropolitan, 274-303
    property rights and, 232
    return of authority to, 284
    See also Local government
Government action, conservative versus
        liberal, 6-7
Governmental regions, 20
Government incentives, location decisions
        and, 52-53
Government role:
    information and, 12
    job creation and, 25
    monopoly regulation and, 12
    See also Public goods
Grants, intergovernmental, 281-285
Gravity migration model, 195
Green, H. L., 85

Hamilton, B. W., 102
Hanson, R. L., 53
Harman, R., 308
Harris, J. R., 194-195
Harris-Todaro migration model, 194-195
Haug, P., 98
Hayward, D. J., 140
Health, poverty and, 23
Heckscher, E. F., 190
Hedonic pricing, 241-242, 269-273
Highest and best use, 212-214, 231
High-tech firms, 315
    amenity orientation of, 141
    employment in, 184-185
    location decisions and, 51
Hill, E. W., 254
Hinterland, 16, 66, 75, 77
    changes and, 79
    expansion strategies, 92-93
    measuring, 84-86
    retail gravitation and, 86-88
Hirschman, A. O., 96
Hoehn, J. P., 270, 271
Home, working at, 230
Homelessness, 23, 154
Homogeneous regions, 19
Hoover, E. M., 56
Housing:
    demand for, 238-240, 244-246, 251, 259
    informal economy and, 264-267

policy, 256-261
prices, 238-241, 251, 272
residential location and, 244-256
segregation and, 255-256, 260
supply and, 238-240, 251
trade-off model and, 248-250
Housing assistance programs, 259-260
Housing economics, 238-244
Houston:
location quotients in, 107
zoning in, 233
Huff, D. L., 85, 88
Human capital:
economic development strategies, 180-181
mobility of, 198
Humidity, quality of life and, 272
Hunches, 14

Ideas, economic growth and, 199-203
Imitation, localization economies and, 99
Immigration, urban development and,
205-207
Impact studies, input-output analysis and,
164-165
Import(s):
indirect, 123
input-output analysis and, 163-164
substitution, 136
Import, marginal propensity to, 130, 138-139
Importance-strength analysis, 157-159
Incentives:
government officials and, 34-37
location decisions and, 60
market system and, 4
perverse, 34-37
subsidies and, 174-180
Income:
demand for housing and, 244-245
economic development and, 14-15
economic growth and, 181
export-base theory and, 127-131
government role in distribution of, 275
informal economy and, 264
labor productivity and, 136
land use decisions and, 220-222
leisure versus, 4, 306
local growth and, 172
money inflows and, 122

nonlocal sources of, 123
productivity and, 135
regional growth and, 170
single-family housing and, 231
suburbs and, 182
temporary increase in, 126
Income creation, 169
Income support programs, 259-260
Income taxes, 52
Individual behavior, economic analysis and,
3-4
Industrial classifications, 104-106
Industrial filtering, 118
Industrial life cycle, employment growth
over, 202
Industrial recruitment, 315
Industries:
agglomeration in, 96, 97-100
external-economy, 103-104
foreign ownership and, 206-207
fostering growth in, 157-159
growth differentials, 146
region's specialization in, 106-112
shift-share components, 145-149
Inefficiency, 176-180
Inertia, location decisions and, 42
Information:
imperfect, 12
prices and, 7-8
work opportunities and, 26
Information asymmetry, 178
Infrastructure, 13
economies of scale in, 100-101
location decisions and, 52-53
policies about, 234
urban access and, 211
Infrastructure assistance, 175, 179
In-migration, 193-197
Inner cities:
informal economy and, 264-265
job creation in, 25
minorities and, 255
unemployment in, 22-27
Innovation:
economic growth and, 199-203
localization economies and, 99
urban, 119
Input, locational weight of, 46
Input-output analysis, 159-166

Interfirm sales, 121
Intergovernmental grants, 281-285
Intergovernmental rearrangements, 293-294
Intergovernmental spillovers, 280-282
Intergovernmental transfers, 296
Interindustry agglomeration, 96, 97-100
Interindustry linkages, input-output analysis
    and, 159-161, 163
Intermediate inputs, 139-140
International commerce, institutional factors
    and, 83
International regions, 15
Investment:
    by nonresidents, 123, 172
    capital available for, 199
    foreign owners and, 206-207
    local, 263
    return on, 13
Invisible hand:
    in government, 37
    public interest and, 34
Isard, W., 95

Jacobs, Jane, 116, 118, 119, 136, 267
Job creation, 25, 169
    cost of, 180
    incentives, 32
    informal economy and, 265
    local programs, 176-177
    local services, 128
    policies and, 203-207
Job training programs, 263
Johnson, S. G., 140
Joint ventures, 141
Jones, B. D., 36, 177-178
Jud, G. D., 253

Kelejian, H. H., 183
Klaasen, L. H., 154
Knight, R. V., 316
Kozlowski, P. J., 155-156

Labor:
    abundant, 190
    amenities and, 51
    business relocation and, 42

demand for, 24-26
mobility of, 172, 192, 193-197
opportunity costs of, 13
preparation programs, 25-26
specialization of, 119
training, 175
turnover of, 24
unskilled, 23-24
See also Employment
Labor costs, location decisions and, 49-51, 61
Labor force:
    highly skilled, 202
    localization economies and, 98
    quality of, 142, 181
    size of, 142
Labor market:
    loose, 169
    metropolitan area, 49
    traditional model, 23-24
Labor-oriented industries, location decisions
    and, 49
Labor productivity, 25
    improving, 136
    regional differences, 49-50
Labor supply curve, 23, 191
Laissez-faire market, 6
    externalities and, 27, 29
    optimal production level and, 29
    public interest and, 34
Land, 141
    demand for, 248-249
    development process, 172, 214-223
    economic development and, 232-236
    productivity of, 210-211
    profit feasibility study and, 218-222
    use of, 209-237
    value of, 209-214
Land developers, 172-173
Land rents, 209-211
Land speculation, 228
Land use patterns, 223-228
Leamer, E. E., 191
Leapfrog development, 228
Legal services, property value and, 224
Leisure, balance with work, 4, 306
Liberal economists, 6-7
Lichtenberg, R. M., 103
Life cycle model, 118
Lifestyle, urban society and, 15

Linkage programs, 234-235
Little, J. T., 246
Loans:
  discrimination and, 256
  low interest, 175, 223
Local capital accumulation, 263
Local economic development, 174-181
Local export sectors, minimum requirements
    technique and, 112
Local financial sectors, 121
Local government, 20
  benefit-cost analysis and, 297-302
  efficiency of, 33-39
  fiscal impact studies and, 295-297
  fiscal problems and, 288-291
  fiscal strategies, 291-295
  scope of, 278-281
  size of, 278-281
Local housing programs, 256-261
Localities, competition among, 169
Localization economy, 97-100
Local leading economic indicators, 155-156
Local services:
  demand for, 138, 170
  job creation and, 128
Location:
  agglomeration economies and, 95-103
  competition for, 102
  demand and, 67-69
  principle of median, 44-46
Locational analysis, 56
Location decisions, 41-65
  business climate and, 53, 59
  competition and, 70
  energy costs and, 54, 59
  formation of cities and, 66
  future factors, 62-63
  government incentives and, 52-53
  inertia and, 42
  infrastructure and, 52-53
  input-output analysis and, 164
  labor costs and, 49-51, 61
  nearness to other producers and, 74-75
  political climate and, 54
  process, 55-60
  production costs and, 47-49, 81
  quality of life and, 51, 61, 62, 269
  site costs and, 53-54
  subsidies and, 175-176

taxes and, 52, 62
transportation costs and, 42-47, 48, 61, 82
Location quotients, 106-112
Longino, C. F., Jr., 197
Los Angeles, location quotients in, 107
Losch, A., 84
Lovell, C., 290
Luger, M., 258
Lump-sum grants, 283

MacDonald, D. N., 253
Machinery, sharing specialized, 98-99
Managers, utility maximization and, 14
Mansfield, E., 24
Manufacturing:
  central business districts and, 226
  government assistance and, 53
  satellite communities and, 17
  spatial cost variations, 81
  transportation costs and, 42-47
Marginal costs, 13
Marginal private benefits, 9
Marginal revenue, 13
Marginal social benefits, 9-10
Marginal social costs, 10
Market(s):
  circular flow model and, 121
  competition for, 69-74
  imperfections in, 26-27
  inefficient, 11
  land use and, 213-214
  logic of, 1-21
  operation of, 7-10
  prices and, 7-8
  profit and, 12-14
  proximity to, 211
  real estate transactions and, 242-244
  rents and, 257-258
  size of, 66, 70, 73-74
Market areas:
  demand and, 66, 67-74
  economic development and, 66-94
  hinterland and, 84-93
  increasing, 79
  locating in center of, 66, 74-84
  overlap of, 74
  radius of, 78
  urban hierarchy and, 66, 74-80

Market barriers, 26-27
Market comparison, real estate value and, 242
Market for jobs, 174-176
Marketing, interdependencies and, 95
Market-oriented producers, business location
    and, 43, 45-46
Market study, land use and, 216
Matching grants, 283-384
Material-oriented producers, business
    location and, 43
Merit goods, 277-278
Metropolitan areas:
    diversity within, 19
    exports, 116-117
    industrial filtering and, 118
    innovations and, 200-201
    labor markets, 49
    land use and, 209-237
    production and, 202
    rapid growth of, 17-19
    roads and, 226
    spreading, 229-232
    transportation and, 79
Metropolitan government, 274-303
Metropolitan statistical areas (MSAs), 16-19
Midwest, rural ghost towns in, 79
Migration, economics of, 193-197
Mills, D. E., 233
Mills, E. S., 102
Minimum requirements (MR) technique, 112
Minimum wage laws, 24
Minorities:
    heavy industry towns and, 185
    inner city and, 255
    unemployment and, 27
Models, economic analysis and, 2-3
Modification, localization economies and, 99
Monetary flows:
    circular flow model and, 120-126
    economic growth and, 127-139
Monetary success, preference for, 306
Money capital:
    mobility of, 198
    supply of, 171-172
Monocentric city model, 224-226
Monopolies, 12, 70, 172-173
Moorehouse, J. C., 258
Moral issues, externalities and, 33
Morgan, W., 61, 62

Morse, G., 53
Muller, T., 295
Multinational regions, 15
Multiple nuclear city, 227-228, 249-250
Murdoch, J., 253
Museums, quality of life and, 51
Musgrave, R. A., 274
Muth, R. F., 248
Myrdal, G., 182

National Housing Act of 1949, 238
Natural resources, 141
Negative externalities, 27, 28-30, 212
Neighborhood(s), 15
    change and, 244-256
    cultural factors and, 250
    economic fallout model and, 254
    filtering-down theory and, 244-248
    growth consequences, 174
    homogeneous, 19
    racial transition and, 246
Neighborhood commercial development,
    261-264
Neighborhood shopping areas, 69, 93
Ness, P., 98
New England, metropolitan statistical areas
    in, 17
Newspaper circulation, hinterland and, 85
New York City, employment concentrations
    and, 103, 107
Nodal regions, 16
Noise, 246
Nonprofit institutions, location decisions and, 55
Nonresidents, business sales to, 122, 123
Norgaard, R., 42
Normative questions, 4-5
North American Free Trade Agreement, 190
Nuclear city, multiple, 227-228, 249-250

Oates, W. E., 253, 278
Ohlin, B., 190
Olsen, E., 247
Open economy, 121
Operating expenses, local governments and,
    296-297
Opportunity costs, 10, 13, 190
Out-migration, 182, 193-197

Output:
    increases in, 9-10
    profit-maximizing level of, 70
    See also Production

Papke, L. E., 52
Parameters, econometric models and, 150
Part-time jobs, 169
Pawlowski, A., 154
Persky, J., 136
Perverse incentives, 34-37
Physical capital, mobility of, 198
Physical improvements, 170
Planned unit developments, 235
Planning:
    development policy and, 310-316
    economics and, 304
    futures studies tools and, 317-320
Police power, 232
Policies:
    administrative regions and, 19
    comparative advantage and, 190
    complex systems and, 185-186
    econometric models and, 153
    economic analysis and, 4-7
    efficiency and, 5-6
    equity and, 6
    filtering-down theory and, 247
    hinterland and, 92
    housing, 256-261
    informal economy and, 265-267
    infrastructure, 234
    job creation and, 203-207
    metropolitan level, 16, 17
    organizations influencing, 177
    planning perspective on, 310-316
    resource mobility and, 203-207
    stages of growth and, 119-120
    targeting activities and, 184
Political factors:
    location decisions and, 54, 55
    urban networks and, 82-83
Political fragmentation, 20
Political issues:
    African American urban areas and, 261
    metropolitan spread and, 231
Political process, business incentive
        programs and, 177

Politicians:
    self-interest of, 34-36
    strength or weakness of, 177
Pollution, 11, 27, 28, 31, 174, 251
Population:
    declines in, 291
    density of, 17
    metropolitan statistical areas and, 17
    migration of, 193-197
Population-income decline, 182
Population size:
    central-place model and, 77
    externalities and, 30
Porell, F. W., 247
Positive externalities, 27, 29, 32, 212
Positive questions, 4-5
Poverty, causes of, 23
Precision operations, 184-185
Pred, A., 80
Premus, R., 207
Prices:
    commodity, 190
    customer location and, 82
    demand and, 7-10
    government goods and, 37-38
    hedonic models, 270
    housing, 238-241, 251, 272
    immigrant labor and, 205
    law of demand and, 2-3
    market, 7-8
    profit-maximizing level of output and, 70
    resource, 10, 190
    supply and, 7-10
Pricing, hedonic, 241-242, 269-273
Primary metropolitan statistical area, 18
Private benefits, marginal, 9
Private sector job development, 169
Privatization, 292-293
Producers, nearness to other, 74-75
Product:
    locational weight of, 46
    market area and, 66, 67-74
    spin-offs, 119
    vaguely defined, 178
Product differentiation, 83
Production:
    comparative advantage and, 190
    concentration in, 103
    economies of scale in, 67, 73, 79

efficient, 5
interdependencies and, 95, 96
location decisions and, 41-65
market-oriented, 43
material-oriented, 43
metropolitan areas, 202
metropolitan spread and, 229
negative effects of increased, 174
optimal level of, 29
prices and, 7, 8-9
Production costs, 10, 118
location decisions and, 47-49, 81
profit formula and, 12, 13
spatial differences on, 81
Productivity:
improving, 136
income and, 135
labor, 25, 49-50, 136
of land, 210-211
measuring, 26
progressive sector, 289-290
Profits:
excess, 69-70
formula for, 12
land use and, 213-216, 218-222
location decisions and, 55, 56
market economy and, 12-14
maximizing, 13-14, 70
monopoly, 173
normal, 70, 72
reinvesting, 199
transportation costs and, 73
Property, 209
Property rights, 178, 232
Property taxes, 52, 170, 252, 287
Property values, 291
Proximity to markets, 211
Public assistance, land development and,
222-223
Public choice perspective, decision making
and, 34-37
Public construction projects, 126
Public finance issues, 274-278
Public goods, 11
economies of scale and, 100-101
property values and, 251-253
pure, 275-276
quality of life and, 51
user fees and, 37, 292, 294-295

Public land planners, 235
Public-private partnerships, 293
Public sector:
improving, 33-39
job creation in, 25, 169
Public sector employees:
self-interest and, 36
wages and, 38
Public utilities, regulation of, 12

Quality of life:
attracting business and, 14
cities and, 307
economic development and, 15
externalities and, 27
location decisions and, 51, 61, 62, 269
migration and, 193

Race, attitudes toward, 306-307
Racial transition neighborhoods, 246
Radical economic analysis, 7
Random variations, averaging, 101-102
Range, threshold demand and, 72-73
Ranney, D., 136
Rationality assumption, 4
Real estate taxes, 52
Redlining, 246
Region(s), 15
administrative, 19-20
exchanges with rest of world, 121
feedbacks and, 137-138
functional, 16
governmental, 20
homogeneous, 19
industry specialization, 106-112
innovations and, 201-203
metropolitan statistical areas, 16-19
migration between, 195
nodal, 16
pro-growth, 174
quality-of-life index for, 269-273
resource mobility among, 191
small versus large, 137
underdeveloped, 96-97, 163, 182
Regional economic development, 116-144
Regional exports, location quotients and,
108-112

Regional growth:
  circular flow model and, 120-126
  econometric models and, 150-155
  economic development and, 116-144
  export-base theory of, 127-139
  shift-share components, 145-149
  stages of, 116-120
  supply versus demand approaches, 142
  supply-side approaches, 139-142
Regional income, factors determining,
  130-131
Regional interaction models, 189-193
Regional interdependence, 137-138
Regional multipliers, 161
Regional structure, input-output analysis and,
  163
Regulation, 7, 12
Regulatory relief, 175
Reilly, William J., 86-88
Relocation costs, 191, 193-194, 196
Rents, 240
  hedonic models, 270
  land, 209-211
Rent bid functions, 224
Rent control, 257-258
Research and development activity, 118, 185
Residential areas, 16
Residential location, 244-256
Resource allocation:
  efficiency and, 5
  externalities and, 28-30
Resource flows, 189-208
Resource market, 121
Resource mobility, 191-193
Resource prices, 190
Resource supply, characteristics of, 171-173
Retail activities:
  central business district and, 225
  outlying clusters, 228
Retail gravitation, Reilly's law of, 86-88
Retiree-migrant development strategy, 197
Retirement communities, 83
Revenue(s):
  altering, 13-14
  elasticity of, 288
  estimation of, 296
  marginal, 13
  profit formula and, 12
Rewards, market system and, 4

Ribbon development, 227
Ricardo, D., 210-211
Richardson, H., 80
Right-to-work laws, 50
Roads, 80, 211
  axial development and, 226-227
  location decisions and, 46
  quality of life and, 51
Roback, J., 51, 270
Romans, T., 52
Rosen, S., 270
Rubin, H. J., 184
Rural areas, 75
  capital and, 199
  expanding hinterland and, 92
  retirement to, 197
Rural ghost towns, 79
Rusk, D., 231, 255, 294

Sabrahamanyan, G., 52
Sale-lease backs, 175
Sandoval, R. M., 205
Sargent, S., 306
Sarkissian, W., 250
Satellite communities, 17
Satisfaction, maximizing, 3-4
Scenarios, futures studies and, 319
Schmenner, R. W., 42, 50, 52, 56-57
Segregated housing, 255-256, 260
Self-interest, 1
  elected officials and, 34-36
  location decisions and, 55
  public interest and, 34
  public-sector employees, 36
  social interest and, 6
Service(s):
  duplication of, 119
  economic development and, 128
  economic growth and, 117
  export earnings and, 128, 137, 138
Service employment:
  export employment and, 151
  suburbs and, 182
Service improvements, 179
Shift and share analysis, 145-149
Shipping costs, 43-44, 46
Shirking, 24
Shlay, A. B., 256

Shopping:
  comparison, 99-100
  hinterland and, 85, 86-88
  neighborhood areas, 69, 93
Shopping centers, 92-93
Siegan, Bernard, 232-233
Simulation models, 149-150
Site assistance, 175
Site costs, location decisions and, 53-54
Skill levels, job creation and, 25
Skilled operations, 181
Skoro, C. L., 59
Smith, Adam, 3-4
Social benefits, marginal, 9-10
Social change, urbanization and, 15-16
Social concerns, economic development and,
  22-40
Social costs, marginal, 10
Social interest, self-interest and, 6
Socially homogeneous neighborhoods, 250
Social scanning, 319-320
Southeast, hierarchy of cities in, 80
Southwest, immigrant labor and, 205
Spatial economic models, 3
Special interests, economic development and,
  35
Specialization, coefficient of, 112-113
Speculation, land, 228
Spillovers, 27, 103
Stabler, J. C., 79
Standard Industrial Classification (SIC)
  system, 104-106
Statistical analysis, 150
Stein, J., 200
Sternal, B. K., 128
Sternberg, E., 98
Stockholders, utility maximization and, 14
Storey, D. J., 140
Strategic planning, 314
Subsidies, 13, 174-180
  cost versus value, 179-180
  discretionary versus entitlement, 180
  excessive, 36
  federal, 178-179
  location decisions and, 52-53
  over-, 176-180
  positive externalities and, 32
Suburban shopping centers, 92-93
Suburban workforce, 230, 255

Suburbs, 83, 231
  annexation and, 294
  central city services and, 280-281
  income and, 182, 244-246
  lifestyle in, 230
  metropolitan statistical areas and, 17
  percentage of residents in, 19
  service jobs and, 182
  trade-off model and, 248-250
Sunbelt cities, 141
Supply:
  efficiency and, 9-10
  externalities and, 28-29
  housing and, 238-240, 251
  land use and, 217
  prices and, 7-10
  rents and, 257-258
Supply curve, 8, 28-29
Surveys, location decisions and, 61
Sveikauskas, L., 191
Swaney, J. A., 33, 174
Systems orientation, 308-309

Targeting decisions, input-output analysis
  and, 164
Targeting development efforts, 184-185
Tax(es), 7, 168, 232
  efficiency of, 285
  equitable, 282-283, 285-286
  externalities and, 31, 251
  housing demand and, 251
  location decisions and, 52, 62
  property, 52, 252, 170, 287
  revenue elasticity, 288
  shifting, 286-288
Tax abatements, 175
Tax incremental financing, 262
Tax sharing, 38, 169, 293-294
Technical assistance, 175
Technological change, 307-308
  input-output analysis and, 165
Technologically oriented activities, 181
Technologically progressive activities,
  289-290
Technology, 315
  location decisions and, 63
  metropolitan spread and, 229
  transportation costs and, 48

Testa, W. A., 203
Thibodeau, T. G., 247-248
Thompson, P. R., 184, 185
Thompson, Wilbur, 37, 116, 117, 136, 184, 185
Threshold demand, 72-73
Tiebout, C., 127, 251-254, 276-277
Tiebout model, 251-254, 276-277
Tobin, C., 290
Trade:
  among cities, 74
  barriers to, 82-83
  flows, 189-193
  functional area and, 16
  hierarchical system of, 16
  interindustry linkages and, 97-100
Trade-off model, housing and, 248-250
Training:
  demand for labor and, 25
  productivity and, 26
  skilled labor and, 202
Training programs, 175, 263
Transactions table, 159-160
Transportation, 15
  access and, 211
  location decisions and, 63
  metropolitan areas and, 79
Transportation costs, 68, 69
  changes in, 79
  geographic features and, 82
  location decisions and, 42-47, 48, 61, 82
  main arteries and, 226-227
  metropolitan spread and, 229
  profits and, 73
  technology and, 48
Transportation sector, urban infrastructure
    and, 101
Transshipment points, 44
Terkla, D. G., 207

Unemployment, 22-27
  African Americans and, 27
  local growth and, 172
  probability of, 194
  structural, 263
Unions:
  location decisions and, 50-51
  tariffs and, 190
  wages and, 24

Universities, quality of life and, 51
Unrestricted grants, 284
Urban areas, 15
  change and, 79-80, 228-232
  external-economy industries and, 103
  growth and, 228-232
  hierarchy and, 66, 74-80
  housing programs and, 256-261
  unemployment in, 22-27
  See also Cities
Urban density, externalities and, 30
Urban development:
  immigration and, 205-207
  influences on, 66-94
Urban diseconomies, 102
Urban econometric models, 152-153
Urban goods, maximum access to, 224
Urban grants, 154
Urban innovation, 119
Urbanization economies, 100-102
Urban planning, economics and, 304
Urban problems, externalities and, 27-33
Urban size ratchet, 117-118
Urban systems, circular causation and, 182
User fees, 37, 292, 294-295
Utility, maximizing, 3-4

Values:
  changing, 305-307
  economic analysis and, 5, 6
  suburban lifestyle and, 230
Van de Berg, Leo, 186
Variables, models and, 2, 150
Venture capitalists, 141
Voith, Richard, 231
Volunteers, government services and,
    292-293
Voters:
  government scope and, 280
  public workers as, 36-37
  "voting with their feet," 253, 276
Voucher systems, 37, 259, 260, 292

Wages:
  above-equilibrium, 24
  central-city residents, 272
  demand for labor and, 25

expected, 194
government workers and, 38
immigration and, 205-206
labor movement and, 49, 132, 192
location decisions and, 49-50
low, 22-27
migration and, 193
region's prevailing, 49-50
unions and, 24
Warner, P. D., 181
Wasylenko, M., 52
Weather:
    quality of life and, 51
    urban growth and, 141
Weicher, J. L., 247-248
Weiss, S. J., 151
Welfare, 275
    economic development and, 14-15

economics of, 259-260
    work rules and, 266
White, H. L., 253
Wiewel, W., 136, 262
Williams, P. R., 79
Wire connections, 80
Women, heavy industry towns and, 185
Work:
    developing new kinds of, 118-119, 267
    leisure balance, 4, 306
Worldview, of economists, 1-7

Yinger, John, 256

Zero-sum games, 175-176
Zoning, 232-234

⋈ About the Author

John P. Blair is the Belinda A. Burns Scholar and Professor of Economics at Wright State University. He received his doctorate in economics from West Virginia University. Prior to joining the faculty of Wright State, he taught in the Department of Urban Affairs at the University of Wisconsin—Milwaukee and also served for two years as a policy analyst in the U.S. Department of Housing and Urban Development where he worked on national urban policy. His work in the field of economic development has been published in such journals as *Urban Affairs Quarterly, Review of Regional Studies,* and *Economic Development Quarterly.* He has served as a consultant to businesses and governments and is a member of the Montgomery County Planning Commission.